What Others Are Saying...

With the framework of the Three As—being Aware, Advancing, Authentic—Caitlin Krause has crafted a wonderful book for educators that shares her teaching experience and deep inquiry as a scaffold for integrating mindfulness into the classroom. This book skillfully provides an informed and practical set of guidelines and exercises for designing mindful experiences for the benefit of teachers and students.

—Philippe Goldin
Director, Clinically Applied Affective
Neuroscience Laboratory
University of California, Davis

Mindfulness is beyond optional; it's imperative in today's society, be it the culture of business, learning, or personal life. By illuminating ways to apply the "intentional use of attention" to our active daily lives, Mindful by Design *is a guide to well-being, a practical resource, and a creative call-to-action, as Caitlin Krause helps readers to bridge the gap between prioritizing true connection and achieving it.*

—Leah Weiss
Author of *How We Work: Live Your Purpose,
Reclaim Your Sanity, and Embrace the Daily Grind*
Lecturer, Stanford Graduate School of Business

Mindfulness is key to effective learning, whether it's a classroom of students or a workplace full of adult learners. Caitlin Krause shares valuable strategies that will help any educator, coach, manager, or learning professional bring out the best in those they serve.

—Dorie Clark
Adjunct Professor, Duke University's Fuqua School of Business
Author of *Entrepreneurial You* and *Stand Out*

In a world that seems more turbulent, more distraction-filled by the day, students and teachers need the restorative power of breathing and mindfulness as never before. Caitlin Krause's Mindful by Design *is a valuable and inspiring guide, offering generous insights and practical advice for those seeking to center, strengthen, and clarify their efforts both in and outside of the classroom.*

—Dinty W. Moore
Author of *The Mindful Writer*

MINDFUL
BY DESIGN

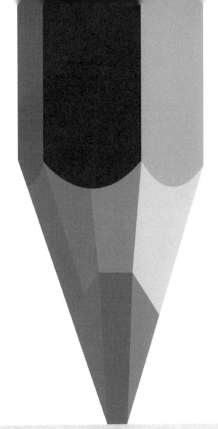

CAITLIN KRAUSE

MINDFUL
BY DESIGN

A Practical Guide for Cultivating
Aware, Advancing, and Authentic
Learning Experiences

FOR INFORMATION:

Corwin

A SAGE Company

2455 Teller Road

Thousand Oaks, California 91320

(800) 233-9936

www.corwin.com

SAGE Publications Ltd.

1 Oliver's Yard

55 City Road

London EC1Y 1SP

United Kingdom

SAGE Publications India Pvt. Ltd.

B 1/I 1 Mohan Cooperative Industrial Area

Mathura Road, New Delhi 110 044

India

SAGE Publications Asia-Pacific Pte. Ltd.

18 Cross Street #10-10/11/12

China Square Central

Singapore 048423

Acquisitions Editor: Ariel Curry

Development Editor: Desirée A. Bartlett

Senior Editorial Assistant: Jessica Vidal

Production Editor: Amy Schroller

Copy Editor: Talia Greenberg

Typesetter: Hurix Digital

Proofreader: Ellen Brink

Indexer: Judy Hunt

Cover and Interior Designer: Janet Kiesel

Marketing Manager: Margaret O'Connor

Printed in the United States of America

Library of Congress Cataloging-in-Publication Data

Names: Krause, Caitlin, author.

Title: Mindful by design: a practical guide for cultivating aware, advancing, and authentic learning experiences / Caitlin Krause.

Description: Thousand Oaks, California : Corwin, [2019] | Includes bibliographical references and index.

Identifiers: LCCN 2018037330 | ISBN 9781506388656 (pbk.: acid-free paper)

Subjects: LCSH: Affective education. | Mindfulness (Psychology) | Social earning–Study and teaching (Secondary) | Self-actualization (Psychology)

Classification: LCC LB1072 .K73 2019 | DDC 370.15/34–dc23 LC record available at https://lccn.loc.gov/2018037330

This book is printed on acid-free paper.

SUSTAINABLE FORESTRY INITIATIVE

Certified Chain of Custody
At Least 10% Certified Forest Content
www.sfiprogram.org
SFI-01028

19 20 21 22 23 10 9 8 7 6 5 4 3 2 1

Contents

Part III

 Visit the companion website at **caitlinkrause.com** for additional resources.

Acknowledgments

Many people have contributed to the making of this book—directly and indirectly. You might find yourself here in the pages somewhere, even between the words. I am grateful for the following people, who helped to bring the messages to life:

My own teachers and mentors, including George Thoms, Melissa Malouf, Ron Butters, Captain David A. Lott, Robert J. Bliwise, Natalie Cohen, Michael McGarty, Susan Feeney, Deb Fitzpatrick, and Mitch Grosky, each of whom instilled in me a passion for discovery, a love of words, and a reverence for mindful learning models. Colleagues, friends and co-learners, especially Lynn, David, Brother Fred, Kristen, Sheena, Kendra, Dave, Rose, Jean, Leanne, Don, Brian, Megan, Ken, Elissa, Ben, and Steve at LaSalle Academy; Ben, Karen, Jean-Louis, Pam, Steph, Martine, Dennis, Natalie, Robert, Ven, and Adam at St. John's International School; and Diya, Ben, Bill, David, Katie, Brook, Leslie, Tara, Kimara, Dale, and Elizabeth at Zurich International School. When George Thoms told me, "Do not walk, *run* to teaching," it couldn't have been more true.

Thank you to the mentors and cooperative community who have enthusiastically shared thoughts about each other's art, poetry, and prose, including Cameron Marzelli, Janet Sylvester, Teresa Cader, Rafael Campo, the late Wayne Brown, K. B. Ballentine, Howard Rheingold, Gretchen Kai Halpert, and Amaury Moulron, who initially told me to write the book I would want to read. Special thanks to DeWitt Henry, whose encouragement, criticism, and camaraderie are beacons. I am especially grateful to my editor Ariel for tirelessly devoting herself to giving feedback along the way that illuminated the text. Thanks to my mother, Kathleen, who is my sounding board and my "first reader"; to my father, Robert, who helped me to fall in love with stories; and to my sister, Emily, in whose values and opinion I trust.

Thanks to Parker J. Palmer, Marcy Jackson, Tara Reynolds, Pamela Seigle, and friends at the *Courage to Lead*, who invited me to seize the day, claim my voice, and take genuine risks in learning and leadership. To Philippe Goldin for embodying mindfulness coming alive in the world of education. To Claude, the Center of Wise Leadership, and the global co-creative community engaged with lighting fires.

The pages of this book were written all over the world, and the writing itself would not have been possible without the support of friends who kindly opened their homes and "created the space to create." I am grateful to Judy, Mark, Nathan, and Fred for beautiful places, by mountains and ocean, that breathe mindful breaths. The practice of writing can be a lot like breathwork. To Kate, Dorie, Miki, Nathan, Wendy, Markus, Jáchym, Tom, Kate, Alex, Andrea, Monika, Boris, Marc, Áine, Sergali, Kristin, Fred, Mark, Charles, Peter, Angie, Jessica, Patrick, Regina, Heinz, Melanie, Jutta, Amy, Dan, Rupert, Jim, Natasha, Rayna, Suzy, Andrew, Tracy, Michael, Starr, and friends in community who are dedicated to building a world that embraces being *Mindful by Design*—it's present in you! Thank you for your daring, joyful inspirations.

I am grateful to my lifelong mindfulness teachers, collaborators, and partners-in-being, for sharing wisdom and grace, allowing curiosity to lead us together.

Thank you to everyone who has contributed to this text—you are here!

For happiness, truth, freedom, peace, and love.

Publisher's Acknowledgments

Corwin gratefully acknowledges the contributions of the following reviewers:

Suzy Brooks, Instructional Technology Director
Mashpee Public Schools
Mashpee, MA

Deanna Brunlinger, Science Teacher and Department Chair
Elkhorn Area High School
Elkhorn, WI

Tracy Crowley, Information Literacy Specialist
and Educational Consultant
Wheeling Community Consolidated School District
Wheeling, IL

Tom Daccord, Director
EdTechTeacher
Dorchester, MA

Rayna L. Freedman, Classroom Teacher
and Instructional Technology Specialist
Jordan/Jackson Elementary School
Mansfield, MA

Marcy Jackson, Co-founder and Senior Fellow
Center for Courage & Renewal
Seattle, WA

Lyneille Meza, Director of Data and Assessment
Denton ISD
Denton, TX

Carol Pelletier Radford, Consultant
MentoringinAction.com
Falmouth, MA

Michael Pennington, Director of Technology
(Public School Administration)
Independence Local Schools
Independence, OH

Leonard J. Villanueva, Elementary School Teacher
Palisades Elementary School
Pearl City, HI

About the Author

Caitlin Krause is a globally recognized learning expert, author, and keynote speaker. In her *Mindful by Design* methodology and through her organizational consulting, she helps individual leaders and teams leverage mindfulness, storytelling, and design principles to connect more deeply with their audiences.

As founder of the MindWise consultancy, co-founder of the Center of Wise Leadership, and a virtual reality and AI specialist, Caitlin contributes to building products and experiences that promote humanity, innovation, and emotional intelligence. She speaks extensively in Europe and North America, leading professional development and learning workshops. Caitlin has more than a decade of experience as a full-time teacher in middle school and high school classrooms, and served as a curriculum designer and department chair, promoting mindful leadership models throughout organizations. She holds a BA from Duke University and an MFA from Lesley University, and believes in embracing creative constraints, living a life filled with moments of wonder, and connecting with passion, purpose, and presence.

For Judy Shannon

Introduction: Making a Difference

[Your calling to purpose] is the place where your deep gladness and the world's deep hunger meet.

—Frederick Buechner (1973)

I felt a deep, clear calling to the vocation of teaching. It felt attached to my own life's purpose, directing me when I made a career change from the corporate arena to education. The larger world seemed to be calling out to me with the message. *Making a difference* is the reason I chose to teach. It could be the reason you did, too. Not only to "do no harm," but actually to promote something good and of value. We want to make a positive difference—in the lives of our students, colleagues, teams, our personal lives, society, and beyond. Sometimes, it's hard to know what effect we've had in the classroom because we're always "on," and the pace of the year can seem too rapid for reflection.

This is how it used to feel for me in the beginning: frantic, frenetic, always receiving multiple inputs and demands on one channel with not nearly enough bandwidth. Between the annual 120+ students, parents, and school community, I knew I could always give more, but my inner resources were sapped. In my first year of teaching, I was intimidated by my own lack of experience. I was confident in my intellectual ability and command of materials, yet I felt it would take a miracle to reach a level of comfort standing in front of a group of teenagers.

Though helpful and positive, it wasn't curriculum planning models that got me through those first days of school; nor was it advice (which I received from more than one person) to *make sure not to smile* (at least, not before the end of the first term!). For me, not smiling was nearly impossible. No, it was a different resource that saved me: Parker J. Palmer's *The Courage to Teach* (1997) echoed my own beliefs about authenticity and wholeness in the classroom, and gave me the strength to act on those convictions.

Tempting as it was to play superhero with my newly appointed authority, I knew in my heart that this form of leadership would be empty and short-lived. In essence, I knew I needed to keep it real in order to be true to myself and teach with integrity. I wanted my students to bloom in their learning, and I had to gain their trust, first, in order for that to happen. My answer was to acknowledge my own fears of being seen as incompetent in my authority. As soon as I did that, I didn't cling so hard—I lost my inhibitions, and began to put myself in the shoes of the learner.

This was a process in empathy, and was the beginning of my use of mindfulness in teaching. I was aware of myself, and my students, choosing openness. I showed them my own learning process, my own passions and joy, favoring a positive, proactive community that could learn together and could understand ourselves even better in the process.

And, guess what? A miracle happened.

During those years, I was teaching in a high school in Providence, Rhode Island. It was a beautiful place to learn and seemed to me right out of a film—rolling green lawns, red brick historic architecture, Latin motto on the façade.

In that school community, miraculous events happened every day because I embraced my own joy of learning and absorbed the fear of failure, letting it become a form of curiosity. I began to understand that students had fears, too, and part of my job was to flip those fears into opportunities. I presented students with choices, offering up all sorts of ways to learn with creativity and confidence. You'll see those opportunities reflected in the exercises in this book, which all stem from values of awareness, empathy, community, and insight.

Starting out, operating on my own convictions about teaching with mindfulness, I had no idea if I would be making a positive difference. I couldn't yet see the results—all I could see was that I was following what felt true, what felt like my calling to merge my own joy in my heart with the world's deep need, just like the Buechner epigraph. Seven years later, on a rainy Thanksgiving holiday during the first year that I was teaching abroad in Belgium, I was surprised and delighted to receive an email from a former student. Part of it read:

> In light of Thanksgiving, I wanted to express my gratitude to you for everything you have done for me. You took a subject that I always found boring and made it my favorite class I have ever taken. Beyond the do's and don'ts of writing, you encouraged us to be free thinkers. From your friendly and engaged approach, I felt more comfortable than ever discussing during class. . . .
>
> So, thank you for all of that, but most of all, thank you for being unique and not just teaching. You did more than taught, you inspired us. I will never quit writing and will always love English because of you, and for that I am grateful.

I felt grateful and humbled, too, to receive such a note. I once read a quote that said, "Teaching is a work of heart," and I believe it. Each day, as educators, we put our full hearts into the process, and our classrooms are such powerful environments, with the capacity literally to change lives. And we can never fully imagine the immensity of the impact we make. It travels.

The email made me think about my own authenticity, as a teacher and human. What I bring each day to the classroom is my true self, with my own set of joys, fears, hopes, and desires. I was happy I had made a difference in this former student's experience, and I knew the impact I was making was beyond the curriculum content, allowing students to recognize broader connections, and to engage with themselves in the process of learning.

I knew, then, that the key variable in my teaching is the presence of mindfulness.

Helping others make meaning out of mindfulness, applying it to everything from tech to storytelling, curriculum design to writing, innovation to empathy and compassion, is where my passion lies. This is what "makes me come alive," in a sense.

Since those early days in that New England high school, I have used mindfulness as part of the core of my teaching (actually, the core of my *being*, since it's undivided), applying it in all sorts of ways, reflecting best practices in a wide arena of interdisciplinary learning. I've taught in middle schools and high schools worldwide, directing programs in international schools, serving as a curriculum coordinator, coaching sports, co-leading Model United Nations, founding creative writing clubs and mentoring student leadership programs, and traveling to present workshops and teach other leaders and educators around the globe. As founder of the organization MindWise, I build bridges and connect ecosystems, as we are entering a new phase of immersive tech that hinges on using mindful awareness and emotional intelligence. It's an exciting time to be human.

I've studied an array of forms and interpretations of mindfulness (see Chapter 1, "Beyond the Buzzword"), including the popular MBSR (mindfulness-based stress reduction) and MBCT (mindfulness-based cognitive therapy). I've also studied emotional intelligence, SEL (social and emotional learning), PBL (project-based learning), blended learning, visible learning, design thinking, and more. I'm a "curriculum mapper" (learning from Heidi Hayes Jacobs and Marie Hubley Alcock [2017]), "understanding by design" (thanks to Grant Wiggins and Jay McTighe [2005]), and I want students to "own the learning" (Alan November [2008]) and adopt a "growth mindset" (Carol Dweck [2006]). Many positive inspirations and influences inform these mindful practices, driven by constant curiosity. I'm up on the various learning styles and colors; I'm down with what it's like to be a TCK (third culture kid) with a TFK (thirst for knowledge). I'm fascinated with the rapid rate of developments in neuroscience, revealing more to us about "the way things work" in the brain, beyond the machinery of David Macaulay's wildest dreams. This could all be freestyle poetry right here, all lightness with a core message to be mindfully adaptive, receptive, reflective, and open.

Underneath it all, true mindfulness is the glue that makes all of the methods above stick; it's the lens of nonjudgment that allows us to see more clearly, invent with abandon, and make better rational sense of things; it's the anticloak of authenticity (a cloak that reveals instead of disguises) that allows us to be real; to be understood; to seek to understand others.

True mindfulness is the glue that makes all of the methods above stick; it's the lens of nonjudgment that allows us to see more clearly, invent with abandon, and make better rational sense of things; it's the anticloak of authenticity (a cloak that reveals instead of disguises) that allows us to be real; to be understood; to seek to understand others.

This book invites each reader to try out various ways to involve mindfulness in daily life, in and out of the classroom. It's personal, real, approachable, and fun, making sense of a term that, while trendy, can seem abstract and elusive. With practical, accessible explanations and applications, this book demystifies mindfulness and allows readers to use it in many ways, to spark powerful learning environments and improve personal well being.

Overview of the Book

We'll dive more deeply into mindfulness and its myriad applications in the following chapters of this book, exploring concepts related to mindful teaching and learning. This collection of mindfulness exercises can be used in different ways: as a professional support tool, as a classroom lesson planning guide, a toolbox for the classroom, and even a way in which to consider some bigger questions and recent educational research and advancements. The questions are often bigger than the answers, pointing us in new directions. It's an ongoing dialogue with ourselves and with the world.

This book is an invitation, giving readers the chance to learn about the concept of mindfulness and to apply mindful learning techniques to their personal lives and learning environments, *if they wish to*. It's not a mandate—it's simply one option that has many benefits, including increasing focus, resilience, empathy, compassion, health, and overall happiness. I can't imagine a better set of motivations; for me, incorporating mindfulness into my daily practices was intuitive, engaging, and the most rewarding step of my multidimensional career.

While this book is written with learning communities and education experiences in mind, it serves everyone, as its intention is to reframe the way in which we think about thinking and learn about learning in regard to our relationship with ourselves and with others in community.

Part I

Chapter 1, "Mindfulness: Beyond the Buzzword," defines mindfulness in clear terms, highlighting problems and pain points that mindfulness helps to solve. This introduction shares some of the inspiration behind the mindfulness movement in education, also addressing mindsets, misconceptions, scientific research, and connections to education, including standards and models.

Chapter 2 gives an understanding of the architecture of a mindful learning environment, looking at the classroom setup and planning design in three key arenas: classroom physical structures, tools, and routines that teachers can use when envisioning their own classroom spaces and dynamic mindful learning experiences. It all starts here, with planning and vision. This chapter illuminates the intentional choices involved in structuring mindful classroom settings, with the focus simply on how to design a mindful learning space.

Part II

Chapter 3 includes detailed examples of mindful exercises that teachers can practice on their own, in and out of the classroom. It builds the base, and offers fresh takes on mindfulness, so that even those who are familiar with the practices and traditions will find something new to appreciate.

Chapter 4 is all about what mindfulness looks like when it's actively embedded in curriculum. There are sixteen detailed classroom lessons that incorporate mindfulness, applying it to all curriculum areas. With step-by-step guidance, and also examples of ways that students engage with the exercises, this chapter breaks concepts down and makes them approachable, practical, and engaging.

Part III

In conclusion, we'll address "The Future of Mindfulness" in **Chapter 5**, which points the way toward innovative learning, which is co-evolving alongside our deeper understanding of collaborative education environments that hinge on emotional intelligence, adaptation, and relational trust. We'll take a brief look at some of the ways in which the modern learning landscape can embrace digital revolutions and stay focused on mindful connection, inside and out.

Interspersed throughout the book are direct quotes from students about their experiences and reactions to mindfulness in the classroom.

There are also additional resources, tips and tricks, quotes and poetry included along the way. This book provides ideas for continuing to build mindful learning, extending to a global network of additional resources, including helpful websites and community groups that will broaden the scope of mindful learning. As Howard Rheingold (2000) says, it's a "virtual community."

Feel free to jump around this book, using it as a workbook, a toolkit, a place for reflections and discoveries, and an interwoven set of personal stories. In some sections, there are quotes, reflections, and exercises, which serve to sustain and motivate teachers and students alike.

I'm wishing each reader (you!) an enjoyable journey through the book, discovering along the way certain aspects of mindful practices that resonate with you. It's personal rather than prescriptive, and I think you'll see that my own stories and pathways are anything but ordinary! It's with openness and joy that I share my journey and my students' journeys with you. I have great respect for the impact that mindfulness can have, and I honor each individual learner, and the trust they place in collective, collaborative communities. They are the true voices of mindfulness, helping to share ways in which personal connection and mindful learning environments ignite.

PART I

CHAPTER 1

Mindfulness: Beyond the Buzzword

So, what's the buzz all about? The term *mindfulness* has popped up everywhere, from training regimens for Olympic athletes to keynote talks at the World Economic Forum in Davos, Switzerland.

One summer workshop I gave used it in the working title ("Mindfulness: Beyond the Buzzword"), and the room was so packed that people had to sit on the floor. I thought this was great—everyone was so eager to hear about "mindfulness," a topic that had been somewhat obscure in previous years. While this was encouraging to me, I realized it could be seen as a harbinger of the word's abstract vagueness, adding confusion to complexity— if a word grows into a buzzword, it runs the risk of being commodified, exploited, misinterpreted, and ultimately misunderstood. I'm no purist, yet I'm motivated to promote and maintain the integrity of something as resonant and important as mindfulness.

It's not too bold a statement to say that mindfulness has powers to change the entire learning environment and experience; it's an effective change-maker that is scientifically proven to make a huge difference in quality of life. I wanted to simplify it, to demystify what was happening with the rise in popularity of the term. When someone asks me to explain what mindfulness is, I usually respond that it's a building of three capacities: Awareness, Advancement, and Authenticity. And it's truly nothing but a concept—*until we apply and embody it.*

A Practical Definition of Mindfulness

It's a common practice to define mindfulness as a "focused awareness." University of Massachusetts researcher Jon Kabat-Zinn (2005), famous for helping to develop mindfulness programs through his use of MBSR (mindfulness-based stress reduction), calls mindfulness "awareness of the present moment on purpose without judgment."

There are other popular definitions, too. In their co-authored book on mindfulness, aptly subtitled *A Practical Guide to Finding Peace in a Frantic World*, Mark Williams and Danny Penham (2011) call it a "simple form of meditation" that is all about "observation without criticism; being compassionate with yourself."

> The simple definition of mindfulness that I've created is "a way to be in the world, using Three A's: Aware, Advancing, Authentic."

It starts on a personal level, and has amazing results, with the potential to reach many others through this presence. Because the focus is on a state of being, the simple definition of mindfulness that I've created is "a way to be in the world, using Three A's: Aware, Advancing, Authentic."

Aware

of self; of others; of senses and context

Being aware involves increasing your focus and knowledge about the current situation, surroundings; emphasis on questions over instant answers, projecting outward, seeing all angles and factors. Sharpening listening skills and techniques. Awareness of multiple perspectives.

Advancing

active, curious, insightful stretching, outward and inward

Advancing involves using trends and methods to test assumptions and chart a course, resilience-building; adaptability. Looking at a system and seeing influences. Prioritizing the goals that have more to do with the "why" objectives. Purpose-driven organizational change. After addressing the "why," moving outward to the "how" and then the "what."

Authentic

accepting of self and others, without judgment

Being authentic involves developing a true voice and presence, applied to speaking, writing, and all levels of innovation and design. Questioning assumptions and judgments. Using terms that MIT's Otto Scharmer (2009) uses, employing *open mind* (nonjudging), *open heart* (noncynicism), and *open will* (release of fear), this is the stage that allows for the greatest leaps in social awareness, empathy building, and rich compassion. Major personal and organizational shifts are possible here (Scharmer and Kaufer, 2013).

This approach shapes mindfulness as a choice about how to be in the world, using the three core principles of "Aware, Advancing, Authentic" as guides and a framework to turn embodiment into action. It puts the power in the individual's hands, giving back agency, ownership, and true freedom. It's purposeful presence with trust. For learners, this has huge impact.

Throughout this book, the mindfulness exercises are connected to the Three A's, with details about each principle and how it directly connects to outcomes and strengths built as a result.

Mindfulness has applications in every discipline imaginable. It's not just insight that directs inward—it's also an expansion outward, with curiosity and care, addressing other cultures and environments. Imagine the possibilities for education, in designing curriculum that spans the globe.

When I incorporate mindfulness into my daily life, inviting it into the classroom, I focus on both the definition of mindfulness as a way to be, and its Three As in active application, using it to actualize many benefits, including:

⬤ promoting presence (Aware)

⬤ increasing focus (Advancing)

⬤ boosting connection capacity for relational trust (Authentic)

Aware

of self; of others; of senses and context

Advancing

active, curious, insightful stretching, outward and inward

Authentic

accepting of self and others, without judgment

Since we had all built up a sense of trust and motivation between ourselves, it was easy being open about thoughts. I thought that everyone was able to share their ideas without being criticized for them, and it helped the overall classroom experience and how we collaboratively tackled problems.

I believe that an open environment is one of the best to have in a classroom as ideas are exchanged and people learn to work together on different topics that they would maybe not know how to tackle themselves. Therefore, openness and communication are key to ensure collaboration.

—Rafael, *former student*

In the different exercises in this book, I explicitly point out some of the ways the exercise enhances each of the Three As to illuminate the deliberate, intentional connections. Mindfulness sets a stable ground for learning and expanding, allowing teachers and students to connect with themselves and with others. We are more empathetic, and more compassionate—less rigid and fixed. While the word can seem vague and abstract on its own, we see mindfulness in action in engaged classrooms, and we know when mindfulness is absent from the environment and state of mind.

Thus, *what it is* also involves *what it isn't*.

To clear up some myths and misconceptions, here are some of the useful (and surprising) discoveries I've made about mindfulness along the way:

> Mindfulness involves mental focus and training. It is not a religion, though the word mindfulness has origins in Buddhism. In a secular way, it is truly addressing the mind itself and a way of heightening awareness.

> Some exercises related to mindfulness incorporate meditation, and many of the mindfulness meditation activities will focus on the breath as a guide and a focus. You don't have to sit on the floor or assume any special physical position in order to exercise mindfulness—it can happen anywhere, anytime.

> Using mindfulness does not result in a weaker willpower, and it does not make you more passive or happy-go-lucky. In fact, mindfulness deepens the clarity with which you see the world and engage with it. It helps with everything from goal-setting to learning—with passion!

Scientific findings, as well as Jon Kabat-Zinn's successful and well-regarded MBSR courses (mentioned earlier), have caused mindfulness to gain attention over the past few decades, and its many applications continue to be a topic of curiosity and enthusiasm in many different societal institutions and learning environments.

Mindful Qualities of Learning

When educators incorporate mindfulness into learning, amazing things start to happen. Lessons that incorporate mindfulness offer chances to build mental focus so that students and teachers are able to make authentic connections, responding to a dynamic environment that is neither rigid nor static. Research shows that mindfulness practices decrease toxic stress and anxiety, improving connections, relationships, and levels of attention. Adopting a mindfulness practice also has great benefits in social-emotional arenas, linked to compassion and empathy, among other beneficial traits. Students will be aware of this quality of mindfulness, which increases our ability as educators to dwell in the present moment, holding space for what arises and what is needed, connecting with students, and establishing relational trust in community.

> *You made the classroom a safe space to share thoughts. I remember looking forward to not only sharing my ideas but hearing everyone else's. I know sharing is difficult at times. I've struggled with speaking in front of people, but never in your classroom. I would volunteer to share ideas and then listen to others. I felt confident in my ideas.*
>
> —Claire, *former student*

Mindfulness implies being more flexible and open; this requires a certain breathing space and mental acuity that we can adopt first, as educators, and then stretch to bring to our classrooms.

The benefits of mindfulness that are especially powerful for educators to consider include the following four arenas:

1. Attention management, greater awareness

2. Increased focus and concentration, less attachment and reactivity to emotion

3. Health and well-being, including calming abilities in stressful situations

4. Conscious decision-making and greater compassion for self and others

Benefits of mindfulness in education are vast, and a greater number of scientific studies, with foundations in neuroscience research and findings, are published every year. I keep up to date with the latest findings and continue to publish them online, also following others' research and posts. Many of the current scientific findings are available on the Mindful Schools research page, which reports (with further citations online) that "When teachers learn mindfulness, they not only reap personal benefits such as reduced stress and burnout, but their schools do as well. In randomized controlled trials, teachers who learned mindfulness reported greater efficacy in doing their jobs and had more emotionally supportive classrooms and better classroom organization based on independent observations" (Mindfulschools.org, 2018).

Regarding studies relating to mindfulness exercises and student benefits, the Mindful Schools site reports, "Studies find that youth benefit from learning mindfulness in terms of improved cognitive outcomes, social-emotional skills, and well-being. In turn, such benefits may lead to long-term improvements in life. For example, social skills in kindergarten predict improved education, employment, crime, substance abuse and mental health outcomes in adulthood" (Mindfulschools.org, 2018).

It starts in the classroom, and grows from there. There are new applications for mindfulness springing up across a wide variety of industries, including:

- Engineering
- Politics
- Economics
- Business
- Technology
- Education
- Science
- Health

While it's hard to pinpoint exactly what mindfulness looks like in practice, because it's not formulaic, we can all envision what a person who embodies mindfulness in day-to-day life might represent, in traits and behavior. Over years of leading mindfulness and leadership seminars and dialogues, participants and I have had discussions that aim to define some of the characteristics of mindfulness—without trying to be limiting. This is one list example recorded during a group roundtable that took place at a "Mindful Leadership" meetup:

A mindful person is . . .

- aware
- advancing
- authentic
- resilient
- focused
- committed to
  social good
- loyal
- charismatic
- passionate
- present

- listening
- approachable (not arrogant)
- has flaws and is authentic about
  showing them
- selfless
- caring
- honest
- positive
- open-hearted
- open-minded
- open-willed

I reference this list again in this book, in the exercise for teachers about values, called "Prime Values, Purpose, and Presence." When we look deeply into how our actions connect to our core beliefs, we might find that our values are connected to our sense of purpose, our "why" that gives us a reason, even if that reason is intuitive. Once these values are realized, they can manifest in better quality of health, increased satisfaction and engagement, improved focus and awareness, and many other measurable statistics shown by scientific studies. In tremendous, life-changing ways, often surprising, the benefits are limitless . . . it takes beginning with enthusiasm and open curiosity . . . and it leads to better presence, which impacts the outer world.

Four Cornerstones of a Mindfulness AAA Mindset in a Learning Culture

Being "mindful," embracing and embodying mindfulness, means you have a "Mindfulness AAA Mindset"—you are Aware, Advancing, and Authentic by nature. It's the lens from which you look, the mindset from which you operate, the way you choose to be in the world. AAA is, by definition, about simplicity over complexity. It's a way of being.

Now, the question is, once you decide you would like to choose that way of being, what could happen? What would you perhaps see around you, in quality and form, that would then be linked to this foundation, with our vocation in mind? Four prime values emerge that serve as cornerstones. These four cornerstones, foundational values, and elements manifest in every individual and organization that identifies with a Mindfulness AAA Mindset. We might even view them as related to the culture of the classroom—they are *culture cornerstones*, pointing to the values of what we stand for, as mindful leaders. They are: Dignity, Freedom, Invention, and Agency.

These four prime elements are visible and celebrated in every *Mindful by Design* environment—natural cornerstones that become visible when one chooses mindfulness. The AAA is the definition of mindfulness itself; the four culture cornerstones of

Dignity, Freedom, Invention, and Agency are what it means to apply *Mindful by Design*—what emerges as part of the classroom culture. In evident ways, they are the embodiment of a learner in action. While they are linked, each has its own distinguishing traits that are embodied in different ways, showing themselves through classroom interactions, mood, experiences, and ultimately, outcomes.

Dignity is at the core of my classroom, and is present throughout this book in different "For the Classroom" exercises. It involves actionable, palpable respect and care for each individual in the group. Students feel that you, as a teacher, are treating them with dignity—often, they will articulate this as feeling "respected." The art of listening, holding spaces, sharing with a mindful reverence for the "other" as a source of insight, building awareness of connections rather than separations, embodying and acting out of respect for self and others— these are all inherently part of dignity. I want students to expect the best from themselves and from each other, and this is also what dignity represents.

Freedom, when operating from a place of dignity, means that each individual has a voice; each student is recognized and welcomed. It's a freedom to create new connections and form understanding and inferences, as well. This means that students can personally reflect and connect, sharing ideas, thoughts, and reflections in community with others, building social and emotional learning capacities. I think, often, we might bypass and/or overlook this phase of deep self-awareness and social-awareness, which have a lot to do with feeling endorsed and welcomed from the beginning—to be free, in many senses, to investigate what it means to be curious learners at this particular place and time. What do we need to spark this level of engagement?

On Dignity

Often, it seems like a statement that is just placed in the syllabus ("Respect each other"), discussed the first day, and then never thought of again. The teacher needs to model that respect for their students, and then in turn, the students can really respect one another. You were able to accomplish this by really listening to what each of us contributed to the conversation and validating and building upon our opinions to encourage further discussion by others in the class.

—Charlotte, *former student*

It reinforces how you treat a classroom, that students are not numbers. You saw us all as individuals, and you treated us all with respect and care.

—Viki, *former student*

On Freedom

The biggest help for me was learning and experiencing enough to see that ideas come from the connections we make through learning, not directly from the source from which we learned. Source material can create a spark, but it can't get you all the way there, not when your unique perspective is fundamentally different from anyone you're working with. Learning to do things like brainstorm uninhibited, to present ideas that may not be the best fit at first, and understanding that to be wrong is to accept a challenge rather than accepting defeat—that sparks the critical thinking needed to pare the ideas down, and bring the successes to completion.

—Ellen, *former student*

On Invention

The thing that I feel makes the biggest difference in innovative learning is understanding that no idea is a bad idea. The only way to be truly innovative is to come up with hundreds of ideas and then weed them out one by one until you come up with something innovative. . . . If we didn't put so many ideas on the board (say, we only came up with ten) then I never would have come up with the idea that eventually won us the competition. Like I said, it made me realize that no idea is really a bad idea.

—Joseph, *former student*

On Agency

I finally learned how to seek out my own learning. I wish I had more classes like that as a child. I didn't feel exhausted or burnt out. Though the curriculum was set to some extent, I learned a lot about making connections and finding ways to integrate passion into purpose. I found the things I loved learning about.

—Ellen, *former student*

Invention comes from *"What if . . . ?"* questions and opportunities to design possibilities. With a base of dignity and freedom in place, the cornerstone of invention is about mindful problem-solving, creativity, and meeting real-world challenges with feelings of optimism, inclusion, compassion, and commitment. As inventors, students carry with them all of their amazing insights, ideas, and dreams. As W. B. Yeats says in his poem "The Cloths of Heaven," "Tread softly because you tread on my dreams." The mindful inventions that come forward from here have the power to change the world.

Agency is the sense of creative power—the pride and ownership of learning—that students carry with them. It is what they will take far into the future, spanning beyond the four walls of our classroom space. Agency couples with identity, and turns to mindful act. It also affects approaches to assessment. Depending on the complexity, I start by guiding students, using questions and models to make learning visible. Eventually, students develop their own personal agency, and this is when relational trust meets evident action, reflecting the four culture cornerstones together in consonance (*such alliteration!*). To have a sense of agency is to belong, and to understand the connection to a larger system, with understanding and empathy for the value of each perspective and contribution. When students feel a sense of agency, working in tandem alongside dignity, freedom, and invention, what sort of learning environment will this be? How will it feel to be a teacher and student in that mindful space?

Presence: The X Factor

Teachers know it when they experience it: the raw confrontation of facing a classroom of students for the first time. Everyone comes into a classroom with their own set of histories, perhaps a set of fears. It can be an intimidating moment: the energy of thirty adolescents packed into the room, legs and arms spilling out over the desks, pencils tapping, feet moving, bodies rocking, a mass of fifteen-to-eighteen-year-old enthusiasm, anger, frustration, confusion, desperation, wit, joy, impulse, and deliberation—it can all become undeniably chaotic and adrenaline-inducing, all at once.

I entered the high school classroom for my first day of teaching with absolute verve, remembering all of the *education about education* that I had received. I had every lesson printed, every minute decided. I had clipboards with attendance rosters and journals with labels of my students' names. I knew how to differentiate instruction—in theory, at least; I knew about different learning styles; I intellectually *knew* what it meant to teach. The trouble was, I hadn't done it yet, and it scared the heck out of me. I was more nervous as a first-year teacher than I had been as a student entering high school, and I tried to deny my fear, letting it become absorbed by the constant action surrounding me.

I hit the ground running, with detailed plans and clipboard in tow, but it didn't always go as expected. Unforeseen events in a classroom not only caught me off guard but also seemed to undermine my entire authority. While I tried to maintain complete control, I found that when I let myself instead focus on the purpose of my teaching—supporting my students— that's when my ego began to dissolve, and I allowed myself to truly inhabit my role as a guide and mentor. My presence allowed me to invite reflection, to foster connections, and to truly recognize my students, inviting dynamic exchanges that were authentic and meaningful.

Gradually, I came to understand that the number one quality that impacted my students' experience in my classes was something I could effectively change at will: my presence. I had ample book knowledge, skills at my craft, energy spent in preparation, and as much curiosity as the most vivacious student; yet it was my ability to be fully present that made more of a difference than anything else.

> *I was a person who was always afraid to be wrong . . . yet in our class, it was about reflecting. We shared and discussed.*
>
> —Viki, *former student*

> *Something that I appreciated then, and even more so as adult, is how you invited people/students to have a conversation rather than speaking to them. That conversation that a teacher has with a student allows the student to open up and think in ways that she might not have even thought of before. Making the student an equal in a conversation not only challenges them, but it gives them more confidence and encourages them to speak and think for themselves. Turning a lecture into a dialogue makes a world of difference.*
>
> —Molly, *former student*

Once I discovered this, it was the most wonderful "aha!" moment, and also the most frightening challenge. All other criteria were within my ability to control; presence was the most elusive, and yet I knew it would be the key to being able to connect with students, and to serve as an effective teacher.

I knew what my presence looked and felt like, and I could see its effects. When I was present and fully "in flow," I would walk into a room, and I could sense subtle details surrounding me. I could see who was having a good day and who wasn't, and I could quickly decide when to move on from one exercise or discussion to a new point. I was actively listening, and the students were responsive.

It was as if a form of magic had descended upon the room. We were all aware of it, yet no one could actively pinpoint what it was. The trouble was, this presence that I had established was fleeting, not a stable certainty.

On a good day, I knew that teaching would be my life's passion. I could tell when a class was "with me" and enthralled by certain parts of the material and discussion; like this, I could teach for a lifetime. On the days when I was not engaged, it was as if I set the tone for the entire class: I would walk in uncertain or in a slightly "off" mood, and calamity would result.

I taught all levels of courses, from honors to a group thought to be the most challenging from a disciplinary standpoint—the lowest in "academic achievement." It turned out to be this group that was often the most rewarding and creative in mindset and approach. The subjects were British and American literature. I was given a textbook, key objectives, and outcomes, yet I also had free rein to design parts of the curriculum according to my choice of independent readings. There was a lot of freedom, and this open approach made such a positive difference for me: the chance to craft my lessons.

> I felt so endorsed and encouraged every time I shared a poem, whether it was in class or in poetry club. Ages fourteen and fifteen are really hard, and I think it is a time in a teenager's life when they really need teachers to believe in them, especially if they are not getting that at home. If it wasn't for your belief in me, I don't think I would be in college pursuing a degree in writing, especially with a concentration in poetry. Teachers can make such an incredible impact and I don't think they always realize that.
>
> —Charlotte, former student

I learned how to hone my own *presence,* how to shape it in the best way to engage students, how to use it to keep myself sustained and whole in the process. I was there to attend to students, and that was my purpose: to convey that everyone has significance, and every voice matters. That special evolution is distilled down into practices in this book, beginning with the "Mindfulness for Teachers" exercises, there for you to try out and experience for yourself.

Each time I focused on presence, I was practicing what I now recognize as the core of mindfulness. I was able to grow in a new way, which is true to this day. The growth and learning are constant. Much evolved and changed over the course of the next decade, in which I was given the chance to lead and develop curriculum models across all subjects, in international schools around the world. As I sought to develop the pedagogical practice that would make the best sense, I was constantly experimenting, shaping, and reshaping what would be most effective for the students who came to my classrooms every day.

Not just any students. *These students.*

I reached mindfulness in teaching through this daily practice, which is the balance of presence and focused mindfulness. In their book *Collaborative Intelligence: Thinking with People Who Think Differently,* Dawna Markova and Angie McArthur say that "attention, intention and imagination form the connective tissue of the human mind" (2015).

These three qualities, in education and beyond, are foundational elements of mindfulness. Attention, intention, and imagination. With mindfulness in mind, the attention is building awareness; the intention is toward growth and advancing; the imagination is to dream and seek that level of internal and external truth—that deep authenticity. I am again led back to mindfulness and the Three A's: Aware, Advancing, Authentic. Once they are there, presence and purpose are naturally involved in a seamless way.

While I can work to ensure that I adopt these qualities, students also need to be allowed to form their own understanding of purpose, their embodiment of presence, and their understanding of what the Three As mean—that's part of their journey, and their ownership and appreciation of learning.

On Mindset: Growth versus Fixed

There's great news to be had here. In the past, intelligence might have been thought to be static, an assessment based on one aptitude test—an ability that can apply itself in different ways, but the raw intelligence itself cannot shift. This was the thinking behind a "fixed mindset," and it created an educational world of labels and limiting beliefs. Now, with the advent of greater understanding of the brain through neuroscience findings, cognition labs, and long-term research studies, we find that intelligence itself can be altered through training and experience. And understandably, the mindset and approach that an individual has to this type of adaptive learning make a difference!

The brain becomes stronger when we learn something unfamiliar, when we seek out challenges, and when we recognize patterns and relationships between what we are learning and what we have already learned, placing it in a context that leads to even greater understanding and application possibility. We form new networks and new relationships in the brain, and we seek out even more related knowledge.

Carol Dweck (2006), in her work at Stanford, looks at motivation and mindset, investigating how different ways a learner approaches the mindset toward learning itself have big impact on outcome. Her studies found that emphasis on praising fixed achievements had less positive impact than focusing on positive feedback toward the efforts and skill development that were used in the process. In a sense, it's process over product, and the challenge along the way is a signature of growth; therefore, the challenges themselves are something to be embraced.

> *I think that having an open atmosphere is one of the best contributors to learning and growth. If you can trust yourself and anyone else with almost everything, learning opportunities tremendously increase and risks can be safely taken. I loved this type of atmosphere. Other classes felt tight and the mindset wasn't as flexible.*
>
> —Rafael, *former student*

Growth mindset, and the knowledge that intelligence is not fixed—that there is plasticity—represent liberating discoveries and a challenge to educators, as we look at how we want to shape our own classrooms. The more open and positive the environment, focusing on the invitation to explore, to grow, to challenge, and to learn through making cooperative, connected associations—this is all rooted in the values of mindfulness.

> Growth mindset, and the knowledge that intelligence is not fixed—that there is plasticity—represent liberating discoveries and a challenge to educators, as we look at how we want to shape our own classrooms.

There was an openness to thoughts and ideas. No matter what your view or stance, there would be no judgment. There would always be agreement and disagreement, and we would have a respectful and challenging discussion.

—Joseph, *former student*

Yes, it's a marvelous discovery, when we step back to think about it, underscoring emphasis on the quality of the learning environment we cultivate for ourselves and others. We want to nurture a "fail-forward" mentality, one that embraces risk and growth, and we can do this through being *Mindful by Design.*

As we'll see in the investigations of standards and models, having a Mindfulness AAA Mindset, one that incorporates growth mindset with Awareness, Advancement, and Authenticity—this is the base from which the best standards and models can be applied in a positive, successful way.

Next steps to explore:

How does mindfulness look in action, and how can these strategies fit the frameworks of current education standards and models?

Mindful Methods: How Mindfulness and *Mindful by Design* Methodology Link to Core Standards and Models

It's all about intention. Then, the form will fit the function.

—Caitlin Krause

I'm quoting myself. I've always had what I considered a good reason for teaching what I taught. More important, I always had a good reason for teaching *in the way* I taught. And, most important, my students always were part of the process, understanding why we were learning in a certain way, using a certain method.

At the beginning of my teaching career, I was often reminded that my curriculum goals, as a learner and as a teacher, should consistently be linked to outcomes. In education, this was called "backwards planning" or "backwards design": teaching toward the goals. Then, I discovered that the process, if also based in values that support the outcome goals, will naturally reinforce the outcome, too. *Outcome-driven, process-proven.*

Effective learning is rarely about the "what" endpoint—it's about the intentional "why" underneath, and the "how" defines the experience that will make the process of understanding possible. There's a great TED Talk by Simon Sinek (2009) called *How Great Leaders Inspire Action* that features the famous phrase "Start with the why." As we begin to design our teaching practices, acting as Mindful Designers, we're thinking about the reasons behind what we're choosing to use in lessons; the intentionality—which gives us the agency and empowerment to choose how to make it happen in pursuit of our learning goals. It's a rich, malleable process with its own life in it.

Where do standards and models fit this equation, then? Standards can serve as useful guiding points, giving us tools and a language to gauge progress and recognize certain societal values that are attached to learning outcomes. We can use this language to share ideas and set goals with students as active participants in the process. Ideally, standards and models give us a common language, acting as supporting structures for our learning.

> **Standards can serve as useful guiding points, giving us tools and a language to gauge progress and recognize certain societal values that are attached to learning outcomes.**

Standards and models do not replace deep learning goals. The larger intentional goals of our education systems relate to values and intention. These values link back to mindfulness practices, which invite that deeper reflection. See Chapter 3, "Mindfulness for Teachers," to effectively initiate a personal practice in which you compare your own system of values to your teaching practices. This is the driving force, and the essential passion behind what you are doing. Students have these, too—and your classroom and school share a larger set of values, which can become the culture of the organization.

Standards and models, then, are not a replacement for these values, nor are they the reason behind the learning. They can serve as useful tools for reflection about teaching and learning practices, and they can often drive us to think even more deeply about the intentionality behind our education designs.

A Note on Formative and Summative Assessment

Conversations about standards seem inevitably to link to considerations of evaluation methods. Some assessment forms are up to us, as educators, to choose—others are delivered and required by mandate. In either case, students take their cues from us about how we interpret and use the assessments, whether we approach them as guideposts for growth or endpoints for judgment and critique. We can incorporate them and give assessments attention as we see fit.

In essence, summative assessments don't always seem to convey mindfulness values because they can be high-stakes, stress-inducing, and also static judgments of ability, which students might construe as measures of their own self-worth. Note that this doesn't have to be the case, though—both formative and summative assessments can be used in mindful ways if students are given enough support, feedback, explanation, alternatives, and reflective time to use the assessment as a tool for their own learning. As with everything, it's more about *why* and *how* we decide to approach the method.

Formative assessment is designed to give groups and individuals guidance toward future growth, goals, and progress. As Stephen and Jan Chappuis (2008) note in a concise overview of assessment purposes in the January 2008 issue of *Educational Leadership*, "how the results are used is what determines whether the assessment is formative or summative."

If most effective learning is judged to be formative, with supportive feedback, then summative feedback (including high-stakes testing and certain grading strategies) can be augmented/replaced with methods that give students more active, conversational feedback, authority, agency, and inclusion in the evaluation methods. This allows students to have the ability to play a role in articulating their own growth strategies.

I mention this because, in the current education landscape, with rich access to both online resources and in-person learning, we have the opportunity to reshape classrooms, creating the ideal atmosphere for student-driven inquiry, using a teacher as a curator, mentor, guide, and reflective co-creator—a modern Socrates!

Let's take a look at some of the commonly used standards and models to see how they are in consonance with our "Mindfulness AAA (Aware, Advancing, Authentic) Mindset." For this book's purposes, we're introducing and addressing examples of standards and models in this chapter, expecting that the assessment landscape will continue to adapt and change. Therefore, good advice is to follow current news and online updates from your mindful "PLN" (personal learning network), as well as the companion website, **caitlinkrause.com**, to access the best, most current external links, practices, measures, models, and ever-evolving lingo!

Each exercise in Chapters 3 and 4 can also be linked to these standards and models. Since specific standards vary by grade level, and the geographic location and type of school culture/pedagogy often play a role in selecting standards to align with, each individual user of this book will be able to map the alignment that best suits their individual conditions. The specific alignment will be context-dependent.

The classroom exercises are designed to be able to be modified to suit your specific curriculum needs, and they are linkable to the standards, and relatable to models. Let's jump in and explore several that are especially prominent, linked to the Mindfulness AAA Mindset and *Mindful by Design* methodolgy.

Standards and Models

Common Core Standards

Operating with an AAA Mindset means recognizing where there are areas for learning growth, and the Common Core Standards are used (in the United States) as one effort to "define expectations for what students should know and be able to do by the end of each grade" (2018b). The goal of the Common Core is to prepare all students for success in college, career, and life. Each state leads its own efforts in adopting, implementing, and measuring the standards, as an interactive map on the website displays.

Addressing frequently asked questions, the website reads: "The Common Core is *not* a curriculum. It is a clear set of shared goals and expectations for what knowledge and skills will help our students succeed. Local teachers, principals, superintendents, and others will decide how the standards are to be met. Teachers will continue to devise lesson plans and tailor instruction to the individual needs of the students in their

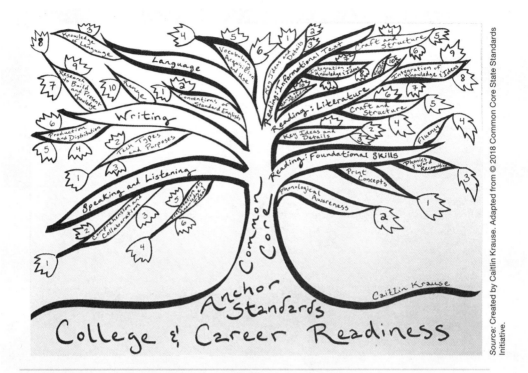

Figure 1.1 • Common Core ELA/Literacy Anchor Standards Tree

A metaphor for connected skill-building across grades and content areas, this tree illustrates the main six branches reflecting strands, with sub-branches representing themed groupings of standards. The number on each leaf signifies the specific standard, attached to its focus area, to show links and support structures for developing each standard and strand from the ground up. For more details, please visit **caitlinkrause.com.**

classrooms." The Common Core doesn't replace teaching, and it doesn't replace each teacher in a classroom having the ability to envision, build, and synthesize curriculum. The mindfulness exercises in this book offer great ideas and also freedom for teachers to address the standards and personalize their approaches to curriculum, with mindfulness values embedded.

> The Common Core doesn't replace teaching, and it doesn't replace each teacher in a classroom having the ability to envision, build, and synthesize curriculum.

Although the Common Core is a set of standards in mathematics and ELA (English Language Arts)/Literacy, they can be applied to different areas of curriculum, and many educational institutions have applied the standards in different ways, recognizing inter-disciplinary links and overlaps. Figure 1.2 shows Tina Cheuk (2013) and the Stanford Graduate School of Education's work to demonstrate overlaps in pedagogical approaches to the Common Core State Standards (CCSS) in Math and ELA, also overlapping with the NGSS (Next Generation Science Standards) science and engineering practices. The exercises in *Mindful by Design* involve the deep, complex reasoning, engagement, expression, and analyses that the CCSS and NGSS encourage and articulate across the curriculum.

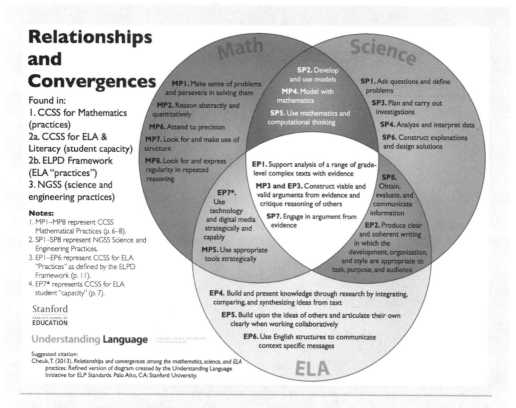

Relationships and Convergences

Found in:
1. CCSS for Mathematics (practices)
2a. CCSS for ELA & Literacy (student capacity)
2b. ELPD Framework (ELA "practices")
3. NGSS (science and engineering practices)

Notes:
1. MP1–MP8 represent CCSS Mathematical Practices (p. 6–8).
2. SP1–SP8 represent NGSS Science and Engineering Practices.
3. EP1–EP6 represent CCSS for ELA "Practices" as defined by the ELPD Framework (p. 11).
4. EP7* represents CCSS for ELA student "capacity" (p. 7).

Stanford
GRADUATE SCHOOL OF
EDUCATION

Understanding **Language**   Language, Literacy, and Learning in the Content Areas

Suggested citation:
Cheuk, T. (2013). *Relationships and convergences among the mathematics, science, and ELA practices.* Refined version of diagram created by the Understanding Language Initiative for ELP Standards. Palo Alto, CA: Stanford University.

Math

MP1. Make sense of problems and persevere in solving them
MP2. Reason abstractly and quantitatively
MP6. Attend to precision
MP7. Look for and make use of structure
MP8. Look for and express regularity in repeated reasoning
EP7*. Use technology and digital media strategically and capably
MP5. Use appropriate tools strategically

Science

SP2. Develop and use models
MP4. Model with mathematics
SP5. Use mathematics and computational thinking
SP1. Ask questions and define problems
SP3. Plan and carry out investigations
SP4. Analyze and interpret data
SP6. Construct explanations and design solutions

EP1. Support analysis of a range of grade-level complex texts with evidence
MP3 and EP3. Construct viable and valid arguments from evidence and critique reasoning of others
SP7. Engage in argument from evidence
SP8. Obtain, evaluate, and communicate information
EP2. Produce clear and coherent writing in which the development, organization, and style are appropriate to task, purpose, and audience

EP4. Build and present knowledge through research by integrating, comparing, and synthesizing ideas from text
EP5. Build upon the ideas of others and articulate their own clearly when working collaboratively
EP6. Use English structures to communicate context specific messages

ELA

Figure 1.2 • Common Skills Developed among Science, Math, and ELA, Relationships and Convergences: Intersections between CCSS and NGSS

In addition to the grade-level standards, the Common Core profile of a learner links well with *Mindful by Design* exercises and overall values. As the Common Core website states, "Students who are college and career ready in reading, writing, speaking, listening and language" are able to exhibit these capacities:

▶ They demonstrate independence.

▶ They build strong content knowledge.

▶ They respond to the varying demands of audience, task, purpose, and discipline.

▶ They comprehend as well as critique.

▶ They value evidence.

▶ They use technology and digital media strategically and capably.

▶ They come to understand other perspectives and cultures.

Source: ©2018 Common Core State Standards Initiative.

A learner who is developing traits and capacities associated with the Common Core State Standards is certainly using a future-forward mindset—one that is Aware, Advancing, and Authentic in nature, reinforced by active practice in a learning environment.

ISTE Student Standards

Released in 2016, the International Society for Technology in Education (ISTE) Student Standards reflect the commitment of the organization to promote developing a broad range of skills and attitudes, including agility, adaptability, and empowered curiosity, to ensure that students are future-ready. It's a universal web, well displayed as a seven-part map, shown in Figure 1.2. The *Mindful by Design* student exercises can each be correlated with several of the ISTE standards, encompassing all of the values.

Here are some of the *Mindful by Design* classroom exercises from Chapter 4, used to illustrate the complements between mindfulness and the ISTE Student Standards:

Empowered Learner: Confidence and capability are part of the *Mindful by Design* approach. Thinking about the four cornerstones—Dignity, Freedom, Invention, and Agency—what could be more empowering than having these as foundational elements and cultural values in a learning community? We can smile and embrace our identities as mindful individuals, empowering ourselves and fellow learners on a lifelong journey. As illustrations, the exercises "Story of My Name" and "Storytelling, Empathy, and Kindness" are just two examples of ways that learners feel more recognized, welcomed, and empowered in our classrooms.

Global Connector: Connection and a global mindset are key aspects of a mindfulness outlook and approach to learning. Our AAA mindset spans the globe, and the curiosity with which we approach broad topics and systems is what helps to serve as a guide. In the exercise "The Danger of a Single Story," for example, we cultivate our skills as global connectors, recognizing the multiplicity within cultures and identities and increasing our awareness about complexity and connection.

Creative Communicator: The ability to communicate effectively, with clarity and precision, cannot be stressed enough in the modern environment of quick transmissions and multiple ways of connecting and learning. Our goal, as *Mindful by Design* learners, is to amplify humanity as we connect with care, with creativity, and with a natural joy that motivates us to explore and express. You can find examples of how we practice creative communication in "Great Debates: 'Fire and Ice,'" "Mindful Journaling," and "Out of This World," among others.

> *Our class was my first experience in seeing words beyond a textbook definition. Previously, I read to regurgitate. Tests, book reports, cold calls in class. The class helped me understand that the reality of words and communication had a lot more depth to it. It was a step beyond an educational "system," offering an approach that would drive lifelong creativity.*
>
> —Ellen, *former student*

Digital Citizen: The fact that there is an exercise titled "Digital Mindful Citizen" in Chapter 4 is a testament to the importance of this topic. Notice that the "digital" is modifying the identity "Mindful Citizen." With a Mindfulness AAA Mindset, we view a digital citizen as a mindful citizen, and the digital applications stem from those core values and ways of being. It gives great consonance to what we do, and to the care we see in and beyond the physical classroom learning space. There is a SEL (social and emotional learning) component here, too. As Matthieu Ricard (2018) has said, mindfulness should be called "kindfulness," and this is applied kindfulness to all that we learn, giving us even greater presence and purpose.

> *I think learning is about ownership in the sense that a teacher can give a student all the tools to succeed and to learn, but it is still up to the student to use these tools. A student can't be forced to learn; they really need to want to learn and put the effort in. With the right balance, I believe that both the individual and the group can be encouraged. Especially when working in a group, I think a teacher can emphasize that a group works best when each individual brings their own talents and ideas to the table.*
>
> —Charlotte, *former student*

Knowledge Constructor: Part of constructing knowledge is about noticing detail, and about distilling information, giving it context and meaning. Having the ability to do this, smoothly, rationally, and with a powerful AAA mindset, is what *Mindful by Design* methodology supports and enables, through practice and application. One exercise example that shows this in action is "Four P's: Projects, Passion, Peers, and Play," which looks at how knowledge is gathered, researched, and then applied to build a meaningful, creative invention. As ISTE.org (2018) states, "Students build knowledge by actively exploring real-world issues and problems, developing ideas and theories and pursuing answers and solutions." That comes to life in the Mindfulness AAA Mindset, *Mindful by Design* methodology and exercises.

Innovative Designer: *Mindful by Design* is all about having a designer's mindset, and all of the exercises showcase this in different ways. "Nature as Teacher: Bold Biomimicry and Design Thinking," for example, allows learners to look to nature as a model, then design different solutions that are inspired by the purpose and intention underneath. The creativity and freedom necessary to approach these topics is underscored by a Mindfulness AAA Mindset, a way of being that embodies an innovative designer.

Computational Thinker: CT skills involve using digital tools and applying them effectively. Using a Mindfulness AAA Mindset, we are able to have the awareness and empathy for deeper connections and motivations behind what we are addressing in abstract computations. For example, the "Architecture and Virtual Worlds" exercises allow students to apply CT skills with mindful purpose and deeper reasoning. As part of using mindfulness with CT, we can also understand how to use data and processing to innovate solutions that result in contributing to a better world. Thus, the way that students approach everything from coding VR environments to Big Data analyses all involve mindfulness skills and values at a foundational level.

There are detailed descriptions of the ISTE standards, as well as classroom supplements available online at ISTE.org.

IB Learner Profile

Well recognized as a global standard for student learning, the International Baccalaureate Learner Profile describes the characteristics of a globally minded, actively engaged student, addressing the ideal outcomes for international education. It nicely

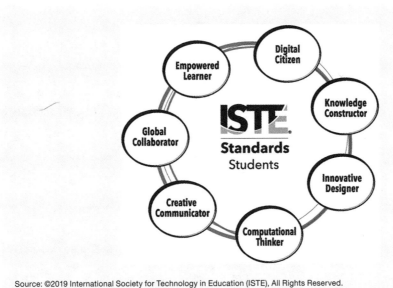

Figure 1.3 • ISTE Student Standards

complements mindfulness values, looking at the context of learning across a wide range of descriptors, each of which represents a component of the core learning principles. The full profile describes an interdisciplinary, modern learner who represents the vision of operating with a Mindfulness AAA Mindset: active, confident, caring, compassionate change-makers who encompass diverse cultures, backgrounds, and beliefs.

The IB Learner Profile aims to develop learners who are:

▶ Inquirers	▶ Open-minded
▶ Knowledgeable	▶ Caring
▶ Thinkers	▶ Risk-takers
▶ Communicators	▶ Balanced
▶ Principled	▶ Reflective

Creative Convergence: "Intersectionality" and a Mindfulness AAA Mindset

Much is evolving in the way that standards are applied in education practices. It's our larger goal, with a Mindfulness AAA Mindset and *Mindful by Design* methodology, to constantly engage with these standards, as if we're standing at the crossing points, incorporating them into our teaching practices in ways that amplify students' appreciation of the intersectionality of disciplines, philosophies, and global goals.

These standards essentially represent what a community cares about; we can reflect upon them in our learning environments, effectively putting them to use in ways that align with our own values and larger objectives. Again—and as ever, starting with ourselves—*starting with the why* makes all the difference.

Next, we'll take a look at what that classroom actually looks like when we give a Mindfulness AAA Mindset and *Mindful by Design* methodology and exercises both our attention *and* intention. How can we envision that space?

CHAPTER 2

Creating a Mindful Learning Environment

Any human anywhere will blossom in a hundred unexpected talents and capacities simply by being given the opportunity to do so.

—Doris Lessing, 1919 (quoted in Chang, 2006)

Teaching in a mindful classroom is about making opportunities possible. It's much like being a skilled conductor—it might not be *apparent*, yet a lot of careful, intentional planning, practice, and preparation go into setting up the right relationship and environment for each musician in that orchestra to play their instrument with passion and joy, in the way it was meant to be played. They might be at the beginning stages of self-awareness, confidence, trust, and curiosity—the discovery of talents and capacities is part of the process. We set up a mindful classroom environment that reflects *Mindful by Design* values in three ways: first, by envisioning the physical environment and how it should evolve over weeks and months; second, by considering tools that foster mindfulness; and third, by attending to the routines that foster the intellectual and cultural environment that we want for learners in the classroom space together.

> I feel that Authenticity was the most important of the Three As. I still remember when you would have us move into a circle and take turns sharing thoughts and ideas. It was important to respect others' opinions and think about them critically, without judgment, in order to have a productive and quality discussion.
>
> —Joseph, former student

The architecture of the physical space sets the stage for learning. Here are some primary suggestions simply to pay attention to, as you design your own classroom space and a workflow that supports your goals to maximize mindfulness.

The Space

Questions to consider about the space, or physical environment, of the classroom:

- How do the temperature and lighting look and feel?
- Can students move around the classroom easily?
- Does the furniture support the types of collaborative experiences you want to create?
- Do students know where to find the materials they might need to access as resources?
- How are the acoustics?
- What's the view like from each student's vantage point?
- Can students easily "switch positions"—or are they always stationed at the same place?
- What is the overall mood of the room? For whom was it created? Who is the intended audience?

I try to keep these questions in mind throughout the year, not just at the beginning, when setting up my classrooms. And we each face different parameters, constraints, and opportunities, which make these questions all the more important. I understand that we don't all have our dream spaces of classrooms, and the idea here is to work with what we have, using it to the advantage of incredible experiences. Sometimes, less is more, and it's about allowing for mindful space.

In my years of teaching, I have taught in countless classrooms, shared rooms, co-taught, and moved up and down floor levels with a rolling cart of supplies, with five minutes of passing time between periods. I have been in spaces that combine indoor and outdoor; I have had a mix of tables, chairs, and beanbags. One room had a walk-out balcony, some had couches, some had desks and tables, and others had fixed chairs with wraparound desks. There have been as many setups as we could imagine, and my mindset is to "roll with it," making each work, even if there are obstacles to overcome.

When I think of how my classrooms have looked across the span of different subjects, grade levels, spaces, and locations, two truths become clear: there are no hard-and-fast rules, and giving learners the chance to "face each other" makes a difference in communication and community-building. It's all about openness and emphasizing connection.

Variation of form and consistent intentionality of values have impact. I like to play around with the setup, and I'm a firm believer that form fits function, and vice-versa. If you create a certain type of feeling in the space, students will respond to it, and you can also enlist them as users in a system. Thinking about the design of your classroom as a living, breathing environment, with students' interactive conversations and reflective practices as focuses, is key—in that way, you can create the best overall experience possible, through using the architecture of the physical space.

For example, while teaching in Belgium, I discovered (to my dismay, as I love morning light and sports!) that the sun doesn't rise in winter months until nearly 9:00 a.m. on some days. Coupled with the perpetual low cloud-cover, this meant we would start the first class when it was still dark outside! In addition, the school community included some middle school students commuting a long distance to attend this English-language international school. By the time they arrived to class, many were still waking up, bleary-eyed, and needing to ease gently into the day's activities, so I began to start my first classes with a lower lighting—not turning on all of the energy-saving fluorescent lights that can be harsh and abrupt in the winter months. Simply listening to community needs had great results. I began to incorporate mindfulness writing and poetry into the morning, easing into more active exercises as fit our natural pace, and this kept the learning fluid, meaningful, and natural.

I suggest the following considerations in the physical space, all of which are ideas I've created myself in response to some of the different space options and desk/table combinations I've had as resources.

Circles—Everyone Sees Each Other

This is useful for certain times, sharing in class, and it's great to get used to including it in the routine. The key here is to make sure that *no one's back is to another person.*

Entrust students with helping you to move the desks into a circle formation, and/or have certain times when you move desks to the side and sit on the floor. Conduct a few systematic classroom restructuring times when students get used to the routine of creating a circle. This helps to make the process smooth and quick. Believe me, it makes such a difference when students are sharing! There's research to support this—just look into "Circle of Trust Approach" (Center for Courage & Renewal, 2018), "Harkness Method" (Shapiro, 2001), publications by Rachael Kessler (2014), and more. It also simply makes sense that a mindful classroom is one in which students have real, active, "face-to-face time" with each other.

A former student, Viki, reflected on our classroom environment: "I just loved the room itself—it was so open and airy, with big windows, and I think that was perfectly fitting for the kind of environment we had to begin with. . . . And, to easily get in circles, so that we could face each other . . . and talk directly, rather than have everyone face front, looking at each other's backs."

> *There was encouragement, and that makes a difference.*
>
> —Viki, *former student*

> *[Our school] was such a competitive place, and entering your classroom, none of that mattered.*
>
> —Charlotte, *former student*

> *It's a better environment, when a teacher treats everyone as if each person has something to offer.*
>
> —Viki

> *It's about vulnerability, too. We can open up. Even though you didn't force us to always share, you encouraged and invited us to speak our minds.*
>
> —Charlotte

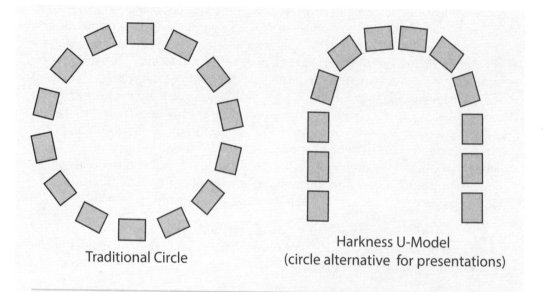

Traditional Circle

Harkness U-Model
(circle alternative for presentations)

Figure 2.1 • Circles

Photo courtesy of Stephanie Slabbert.

Figure 2.2 • Classroom Space Example

This classroom space where I taught had movable "desks," which were individual tables with legs that had wheels at the base, easy to move around. Students could easily form table groups with these desks, which could also form a larger oval shape. See what adaptations are possible to suit your needs and desires! And check out my online resources for guides about where to buy the desks.

Tips: After forming the circle and/or *U*-shape, do a check-in, asking the group if everyone can see everyone else. You can time this, in the future, turning it into a speed competition for circle formation. The point is that, without the extra check-in, some students might be obstructed and/or inadvertently blocked out from the circle, and they will rarely advocate for themselves. Having the group do a "left/right check" lets everyone actively look out for one another.

Desk/Table Groups of Four

Keynote speaker and Tufts professor Chris B. Rogers (2018) talks a lot about ways to encourage open inquiry in education. He announced, "My favorite teaching technology is a table," to the group of teachers with a certain level of humor-meets-candor when he spoke at a recent "Learning and the Brain" conference about engineering mindset. As I've asked different influential teachers and collaborators to share insights about their own classroom architecture and mindful layouts, what come up, time and time again, are opportunities for focus and connection. The raw materials and physical structures set the stage.

Grouping students in desk or table groups of a magic "four" number allows for, mathematically speaking, five basic grouping variations. You can have a group that is "all four" together as a team, all four as individuals, partners along verticals, partners along horizontals, or partners at diagonals. You can also create subdivisions and roles within the groupings, and it's small enough that the table groups develop trust and relationships with one another. No one gets lost in the mix. Everyone has a voice. You're free to create some wonderful complements here, which I discuss in the "Routines" section later in this chapter. I actively aim to mix it up, trying out different groupings along a theme—for example, I would use a table seating for the length of a unit or focus of study and then might switch to a new formation that fits a new theme.

I would not announce the changes days ahead—only on the day of initiating a seating change. Sometimes, students would anticipate a new formation and make a special request to sit near a friend, or sometimes to sit apart from someone they found challenging. What I found, in general, is that creating community means that I look at the whole group, which is the sum of its parts. While I constantly consider mental, physical, and emotional needs when forming groupings, I also try to think more broadly about what could offer the most growth, in mixing familiarity with challenges, in creating diversity of opinion and choice—*and* in fostering inclusion and kindness. This applies to abilities, personalities, gender, culture, language development—every differentiator imaginable. Back to fostering a welcoming community, how can we welcome interactions and shared stories across and beyond perceived boundaries? How can we see multiplicities in each individual? As Walt Whitman said in his poem "Song of Myself," "I am large, I contain multitudes." He was talking about seeming contradictions, about identity being more than one thing; more than one element or trademark we might see and recognize first in another. I apply that concept directly to my teaching. If I taught a student who had been labeled "quiet," for example, I looked to see the fullness of her attributes, parts that were certainly also animating her larger story, even if less apparent at first look. Each of us contains multitudes of stories and backgrounds, and in a classroom, it's critical to see learners' behaviors, identities, and traits as diverse and plastic. We all need to stay curious and open to hearing each other's many stories.

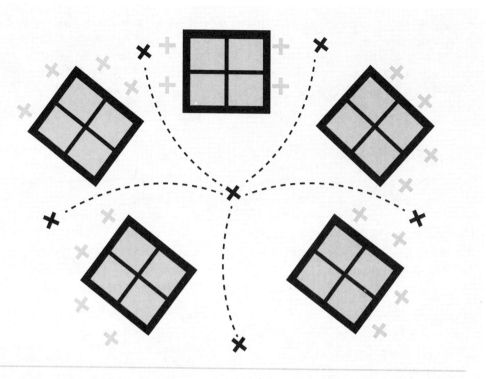

Figure 2.3 • Desk/Table Groups of Four

This is part of the *Mindful by Design* mindset: to stay open and adaptive. What are my overall goals as an educator, in creating teams? I think about all of this. That being said, my groupings have looked like everything under the sun—tables/groups of what might be perceived as all-introverts together, groupings of a mix of introverts/extroverts, groupings of all females or all males, mixes of males and females, variations and similarities in learning styles, and the examples go on and on. We are connectors, in many shapes and forms. You are giving students an opportunity to experience transformation, growth, and variety. To be surprised. You are also teaching them to find joy, challenge, and possibility along the way. In a full world of opportunities, with a wealth of advantages that reflect diversity and change, we need to send a message to learners to embrace multiplicities as an advantage.

Pinball Theater

One of my favorite formations for a class performance or something that might involve a "front" of a room, whether that involves a smartboard, is something I call "pinball theater" because the angle reminds me of a pinball machine, with the gravity directed toward the "front," yet with many ways that a conversation could happily bounce. Essentially, traditional classrooms might have rows and/or columns of desks, and the pinball theater concept reshapes this to have the desks facing slightly inward along a central axis, which can open up to form a large central aisle or runway so that students can turn easily to see each other's faces. It's not distracting, though, away from the focus on the perceived "front" of the room. What it does for me, if I can apply my feeling for a classroom feng shui of sorts, is it moves the energy of the room to flow around the center space. It lets feedback become more inviting, as each student belongs in the space and can easily form partners and small groups, as shown in Figure 2.4. It can also be great for interactive performances and for you, as the teacher, to easily reach each area of the room.

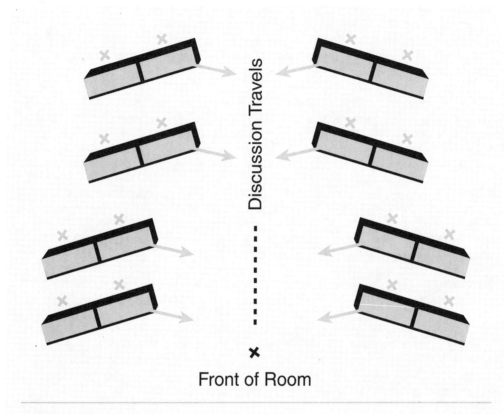

Figure 2.4 • Pinball Theater

On Designing Mindful Learning Spaces

In thinking about the care that underpins (unintentional pun) my own intentional design of effective learning spaces, I reached out to educators who inspire me in their dedication to building mindful environments. I asked them about what they value, and how they go about designing an effective classroom space that promotes a *Mindful by Design* mindset, open to learning, embodying that AAA multifaceted definition of mindfulness.

Ewan McIntosh founded NoTosh (notosh.com) in 2009 as a global consultancy that focuses on innovation and creativity—*thinking differently* and embracing mindful metacognition are fundamental to his work. I asked Ewan to answer one simple yet complex question: *"What do you prioritize when you're designing spaces for learning?"*

Ewan gave the following response: "Prioritize the kind of learning you want to see, to feel, to hear. And then just make the changes in practice before you touch the phone to call an architect, or put out that tender document, or head down to IKEA. In most schools the real innovation I see in space design does not come from adding things—it comes from stripping them away. Schools generally have too much furniture in too small a space, with too many constraints on time to manage much more than what one might call 'traditional' teaching and learning."

It's clear that there's a level of metacognition with space design that takes mindfulness and patience to establish. The true, lasting, effective changes in space design take time, because they evolve as educators consider, prototype, and investigate solutions, allowing the community to drive and experience the transformation rather than have it prescribed. This type of active awareness hinges on communication, trust, risk-taking, listening, and authenticity. Mindfulness is involved.

Another advocate for intentional design is Ben Kestner, an educator, leader, and school designer. He and his wife, Lisa, also an experienced educator, co-founded the Glacier Lake School (glacierlakeschool.com) in Montana in 2013. Based on core values of democracy and freedom, the Glacier Lake School puts children's proclivities, voices, and free choices at the heart of its design.

I first met Ben and Lisa at St. John's International School in Waterloo, Belgium, where Ben served as principal of the middle school and I taught eighth-grade English. Many facets were remarkable about the community that was created and shared there. Three qualities stand out in my memory, contributing to the exceptional nature of our experience: autonomy, nonownership, and curiosity.

Autonomy: As learners and teachers, we had the freedom to create and to influence our own pathways and journeys. In this way, everyone belonged, with great freedom.

Nonownership: No teacher or student "owned" a learning space—even in the classrooms where we taught. There was a sense of co-ownership and mutuality. It was not "my" classroom, nor were any other spaces possessed by teachers. We were not considered the grand "sages on stages" of knowledge; my role was to facilitate learning, opening up opportunities for students to take authority and direction as they were ready.

Curiosity: Along these lines, teachers were also engaged, as students were, in curiosity-driven learning, asking questions, and exploring different resources and links that uncover new meaning. We, as teachers, formed a voluntary group that met weekly after school to learn and share new pedagogical research, findings, and community practices. We talked about values, and our own curiosity drove us to help to shape a school culture in which everyone had a voice.

When I asked Ben about how to plan and design open, flexible learning spaces, he painted a colorful picture:

> As for learning spaces in a democratic free school like ours goes, that's hard for me to explain. When someone walks around a school like ours, they should be able to see multiple opportunities for learning. We don't have designated classrooms as such. So, for example, we have a big multipurpose room with Mixed Martial Arts gym–style mats covering half and the other half, couches, a table and chairs, and some cubbies. At any time of the day, many different things might be happening. Some kids might be doing gymnastics on the mats, while some others sit on the couches reading and someone else might be watching the gymnastics sitting at the table. We do have some rooms which lean toward a particular activity or activities. For example, we

have a craft/art room which also has a long work bench with tools and so forth, and a sewing area with sewing machine and the like. We have a room which looks like a classroom (has the whiteboard and tables and chairs!) but it also doubles up as a music room (has piano/keyboards in it, for example). That's not to say that if the room isn't booked you can't do anything else in it. We have a library which doubles as a quiet room for quiet studying and reading, or napping!

The design of the Glacier Lake School is purposefully free, giving students all the tools they need to explore at their own pace, using their own style and methods. Ben calls it a "learning environment we call school within a philosophy which has self-direction/mixed age learning and democracy at its core. The spaces have multiple uses, since our curriculum is only limited by the imagination of the student." The implicit message in this design is that the community has values of trust and inclusion, in giving liberty for self-direction, with ample support and care. Mindfulness involved in the environmental design helps a student to be able to articulate needs and reflect on their own learning journey.

When educators put this level of mindful attention into the design of the space, the learners can tell, and they feel invited to participate in the process, which helps to make the learning authentic, a hallmark of mindfulness.

Education design specialist Rebecca Louise Hare (2016), co-author of *The Space,* said in an online video, "We spend countless hours thinking about what we're teaching, and very little time thinking about where we are teaching, but the truth is, where our students learn matters. You have to ask yourself, *Are they guests, or are they collaborators?*"

Every teacher, and every student, can be a mindful designer, looking at their own curriculum and being thoughtful and intentional about the living experience they want to create, actively aware of what will enable and empower the most effective learning and thriving! It's an exciting prospect, to consider all the ways to embrace a *Mindful by Design* level of consciousness when it comes to the physical space.

The key aspect I find in all mindful learning spaces is "flow"—the spaces all have some element of allowing movement and collaboration rather than stasis. Each space might be different, with a unique set of constraints, and mindful educators have found ways to transform their environments into collaborative "flow spaces."

There are many more examples and ideas that will spark your own mindful ideas, giving you tips and tricks, allowing you to hack classroom design in the way that fits your needs.

For more resources and ideas, I suggest a few articles on the companion website that can be inspiring and helpful for thinking outside the box—especially if you're feeling as if you teach inside of one! Access the companion website at **caitlinkrause.com.**

There are many ways to consider mindful architecture and space design, keeping in mind that *you* and your mindset are a key element!

The Tools

While I like to say that the best mindfulness tool is an open mind, there are a few staples that add to fostering a mindful environment. And though I could be advocating for specific colors of Post-its, or analog maker kits, or the use of a certain type of 1:1 tablet or computer, or the top twenty learning apps that complement a *Mindful by Design* methodology, those would all make for better blog posts in the future—stay tuned! Here, in this book, the tools I will mention are timeless, and my online posts on **caitlinkrause.com** will reference the "latest and greatest" updates for mindfulness, learning, and *Mindful by Design* architecture and design as they evolve and adapt to changing times. And the truth is, some of the apps and gadgets change, and we should first be prioritizing the values underneath, and then looking at what fits our needs best.

Namely, using *Mindful by Design* tools and approaches in two primary categories, *reflection* and *sharing ideas*, are a strong way to make sure the Mindfulness AAA Mindset and four cornerstones can flourish in classroom culture action. Let's look specifically at the primary tools of journals for reflection, and publication means for spreading ideas.

Journals—A Reflective Space for Exploring

I'm bringing up journals as a prime consideration in classroom formation because they make that much of a difference—they are not an activity or an exercise; they are elemental to the operations of a classroom space. There are whole courses built upon the uses of journals, and ample evidence about the proven benefits of journaling practices, for everything from boosting creativity to stress release to organization to self-esteem. Journalist Clive Thompson (2015), who writes about technology and everyday life, gave a great INBOUND Bold Talk about the power of words and the writing process itself, both handwritten and typed. As a writer and educator, I use journals as a writing vehicle; a classroom staple for collecting thoughts, quotes, snippets, or seeds of information that might later turn into a larger project.

I tell students that journals are our "garden space." Using a term I love from a poet, friend, and mentor, Janet Sylvester, it's all about inviting the "mulch" in our creative space. Our garden needs earth, mulch, twigs, and leaves, as well as water and sunlight—it all works together to help to fuel blooming.

When I come to class, I'll bring journals with me, to show what I mean. In any area of curriculum, they are the garden, because they foster the mindfulness process of *reflection*. They create an open space that invites deep thinking. Encourage students to keep a journal that is devoted to class exercises. Write together alongside students—I cannot overemphasize the camaraderie that is created.

Tips: Encourage students to decorate and personalize journals at the beginning of the year, even dedicating some class time to it together. This encourages the fun nature of it.

Consider having a crate or shelf in class where students can store journals, rather than risk them forgetting their journals at home. The upside is that the journals will always be in class this way. The downside is that students will often get so into the exercises they'll want to have the journals with them at home. In some ways, this is a great problem to have, because it shows they see connections between what's happening in class and the "outside world"! Cheers to the cross-pollination. One solution is to tell students that *you trust them to care for the journals and keep track of them, bringing them to class. An alternate solution, which I favor, is to let students keep multiple journals—so that the one they use "out of class" can become a feeder, which they'll bring to class to inspire the in-class journal exercises. This keeps it simple for you, too, as a teacher keeping track of the journals!*

A great resource on journals and keeping reflective writing exercises is Linda Rief, a teacher who advocates for notebooks in class, to accompany curriculum. It's all about offering choices and challenges that increase students' means of honing voice and expression. In Linda's words, "To write or draw everything you think or feel or believe, because your thinking matters." Journals are an exercise in thinking itself.

Publishing Ideas—Blogging, Vlogging, Sharing!

When students and teachers are using a Mindfulness AAA Mindset, they are focused on presence, looking to connect authentically with each other and the world. This is why giving opportunities for communication that matters—showing awareness, looking to advance, and stretch authentically (AAA mindset)— is part of the design of the classroom space.

If we want students to own their ideas, seeing the authenticity in what they are creating, we can show this by inviting them to share their ideas with more eyes than our own. As teachers and the "assessors" of materials, so often we denigrate the learning process by turning it into a "must pass muster" situation, in which students come to us asking, "Is this good enough?" or "What grade do I get?" If students ask me these questions, I flip them into a conversation about what they see in their own work, and how it relates to what they were aiming to accomplish. I ask them about their intended audience, which is certainly broader than just me! I want them to see that they have impact. Once they see this, a fire ignites. Learning becomes something beyond the confines of the classroom.

Publication reinforces the mindset that the ideas students have are worth sharing. And publishing can be powerful, because it creates connection. When students are able to publish their creations, a live link forms between them and a larger audience, and a certain sense of pride, projection, curiosity, creativity, and identity is evident.

I once had a colleague who avoided the term *showcasing*—in fact, he derided it so much it now triggers a reaction in me, too. I think the aversion came from the connotation of "showcase" as some sort of stage on which to brag, boast, and flaunt. It looks one-sided and lacks the meaningful connection that happens when there is what I think of as "profound publishing"—sharing what one has crafted with purpose and intention; sharing when one *has an audience in mind and cares about the interaction.* Publishing is not showcasing. Publishing is intentional connection.

This doesn't mean that what is published needs to be *perfect*—the opposite is often useful, sharing work that is "off the cuff" or "stream of consciousness"—to connect and gather ideas in a crowd-sourced way. In this way, I firmly believe that "published" online work can be a formative stage of the craft. However, it's not haphazard and slapdash—it shows care for what the student is creating.

Sometimes, students would tell me they believed no one was reading their blog posts, and the posting became the same "busywork" that used to be in the form of the much-maligned *worksheet*—an invitation for boredom and feelings of inconsequence.

Seymour Papert (2018) famously said, "The reason most kids don't like school is not that the work is too hard, but that it is utterly boring." In my view, boredom is a mindset—and anything can be engaging; it's about the approach. Papert (who, by the way, is one of my favorite legendary educators to quote) also emphasized discovery and wonder as being key parts of the process: "The scandal of education is that every time you teach something, you deprive a [student] of the pleasure and benefit of discovery." When students discover something, and recognize its meaning, they will want to articulate that journey in some sort of way of sharing, which is where publication plays a role. And I would take this a step further—if we, as teachers, design publication opportunities that are more chore than game, and less challenge than simply a check-off, then students will view the merit of the process—and perhaps their own personal merit—as meaningless.

The publication is intentional in all cases, just as every well-acted play performed before an audience is one in which the actors care about their audience, and one can feel the sensation of that live energy, distinguishing it from any other medium.

I encourage blogging, vlogging, and sharing—*if it's with intention!* Talk about the intentions and goals as outcomes, and make it clear to students that the publication has an audience and an intention behind the sharing. There are many reasons to publish, including to boost engagement with a wider audience, increase students' sense of pride and ownership in their work, and let them practice ways of adopting different writing voices that align with purpose. For example, if what is being shared is a persuasive piece meant to convince the audience of a point, the writer focuses on rhetorical strategies and authority. If the writing is a poetic expression, the writer might take a daring leap in representing an idea, image, or concept, choosing line breaks, words, and metaphors that capture a certain spirit or mood. Writing is a process in self-development, and exploring the dynamics of intended audience is part of the complexity.

For support and even more ideas about ways to make expression and publication come alive, I suggest talking with IT specialists, and finding a way to build publication opportunities both locally and globally!

It will be equally valuable to foster relationships with fellow educators and student communities in which you are also the audience. Think about peer audiences, as well as other ages with which to interact. The more fun and engaging you make the dynamic, the more students will see it as joyful and motivational, too. We, as teachers, have more power to serve as mentors and role models for this type of active curiosity. You might consider publishing and sharing your work, too—my students always saw it as encouraging that I also "put myself on the line." If we care about what we are producing, it might take great courage to publish and share, and once we do share, it will have the power to change lives. It matters, as do we.

The following are *Five Places to Publish, Five Arenas for Audiences,* and *Five Interactives* (places that serve as both!).

These are general venues—you can choose the medium and specific tech tool that suits your needs. Check out some of my specific recommendations online, as constant updates about mindful ways to connect and share will make platforms more robust, versatile, and user-friendly—hopefully without distracting us from the *meaning* of our messages. The tools will advance, the lingo and slang will shift, yet the ideals and objectives are timeless. These are five ideas for ways to increase student connection, building Awareness, Advancement, and Authenticity.

Five Places to Publish

Vlog: Video blogging, which can record reflection and/or reach out to the audience.

Blog: A place where students can post reflections, ideas, feedback, and more.

Contest: Look for online contests that ask for student submissions, and/or host your own.

Performance: Host a poetry reading, slam, skit, or recreation of a historical moment; perhaps use the hit play *Hamilton* [2015] for your inspiration.

Billboard in school: If your school doesn't already have a venue for students to see one another's work, try asking your administrators if you can create one, to boost spirit and connection to what's happening in classes.

Five Arenas for Audiences

Visit the visual arts fair: Visiting your in-school arts presentations shows active support and cross-curricular interest. Talk with your colleagues before and after, and see if there's a chance to have students practice some "ekphrasis," which is writing in response to art. You can spark dialogue and show students the links beyond your classroom.

Take students to a science exhibit: My most memorable school experiences include the "field trips," undoubtedly—and not just because it was fun for us to spend time together in a change of venue. Interacting with the learning subject gives it meaning. If you don't already have ideas about links to standards and themes, reach out to your Twitter PLN.

Have students observe an online tutorial (such as a student-created lesson on Khan Academy): Make the viewing *active* rather than passive. Let students critique the tutorial. Is it clear? What questions do they have? Using it, could they teach someone else?

Improv/drama class: I tell students that "drama is everywhere," and there are ample opportunities for "improv moments" as part of every class. Tell them about the "yes, and" adage that is a staple of improvisation, mindfulness, learning, and life. You accept what presents itself and "roll with it."

Local cultural festival or museum: You can encourage students to attend a local festival or museum you find has certain links to your curriculum. In addition to the engagement, this adds to their ability to serve as an informed resident at a local level.

Five Interactives

The following five suggestions are more concrete and specific, as they give examples of empathetic collaborative venues in which students can be both creators and consumers of information, with each other as audiences:

- Partner with another school for interactive exercises

- Join online global learning forums

- Partner with Harvard Project Zero (2016) for Out of Eden interactive opportunities

- Check out the UN Global Goals' (2018) Student Interactive Module, as referenced in our "Human Rights" student exercise

- Go to a conference and form a partnership with another teacher, or reach out to your Twitter community seeking opportunities to collaborate

The Routines

There are Three C's that ground the routines of a mindful classroom:

▶ Care (do students feel invited to belong in this space and join in?)

▶ Consistency (are there routines involved that let students anticipate and navigate?)

▶ Clarity (are routines clear and easy to interpret?)

Thinking about how to establish your own classroom routines that incorporate care, consistency, and clarity helps teachers visualize ways to make their spaces more student-centered and mindful. You will see these Three C's in each of the types of routines discussed in this section.

A Note on Consistency

While the concepts of "care" and "clarity" appear throughout these exercises and are intentionally woven into the class design in context, "consistency" seems to ask for an explanation up-front.

Does this word—*consistency*—sound so reliable and staid that it somehow takes on a connotation of less than passionate, or somehow uninspired? I think about the values underneath teaching, and the mentors along the way who have continuously impressed me with their gentle, calm, welcoming spirit, with their curiosity and supply of energy. As a learner, I saw these traits reflected in the spirit of the teachers who made an impression. Theirs were not the loudest voices; they were not explosive or combative. They were supportive, challenging, dedicated, and consistent.

How can we be in our element as teachers, on a consistent basis? Part of this question is answered in Chapter 3, in the "For the Teacher" section that helps us come down from stress and chaos, establishing a balanced base and filling our wellspring. Then we can mindfully address the purpose and design underneath what we bring to each classroom experience.

Consistency, then, is the key to this foundation of experience. It's not necessarily a consistency of *content*, as new ideas, exercises, collaborative efforts, lesson plans, and units continually shift to fit our changing needs. These concrete details will adapt and advance. What is consistent is our approach as mindful teachers—our behaviors, our cycles, and our patterns and values underneath. We allow that consistency to be visible to our learners, and then they will trust us and partner with us in the learning process.

In terms of the learning routines, we don't want students to have to puzzle it out. In addition, we don't want them to be challenged to puzzle *us* out. We can be visibly caring, attending to the learning community by meeting it each day where it is. In all ways, with consistency, we want to be clear and committed to our students. They will meet us in return.

Here, for starting examples, are seven of my *Mindful by Design* consistent behaviors, which I aim to incorporate as steady life practices. I can depend on them, and I make a deliberate effort to practice them. Certainly, more will work their way into future online posts (at **caitlinkrause.com**) and writings, as there are many other applications that can extend from here!

- I choose to consistently practice kindness. To care is human.

- I choose to consistently practice patience. We are all learners.

- I choose to consistently demonstrate relational trust, which reflects my belief in community.

- I choose to consistently give encouragement and to offer choice. These are forms of mutual freedom.

- I choose to consistently invite, and I choose to follow up on my invitations.

- I choose to stay open, using the emerging future to help guide my actions, in support of learning.

- I live as one identity, a Möbius strip where my inner and outer worlds merge. I choose to be whole as I walk my path. I live an undivided life.

Routines for Classroom Motivation
(Otherwise Known as "Discipline")

A frequently asked question is *"Are there rules? What about the discipline?"* Effective, mindful leaders motivate, and they use themselves as role models, sustainers, and supporters. It's about key elements of dignity, respect, and care—a mutual compassion that exists for self and others. They are right beside their team, rather than commanding from on high. They look to let their group community feel valued.

In the *Mindful by Design* approach, the word *discipline* is transformed to *motivation,* and it is framed in a positive light. Why do we often see behavior cues having to do with discipline framed in instructions about what not to do? Instead, we should communicate our expectations in positive words that motivate students to see themselves as active, engaged participants. When students are identified as needing some "disciplinary support," this is often viewed as an intervention. In many cases, the issues are delicate, and a team of support from teachers and staff helps to address the student's needs and creates the best learning environment possible.

My own mindset helped to establish my own way to be in a classroom, which in turn led to a broader three-pillar belief about discipline and expectations.

First, fear doesn't motivate any long-term, sustained behavior change, because fear only stifles a natural impulse, and it implicitly reinforces a belief in the learner that suppression is necessary and that whatever is suppressed must be bad in some way. Otherwise, why would we need to suppress it? When we naturally gravitate toward using fear as a motivator, it just might be our own fears that need addressing. In these cases, Parker J. Palmer's (2009) writings *The Courage to Teach* and *The Undivided Life* can be great resources. What if we show students more of our own true nature, giving them the benefit of revealing deeper compassion and humanity? What if? Sometimes, it takes stepping into this intimidating territory to see what happens when practices change. Many of the exercises in Chapter 3, "Mindfulness for Teachers," invite this form of inner transformation, which then impacts our outer behavior and personality.

Second, your goal as a teacher is not to get students to like you. It seems obvious, yet we have all been products of various systems of education, and the nature of the environment often triggers an animal instinct: we want, first and foremost, *to belong*. Sometimes, we confuse belonging with popularity. If you're chasing a likability index or some reward of popularity, then it runs the risk of becoming more about your ego than about the good of the students. The irony is that adopting a "way to be" that embraces mindfulness just might result in popularity, but it's not the goal. The measures are often unreliable and beyond your control. And eventually, at some point, you will be faced with some decision that you need to make, and you might falter because you've been chasing a false prize of popularity over what is in a learner's best interest.

Third, how do you decide what's in a learner's best interest? How do you make that decision, to weigh those values? This is where the bigger messages underneath mindfulness come into play, and there are incredible rewards—because the messages are about promoting the quality of experience, the love of learning, and the well-being of each individual in our learning environments. When everyone feels whole and welcomed, when they are treated with empathy and care, they will bloom. As the Doris Lessing epigraph that opens this chapter says, "Any human anywhere will blossom in a hundred unexpected talents and capacities simply by being given the opportunity to do so." We need to give students many opportunities to shine. Sometimes, this will happen by giving support. At other times, it might happen by getting out of the way. We will feel what is right and mindful as we listen to our learners and follow the guide of our deeper, mindful intentions.

> *Ms. Krause posed questions to us that challenged our perceptions and made us dig deeper into issues. I always felt comfortable speaking up in class and felt as though I was in a truly welcoming/nurturing environment. It was as though there was an unspoken precedent of respect set that everyone in class adhered to.*
>
> —Eric, *former student*

Routines for Partners, Teams, and Groups

In a mindful classroom, there's a spirit of openness, care, and kindness. Earlier in this chapter, we addressed how to plan the physical environment and seating formations. Here, I will go deeper into ways to keep the routine of how you approach mindful partnerships. This is especially helpful because when it's time to "pair and share" or form larger teams, the whole community benefits when the process is defined and streamlined.

If you can imagine your groupings in advance, this will save some coordination in the long run.

For my classrooms, it works best when there's scaffolding—in the beginning of the year, I have assigned seating and table groups that reflect certain strengths in partnerships or working collaborative groups. I will tweak and play around with these, but there's an intentional structure to the seating arrangements. I have used seating at tables that might look like a modification of Dr. Spencer Kagan's (2009) popular cooperative learning structures, giving chances for partnerships and differentiation, and also employing grouping strategies to wonderful effect. My own mindful teaching methods reflect the same values toward which Kagan points, which is a basis of student empowerment, engagement, and team-building.

Furthermore, I have also created ways to presort partnerships using GroupSort.com (2008), the Team Shake (2016) app, or teaming icebreakers that I can easily set up at the beginning of the year. That way, when I want to start an exercise that involves groups, students know exactly what's needed, and the focus and energy are on the exercise rather than the formation of the group.

Routines for Technology and Social Media

A classroom is a space—physical, emotional, and mental—that promotes learning and growth. It is not solitary; it is not unidimensional. Just as it thrives on connection, the *Mindful by Design* methodology seeks opportunities online for presence and community. Technology and social media can be linked to the design of a mindful classroom, and their use can represent extensions of how we approach the values of our classroom culture.

The following are some maxims that govern how I approach social media and social learning with mindfulness as my guiding anchor. These are my own views, developed from direct experience.

Start With the Why

Ask students to focus on intention first, articulating it to you and others when they use social media.

Make Data Privacy Your COPPA Tea

While subjects like COPPA (Children's Online Privacy Protection Act) might be intimidating at first, get familiar with your school's policies and empower yourself with knowledge about student data privacy and responsibility. A great site to start with is ConnectSafely.org (2015), with a deep network of active educators and digital leaders offering expert recommendations, global news, and insights.

Encourage and Model "Curious Collaboration"

Let students' curiosity be their driver to approach others, acknowledging that there are often multiple viewpoints about a topic. Curiosity invites storytelling and multiplicity.

Express Yourself

Invite students to explore a mindful identity, using social media as a tool for self-awareness, discovery, and social-emotional learning growth. They can approach their own identity exploration mindfully, aware that it doesn't replace their physical IRL ("in real life") interactions and senses.

Voice Your Values

Use social media to amplify voice and expand your network through being a global force for good. In this way, students can see how being a digital citizen is about being empowered. There are many examples of this online, and you can begin by looking at approaches educators take to working with the UN Global Goals for Sustainable Development.

Explore Physical Community Alongside Online Interactions

S-t-r-e-t-c-h to discover your physical environment at the same time you encourage online exploration. If possible, I would take students to a different location in the school for a writing exercise, or even have them do something interactive outdoors for part of the class time, before jumping online for more of a type-driven interaction. You can geocache or get into VR/AR experiences, too, as part of interdisciplinary learning.

Take Tech to the Next Level Through Mindful Democratization

Have student ambassadors who learn a certain tech device/function teach others. In this way, they can broaden learning and spread their understanding.

> I think that learning in a natural space was a great way to improve concentration, and it allowed for our minds to relax and think about the task at hand more clearly. I really like the outdoors, as it just helps me relax and concentrate more clearly.
>
> —Rafael, *former student*

Collegiality Models Collaboration

Find out if other teachers on your team have similar values, goals, or topics to complement your particular area of study (perhaps also using library or media specialists as resources); then consider making this a cross-disciplinary exercise that has the boost of applications across multiple parts of the curriculum. Start by having open conversations with colleagues. Start by listening.

Everyday Routines

Here are some tips I'd like to call "Everyday Routines" because they become the ground of the classroom space, so much so that students will anticipate and appreciate them, too—the key here is that each individual establishes her own routines, based on what works best. There is no formula.

For Entering the Classroom, and in Halls: I use students' names and greet them, taking time to be present. I let us "arrive" together. I ask how they are. I listen. This is true for fellow teachers in community, too. When I began teaching, a colleague, Silas, would stand in the hall, often near the stairwell where we entered the school. His warm greetings of "Hello, so nice to see you" in the morning, along with a genuine smile, were mindful invitations to embrace the day. It made all the difference.

For the Start of Class: Classes have different starts in content and form—sometimes with music, poetry, a quote, a quiet moment of reflection, or a special intention. In all cases, they start with *presence*. I give students and myself time in community, at the beginning, to be present, to see each other, and to join together intentionally.

For the End of Class: The end of class signals a time of appreciation, *not* a recap and not a listing of "to-do's" and assignments for the next class. As class time approaches its end, there is a sense of closure as we leave that includes a spirit of connected reflection. Sometimes, it will be a "pair and share" moment of partner co-reflection; sometimes, a word; and other times, simply a goodbye-for-now greeting. I try to make a point of not feeling rushed in the process—after all, we want to keep the flow!

On Lunchtime/Recess/After School: I purposefully and mindfully get some air, take a walk, write a poem, sing a song. I use the time to enjoy a mindful break. I will host student gatherings if I feel it's manageable with the schedule of that particular day.

Assembly/Event: I will make a mindful effort to attend plays, games, and other school functions, supporting students and community. I'll even get up on stage and perform slam poetry from time to time. If I have personal plans, I keep them. When I'm at a school event, I remind myself to enjoy the time and appreciate it.

For Co-Teaching and In-Classroom Support: I celebrate the art of intentional improvisation. Co-teachers and I support one another, and students recognize this. I am a *"yes, and"* aficionado with my colleagues in community. I involve classroom teachers and other supportive collaborators in the process, letting students see us visibly joining and relating to each other.

For Students with Needs: I meet with students and families, and I will ask students to check in with me regularly to let me know how they are feeling and responding to new ideas and materials. In many cases, students will know how I can best support them, and they have ways of learning best that are individual and special. Honoring them and their voices makes all the difference.

For Parent Calls, Meetings, Conferences, and Interactions: I call families to share good news. I let students lead conversations. We conduct student conferences with the student taking initiative, and students appreciate this. If the student and family speak a different primary language, I will encourage them to lead meetings in this language, and then ask the student to translate for me.

For Giving Student Feedback: I encourage students to self-evaluate and reflect and to tell a story about how they learn and what they appreciate rather than use other methods to evaluate learning. I give feedback about their progress, and point out specific areas for growth, asking them to contribute in goal-setting and tracking progress. If I am using a rubric, I make sure that a student can understand and explain all parts of the rubric, using it as their own tool for growth rather than an external evaluation.

For Email and Written Communication: I am positive in my communication, clear and specific. I make an effort to respond without a delay, and I am mindful to consider that, sometimes, personal phone calls and/or in-person meetings can help support mutual goals and reinforce a sense of connection. I make time to listen and focus on the student's voice as a valuable contribution. In this way, my communication creates a bridge.

In sum, creating a *Mindful by Design* learning environment is all about flow. In setting up a place to "mindshare," it is essentially about adopting a Mindfulness AAA Mindset and designing curriculum as a connective vehicle. It is about getting to know students as individuals, inviting them to experience learning in a new way. Each educator has this opportunity, this chance to connect. It starts with us and our intentions. The student voices we encounter, including the ones present throughout this book, serve as testaments to what is possible. A world opens.

PART II

CHAPTER 3

Mindfulness for Teachers

There's a reason why mindfulness is both popular and powerful: it can effect profound life changes, both for you and your students. Positive practices in your own life will make a significant difference you'll start to notice in little and big ways, and they will spill right over into the quality of your classroom experiences.

Recent research reveals our human brain is an organ that can reshape itself over the course of a *full lifetime*—not just during middle school, high school, and college years. That's good news for each of us, as lifelong learners and creative explorers. This ability to change brain architecture and function is known as *neuroplasticity*, and it has profound implications on our lives and well-being. Evidence from laboratory studies of meditators shows that repeated practices involving mindfulness can influence positive changes in the brain that reflect mental and physical well-being. These effects include greater emotional balance, compassion toward oneself and others, and happiness, as well as increased ability to cope with stress and challenging life experiences in a healthy way (Lutz, Dunne, & Davidson, 2007).

> Positive practices in your own life will make a huge primary difference, and they will spill right over into the quality of your classroom experiences.

There are many reasons to practice mindfulness, and just as many forms that the practice itself can take! This is where it can get confusing: with all of the resources, apps, hashtags, and online fads surrounding mindfulness, how does one really drill down and find a rhythm that will work for the life of a busy teacher?

I understand what it's like to be overcommitted: as a full-time teacher, sports coach, Model UN coordinator, student club moderator, and more, I was "doing it all" as an educator and also aiming to maintain a healthy equilibrium. I used the phrase "maintaining a balance" quite often, yet it took me years before I was able to recognize how mindfulness could help. This was my dilemma: how could I effectively incorporate quality personal mindfulness practices into my daily life, without compromising myself and my sense of wholeness?

This book can serve as a resource for those who are just as busy, and just as uncertain about where mindfulness could fit into the equation. My goal is to offer you options of several varieties of mindfulness, so that you can test them out and see what works best for your style. The key is to get playful, because it's as much about play as it is about work and focus. Mindfulness is not always relaxing, yet it is amazingly rewarding, in giving us many creative opportunities to explore. In fact, we can treat our own minds just as we would our students': with open curiosity and patient kindness. As Jon Kabat-Zinn wrote in his foreword to an MBSR (Mindfulness-Based Stress Reduction) workbook by Bob Stahl and Elisha Goldstein (2010), "Mindfulness involves an elemental and spontaneous openness to experience, grounded in the body, in the timeless, in not expecting anything to happen, a befriending and inhabiting of this present moment for its own sake." When we begin to befriend the present moment, we open up to life—not the life of the future, but the life of right now. We wake up to ourselves.

> When we begin to befriend the present moment, we open up to life—not the life of the future, but the life of right now. We wake up to ourselves.

Much of the inspiration for these exercises has come from my own experiential mindfulness practice, as well as learning in community. I've personalized these mindfulness exercises, adding my own flair and guidance, as a fellow teacher. My full gratitude extends to those who have inspired me along the way. During the exercises in this section, as well as online at **caitlinkrause.com**, I'll make specific references to resources and inspirations that can augment the exercises and let us stretch further.

I'm encouraging you to try each and every exercise, to keep a journal along the way, and to continue to practice, practice, practice. As with everything, continued practice makes it easier, and it's the key to lasting positive effects. We can be gentle with ourselves; we are all on this path together. I'll continue to provide ample supportive resources and extensions, which are a great way to stay connected with a larger community of like-minded fellow educators. After all, it's a journey, and the company along the way enhances the experience.

> I think mindfulness in the classroom has less to do with the academic discipline it's being applied to and more to do with the teacher who is running the classroom. Because at the end of day, the only way it's going to work is if the teacher is applying it to their life and their class. I think teachers need to be open to integrating mindfulness into their lives. If there would be a way to integrate it into the curriculum for those getting an education degree, that would be ideal.
>
> —Charlotte, former student

This chapter contains eight mindfulness exercises, designed for teachers, and useful for everyone looking to explore a personal mindfulness practice that is engaging, adaptive, and purposeful:

Just Three Breaths (Breathing Meditation)

Kiss the Earth (Walking Meditation)

On Listening and Being Heard: Reducing Stress and Anxiety

Grateful Heart and Happiness

Prime Values: Purpose and Presence

Daring Greatly: Three Exercises for Freedom

Building Solidarity

Les Petits Plaisirs: Simple Pleasures for Sustenance

EXERCISE 1

Just Three Breaths (Breathing Meditation)

During the course of an active day, we might not consciously take the time to recognize our breathing. Thank goodness, this process of breathing happens quite naturally, due to our autonomic nervous system. While it's natural to breathe, this doesn't necessarily mean the quality of our breathing is top-notch—when I'm feeling tension or pressure, I take very shallow breaths, and my shoulders rise up, tightening my neck and back. This feeling of tension is common while teaching, as we travel point to point, our attention fully devoted to the task at hand. I built in this activity at the start of my planning period, and/or included it as a quick midday rejuvenator. This exercise takes us back to our core, elemental, involuntary act of breathing, practicing it in a more mindful way.

Mindfulness meditation is considered "insight meditation" (as opposed to concentration meditation, which focuses on concepts and imagery) because it connects the body and mind to the present moment without trying to alter the experience in any way. This simple breathing exercise can be done anywhere, anytime, to bring us back to ourselves. I've also used it in waiting rooms, while driving, and at bedtime before falling asleep. Try it now, and see how you feel!

Mindfulness Skills Taught

▶ **AWARE:** builds awareness of self, breathing, tension levels, and the present moment

▶ **ADVANCING:** allows individual to adopt an insightful, curious approach to breathing; builds sustained focus

▶ **AUTHENTIC:** encourages one to recognize the breath without aiming to change it; leads to a calmer, more reflective state

Practice

▶ Take a few moments to gather yourself and be still. Try to maintain a comfortable position. You can be sitting or standing (you don't have to sit to meditate; you just need to be alert, attentive, and comfortable).

> When you feel ready, bring your awareness to your breath. As you breathe in, quite naturally, just feel the air filling your nose, mouth, neck, chest, belly, or wherever you feel it most prominently in your body.

> Feel the turn, as you slowly let the breath out.

> Experience the ebb and flow of breathing in and breathing out, just like waves, simply noticing the rhythm of your breath, without trying to evaluate anything else about it.

> Mindfully maintain the awareness of your breathing, trying to focus your attention on three successive in-and-out waves of breath.

This way of checking in with yourself is a gentle reminder of mindfulness that you can carry with you anywhere, anytime. It does not need a special time or place, and it might be imperceptible to an outside observer. (You might, however, noticeably change the environment. I was doing this once while waiting for a meeting, and the organization's CEO, who was walking by, stopped to tell me that I looked especially calm and serene.)

Extensions and Additional Resources

If you find yourself enjoying this exercise, try a breathing-focused meditation for fifteen minutes. The longer time is an opportunity to let additional thoughts, feelings, and experiences of awareness come to the surface.

EXERCISE 2

Kiss the Earth (Walking Meditation)

As a long-distance runner, cross country coach, and all-around athletic zealot, I was forced to stop my regular sports routine when I developed a complicated stress fracture in my foot. It coincided with (and certainly intensified) deeper discoveries about mindfulness and meditation. Each day, as I learned to walk again, I felt such appreciation for my feet. As Thich Nhat Hanh (2005) says, I was learning to "kiss the Earth" as I walked, practicing such gratitude for each step, and for my body's improving health.

Even after recovering, I retained that sense of connection to Earth. Many mindfulness practices incorporate walking in some way; there are mindful retreats and expeditions that involve longer pilgrimages. As Valerie Brown (2015), co-author of *The Mindful School Leader,* says in a blog post about mindful pilgrimages, "The road teaches us what we need to know." Brown leads pilgrimages along an ancient path in northern Spain and reflects about the feeling of presence: "In walking El Camino, I trained myself to be present each moment, not thinking ahead to the next hill or the next turn in the road." In just the same way, on a smaller scale, this walking meditation offers a calm way to reconnect with what is local and immediate. We tune in to our own grounding force, processing the artful, sensual journey of walking itself.

Mindfulness Skills Taught

▷ **AWARE:** builds awareness of sensations, surroundings, and presence

▷ **ADVANCING:** trains our bodies to process each step; to see the inner journey, too, and not the destination

▷ **AUTHENTIC:** connects us with our own inner nature, as we also appreciate the environment surrounding us

Practice

▷ Choose a space for this walking meditation, outside or inside. The length of time and distance is up to you.

▷ Begin by taking a moment to stand in place, feeling the body and its connection to the ground or the floor.

▷ Take in your environment, noticing any sounds, sights, scents, tastes— anything that's surrounding you. Also acknowledge how you are feeling emotionally in this moment, and just let that feeling be, as it is.

▶ While standing still, try shifting your weight, subtly, from your left foot to your right, and back again. Feel how that affects your stance and stature; feel from your head, down your spine, down your legs, to your feet, how even small changes in the placement of your weight make you feel.

▶ Now, try lifting one foot, moving it forward, and placing it down. Mindfully shift your weight, lifting the other foot, moving it forward, and placing it down. Continue to walk slowly, at this conscious pace, feeling the shifts and changes in your body while doing so.

▶ Walk with awareness and with focus, one step at a time.

▶ Each time, as your mind starts to wander, reconnect with your feet, your ground, and continue to focus on the sensations of slowly walking, "kissing the Earth."

▶ Walk with this level of mindfulness, taking in your environment, focusing on the awareness of one step at a time.

▶ As soon as you finish this walking meditation exercise, which might be after five or fifteen minutes, depending on what you choose, I recommend taking time to write down any thoughts or feelings in a journal.

Extensions and Additional Resources

The walking meditation is something you can literally take "on the road" wherever you go; it suits any time of day and every environment.

Informally, it can be practiced everywhere. You also don't need to walk at a "snail's pace" to feel a connection; I have tried my own variation of a "foot-strike meditation" while running, really feeling my connection with the trail. Of course, this became easier for me after I had some practice under my belt with slower walking meditations, as I had established a connection with all of the subtle feelings in my feet and body.

It's hard to perform this "insight" sort of meditation while walking with someone else and having a conversation. The next exercise, "On Listening," however, provides ideas for partner exercises, which can be wonderful forms of mindfulness and listening practice. I use them often!

Online, you can find recordings and information about movement meditations and walking meditations. Just as we know that some students are kinesthetic learners, if you find your body wanting to move itself, and seated/still meditation practices are especially challenging for you, this walking meditation offers a wonderful alternative.

I've also created my own variations for hiking, climbing, swimming, and other movements that tend to have their own natural rhythm and pace that connect with mindfulness. Later, I give more details about this in the exercise "Daring Greatly," which challenges us to go beyond expectations and comfort zones, seeing what happens when we step into the unknown.

Enjoy the journey!

EXERCISE
3

On Listening and Being Heard: Reducing Stress and Anxiety

Listening is such a simple act. It requires us to be present, and that takes practice, but we don't have to do anything else. We don't have to advise, or coach, or sound wise. We just have to be willing to sit there and listen.

—Margaret J. Wheatley

When I was part of a leadership retreat led by Parker J. Palmer, we practiced a basic and profound exercise as part of a circle of trust: *we listened to each other.* We really listened. We weren't each thinking of the next thing to say; we did not offer jokes, words of encouragement, or comforts that can sometimes unwittingly serve to pacify or shut down the speaker. We suspended the chitchat and stifled our impulsive murmurs of agreement, favoring instead to surround each other with silent space, *allowing.* Space that is attentive, quiet, and loving, accepting what is there in the present moment. It was simple, sincere, and insightful. It took practice, patience, and trust. In the space that we opened were hidden thoughts, feelings, intuitions, and truths. Discoveries were made, all from listening.

Since that incredible experience, I've engaged in different forms of mindful listening, with friends and colleagues worldwide. One memorable exercise was created and led by Angie Weinberger (2016) in a workshop called "Take a Walk," inviting us to form pairs and practice free expression (and quiet listening) while moving. The results were natural and profound—it freed us up to honor our voices.

> Effective listening is useful in just about every aspect of life.

Effective listening is useful in just about every aspect of life. These are exercises that we can use in class, too, yet we start with ourselves. *LISTEN and SILENT happen to be anagrams.* They are beautiful exercises to combat stress, tension, and anxiety, inviting us back to the quiet, mindful listening space, able to receive our own reflective thoughts again, able to hear our own voices.

You can use these when you need to slow down, getting back to center, away from stress and anxiety. You can also introduce it to friends, colleagues, and students as part of mindful practice. There are three mini exercises, with different angles that all enhance our listening skills, seen as a key trait of leadership, insight, and self-awareness.

Mindfulness Skills Taught

▶ **AWARE:** becoming aware of some of the hidden messages and quiet truths from others that become apparent when we listen to understand rather than focusing first on what we are saying

▶ **ADVANCING:** practicing listening is timeless, encouraging us to stretch and grow beyond what we might have set as preconceived limits

▶ **AUTHENTIC:** reinforcing true connection, practicing the art of open, active listening

Practice

Try out the following listening exercises, taking time to reinforce each with several rounds of practice. In the beginning, parts might feel awkward or forced, which is fine—it's hard to be the speaker, and equally hard to be the active listener, creating the open space. Over time, your ability and comfort level will grow, and amazing connections will certainly unfold. Remember the tenet that we are all linked, essentially.

"I am who we are." This is similar to the South African concept of *Ubuntu,* the belief that we are all connected by humanity, sharing what is collective. We can receive this only through co-sensing, co-listening. This is practice, building that sensibility.

1. Listening to Invite the Open Space: Partner Walking

Try this with a friend, colleague, partner, or teammate:

You both head outside and decide on the direction and walking route.

Decide who will be talking first. Establish that what you will say has complete confidentiality—no Instagram or Tweeting, either. It's an exercise that exists in its own space, protected by the honor of the speaker–listener pact.

Set a timer (or check your watch) for five minutes.

When the time starts, the person whose turn it is to speak begins to talk. The topic is not set, so they could tell a story, they could talk about a challenge, or they could ramble along, following different threads of ideas and trains of thought, for the full five minutes.

For the speaker, your challenge is to keep talking for the full five minutes, without self-critique. "Let the words flow, let the mind go." (Hey, that's my new mantra!) Stop *thinking* as you talk, if you can help it. Instead, dwell in the moment as it emerges and comes into being, allowing your speech to translate more directly from the mind-body-heart connection. This becomes a deeper "consciousness" that is more authentic than self-conscious speech. Our self-conscious "thoughts" are sometimes ironically in the way of our speech, adding commentary or guiding us about what "ought" to be said. True clarity can come when we keep it simple, speaking from a more genuine place, a place that simply speaks "what is" right in that present moment.

> Our self-conscious "thoughts" are sometimes ironically in the way of our speech, adding commentary or guiding us about what "ought" to be said. True clarity can come when we keep it simple, speaking from a more genuine place, a place that simply speaks "what is" right in that present moment.

This, by the way, is intentionally not a set "prompt" to discuss, because the practice is not a filibuster—the speaker's job is not simply to speak in response to a command, as if they are coming up with a good answer for an interview. Nor are they supposed to be entertaining or engaging the listener. It is their time to talk, and the open-ended nature of the subject and topic allows them to tune in more authentically to what might emerge from inside. This includes the emptiness of pure silence. As composer Claude Debussy said, *"Music is the space between the notes."*

For the listener, your challenge is to allow that music of silence, and to defend the space for the speaker. As you are walking, there is no eye contact or other facial gestures, like smiling or smirking at each other, no body-language cues of affirmation (e.g., nodding, hand gestures, pats on the back, hugs, arm squeezes), and no verbal feedback (hums, murmurs, words). Remember that you play a special role in listening. You are giving yourself, and your full attention, to the speaker, without inspection or intrusion. You are inviting the words to come.

At the end of five minutes, if a bell is ringing to alert you of the time, let the speaker come to a natural close.

Without commentary, feedback, or any external conversation, switch roles and begin the same five-minute timing.

This listening exercise is powerful for both people. Whatever you share in this space has the complete freedom to exist of its own accord. After the exercise ends, as you walk back to a group space again (whether a classroom, workplace, or other space), an understanding exists, which should be set from the beginning: no further dialogue is needed about these topics, unless the speaker initiates and wishes to discuss more with the listener.

This listening exercise can mark the beginning stages of speakers finding their inner voices. And it's also incredible practice for listeners to be better leaders.

2. Listen to Understand: Mirroring

This "Mirroring" exercise is similar to the "Open Space" exercise above, yet the partners sit facing each other, and the venue can be anywhere—indoors, outdoors, in any location.

This time, the speaker has three minutes to talk, and it's the listener's job to be attentive, giving space and focus.

Again, the topic can be about anything, though you might want to focus it this time, to home in on a theme, such as "A Challenge Faced and Overcome" or "A Difficult

Decision" or "The True Meaning of Success"—something that's a prompt to get the speaker talking. The listener's job is only to listen.

At the end of the three minutes, instead of immediately switching roles, it's now the listener's turn to mirror back what they have heard. Mirroring is not a chance to offer a solution or advice about what the speaker is saying; if there is a problem discussed, it's not the job of the listener to try to fix anything. The goal is to do exactly as the word suggests: *to act as a mirror*. The listener, then, has the chance to offer points about what they have heard and seen—key phrases, words, and gestures. By illuminating this for the speaker, the listener gives a chance for the speaker to reflect upon what was communicated and articulated, then perhaps seeing how it resonates when mirrored back.

Then the roles reverse, and listener becomes speaker; speaker becomes listener.

This exercise, again, deepens the capacity for capable listening, and reinforces the art of speaking and receiving your own expression reflected back to you, which can be rewarding, affirming, and often revelatory.

3. Listening for Stories: "Freeze" Improvisation Game

This listening exercise is a variation on an improvisation technique used in drama programs, too. It's a group activity that you can use in staff meetings, with peer learning groups and curriculum teams, and also with students. It makes for good classroom listening practice.

For a timed ten minutes, you're playing in a traveling storytelling game. Try to be as visual as possible.

Start out with a group of three actors on "stage" in the center of the room. You start them off with a scene, and perhaps one prop item. You might tell them, for example, to open the scene, that they are a family sitting at dinner together, and they're deciding how to spend their upcoming school vacation time. Make sure they establish character names for one another.

Scene 1: Opening Act: A Decision

As the three actors are talking about this vacation, have others in the group listen for cues about how each is feeling about the decision.

Freeze! After about one to two minutes, freeze the action; replace two of the actors with new people. Make sure they each know which character they're playing.

Scene 2: Development

Continue with the same story, new scene. Tell the actors that in their dialogue they should focus on revealing some details about their character's motivations and emotions. Think about somehow showing this, rather than telling it. Try to make the characters human.

Freeze! After about one to two minutes, freeze the action; replace two of the actors with new people. Make sure they each know which character they're playing.

Scene 3: Conflict

Continue with the same story, new scene. Tell the actors that in their dialogue they must introduce a new place and a topic involving a conflict.

As the actors talk with each other, in their roles, make sure others are listening for story cues.

Freeze! After about two minutes, freeze the action; replace two of the actors with new people. Make sure they each know which character they're playing.

Scene 4: Resolution

Continue with the same story, new scene. Tell the actors that in their dialogue they must somehow resolve this conflict and bring the story to closure.

Freeze!

Evaluation

As a group, actors and viewers included, briefly reflect about what the experience was like here, and how the scene developed and grew. Allow different participants to speak about their experiences—what they found surprising, what they found useful.

Extensions and Additional Resources

These exercises are useful for personal well-being, and also for community. They are a powerful way to connect, bringing people together through true compassion, which seeks first to understand the other, and ultimately to see past any perceived divisions. They also allow us freedom from superior assumptions that our roles are to save one another. In times that can be isolationist, this open invitation to speak and be heard without judgment and without any threat to honor, integrity, and personal freedom—this is a way to bring people back to each other, in solidarity and strength. There are many more ways to hone speaking and listening skills. And there are always good reasons to keep practicing.

Grateful Heart and Happiness

Gratitude is a habit of the heart.

—Alexis de Tocqueville

You've probably heard about a major gratitude movement growing worldwide. Dr. Brené Brown (2010), famous for her TED Talk about vulnerability, speaks about it; Liz Gilbert (2014) writes about it; John Kralik (2011) wrote a book about how spending a full year writing and sending one thank-you note every day drastically changed his life. Being consciously grateful, and acting from that feeling, has the power to transform our perception, our experience, and ultimately, our reality.

The movement is not a fling or fad. Much like mindfulness, the roots are timeless. In an article for *Greater Good Magazine* called "Why Gratitude Is Good," Robert Emmons (2010) describes gratitude in detail, citing two major elements: "First, it's an affirmation of goodness. We affirm that there are good things in the world, gifts and benefits that we've received. This doesn't mean that life is perfect; it doesn't ignore complaints, burdens, and hassles. But when we look at life as a whole, gratitude encourages us to identify some amount of goodness in our life. The second part of gratitude is figuring out where the goodness comes from. We recognize the sources of this goodness come from outside ourselves." Often, I also find that gratitude starts *within* us, too, in the form of self-compassion, which allows us to appreciate the present moment and its opportunities without too much overbearing self-criticism.

We'll explore gratitude by practicing several exercises. First, though, some common questions.

Is gratitude hard to grasp? The key is to start small. Gratitude can take place at any instant. It's curious that sometimes we might think we need to justify being grateful, or reserve our gratitude for "big moments" that might be labeled as incredible and revelatory. Does it seem whimsical to be grateful for the small moments, the ones that might pass by without notice? Actually, these little moments, these seeds of joy and peace and minitranscendences, are exactly what make up a life. To recognize and honor them is part of the process.

> These seeds of joy and peace and minitranscendences are exactly what make up a life. To recognize and honor them is part of the process.

Do I need a reason to be grateful? Along with mindfulness exercises, I decide to willingly (and willfully!) choose to be grateful. I make time for this reflection. Sometimes, at the beginning of my practice when encouraging myself to feel and express gratitude, it felt false, as if I was self-imposing gratitude, giving myself some lesson. I felt self-critical for not being grateful at every point of every day.

To flip that switch, I decided to release any negative thoughts about it. *Any practice takes practice.* To evaluate my beginning practices in gratitude would diminish it from being able to naturally exist, grow, and thrive. I let go of all of these expectations and just let myself gently invite an *appreciation* to unfold—for whatever that present moment of observation offered. *Both the good and the bad.* Practicing this type of intentional gratitude just might hook you as soon as you begin it, without self-critique. The reasons for gratitude are multifold. It's not restricted to massive moments, holiday traditions, or conversations saved for the dinner table.

How to fit it in? Days are jam-packed with action. I try to make a bit of space for gratitude each day. It sounds easy, yet it takes attention and intention on my part. Gratitude is my instant hack to bring me back to myself. It also brought me closer to my classroom. I'll simplify some entry routes here, just giving a way to make it a daily practice, as an invitation that's guaranteed to lead to some unexpected magic.

Mindfulness Skills Taught

- ▷ **AWARE:** builds awareness of the quality of a moment; a detail
- ▷ **ADVANCING:** allows us to set balanced goals for the future, recognizing what the present moment offers
- ▷ **AUTHENTIC:** engages us with our surroundings and our true self that can dwell in appreciation of both good and bad experiences, reframing our own schemas

Practice

These practices are each multilayered, and give a chance to engage with gratitude in three different ways, following the three A pillars of mindfulness. They can be completed in a journal in a few short minutes for each. You can build on them in different ways.

Awareness. Write a description of something that made you happy yesterday. Include as many of the five senses as possible. For example, if you were happy when you went for a hike in the woods, try to describe the temperature, the feel of it, the colors and sights around you. Try to bring yourself back there through the writing. Let loose and just flow with the scene of the moments you recall, using attention to detail.

Advancing. Write down three attributes you have that you value in yourself. These could be any quality, from trustworthy to funny to caring. For each quality, what is a life situation you have experienced—an "anecdote"—that illustrates it in your life? Feel free to think of examples that have humor. Could you practice by sharing this out loud with someone else? Many of these illustrated moments make for great connection points, yet we deny ourselves the right to "own" them and appreciate them. This type of gratitude can translate to powerful self-compassion.

You can also extend this exercise by choosing to focus on another person, writing down the attributes you admire and value in them. After writing them down and reflecting upon how their inspiration has made an impression on your life, consider writing a note to them to let them know your feelings. This shared expression of gratitude can be quite the boost, for the giver and the recipient.

Authentic. Think back to an experience where the time itself was not what you expected in the short term, yet it offered some sort of long-term benefit. Describe the situation in detail, using a "before" perspective (anticipation), a "during" (experience), and an "after" (reflection). What do you appreciate about it now, in hindsight? How do you think it adds some flavor and dimension to your life?

Sometimes, just taking time to record our own reflections and thoughts about these experiences can lend us deeper clarity and insight. For me, building components of grateful writing and storytelling into my mindfulness practice adds an extra layer of appreciation, insight, and what I call "connection capacity."

Extensions and Additional Resources

The "Gratitude Movement" is certainly going global, and there are many ways to build it and share it with friends and colleagues in local and online communities. One example that follows is a minimovement I enthusiastically took part in recently. It might give you an idea for your own extension.

Gratitude is closely aligned with happiness, and hinges on the art of noticing and appreciating. I was recently invited to join a daily "Team Happiness" initiative, hosted online and organized by Andreas Johansson, director of Technology Integration at Kenston Local Schools in Ohio. As Andreas described to me, "We're aiming to re-train our brains for happiness, and promoting folks on a daily basis to take stock about what makes them happy. You in?"

I was "in" in a heartbeat. I like that we kept it simple and didn't overcomplicate the mission. We were discovering more as it evolved. We joined together during that post-holidays time in January, the stretch that can seem the least mindful. Instead of adopting a traditional resolution for the New Year, I opted to chart my "happiness" and reflect together about the journey.

Using the Basecamp 3 app (2018), we were well connected on a digital platform. Thirty-seven of us (a prime number!) jumped online each morning and evening to record our thoughts and read one another's reflections. There was a morning prompt and an evening prompt, detailed in Figure 3.1.

[TH17] What three (3) things made you happy yesterday, big or small?

[TH17] Journal Opportunity: What would you like to explore more, memorialize, or think more about today?

Source: Basecamp 3 at basecamp.com © Basedcamp, LLC.

Figure 3.1 • Basecamp App

Basecamp easily let us jot down thoughts and respond to each other in a community of care. We could gather around a "campfire" to discuss. Talk about motivation! It brightened each day to share these stories, and I found myself enjoying the act of noticing, and also sharing and receiving these gems from an online community. There was no way to "fail" at this—everything we shared was a success in the act itself. The support gave us a boost. Reading about others' experiences reinforced the recognition that hardship, happiness, and gratitude are universal.

Online, there are many of these types of supportive tech resources for gratitude and happiness motivation. All you have to do is start practicing it, and this exercise starts taking on a life of its own—and it spreads like wildfire. Ready to start building your own Team Happiness?

Prime Values: Purpose and Presence

If we are to achieve a richer culture, rich in contrasting values, we must recognize the whole gamut of human potentialities, and so weave a less arbitrary social fabric, one in which each diverse human gift will find a fitting place.

—Margaret Mead (1935/2001)

Our values rest at the core of who we are. They give us a sense of purpose, and our mindful presence stems from there. Rather than a map, the values provide the compass, guiding us even when we're in unknown territory. Our values, too, are what bind us to the rest of our community, uniting us in a shared vision. Values create culture, shaping a better, more inclusive, and expansive world.

In my first days of teaching high school, I was not as concerned with promoting my values as I was with exercising control. I exhibited my "class rules" on a poster board, prominently displayed, front and center. There were three key commands: *Be on time; No talking; No hall trips.* In retrospect, I understand where I was coming from: I was a teacher who wanted to establish order, above all else. *We would not be running wild under my watch.* Each day, I was maintaining stability, with each row properly in alignment, each student sitting in alphabetical order, uniforms in regulation, ready to learn. Say what they might, no one could call my class disorderly. What I was missing here were our collective *values.* I was missing the chance to express my core beliefs, and my students were missing the chance to express theirs, too. *But no one questioned the system—they dutifully followed my command, because their goal was to comply.*

Systems of devoted, blind obedience are short-lived. I soon realized we were lacking the essential human component of learning, which was to know that our mutual time together rested on community. Thank you to George Thoms, an education teacher of mine, who placed the word *community* on the floor in the center of our classroom on the first day of our graduate course together. Our desks had been arranged in a circle. Everything served as a visible, tangible reminder that every part of interaction, understanding, connection, and learning stems from community, and community rests on values.

Over a short period of time, my priorities shifted as I intentionally structured a community based on values related to mindfulness. Students noticed. Community, connection, and learning flourished. The classroom experience was transformed.

In this exercise, we're encouraged to take time to think about our values, which serve as a guiding force. Our sense of values restores and renews us in trying times, reminding us of our own sense of purpose—our presence that reaches out to connect with others.

Mindfulness Skills Taught

▶ **AWARE:** builds awareness of how values affect us in a foundational way

▶ **ADVANCING:** allows us to use values as a base from which to stretch and grow

▶ **AUTHENTIC:** values are communal, personal, and collective, meaning more when embodied

Practice

1. Characteristics of Your Mindful Self: Journaling

In a journal, just for yourself, jot down all of the traits you believe are the ultimate values for a mindful individual, with the Mindfulness Aware, Advancing, Authentic Mindset in mind. In other words, picture your "best self"—what qualities do you value, and/or what qualities do you value in others?

The goal is for quantity, to get down as many as possible, without edits or too much critique. Later, you can rank them, going through and accepting some as your top choices.

In classes, you can have students do the same; then each chooses a tag-word for one of their prime values for the classroom. Combine the keywords on a display in class, representing everyone's contributions. When I did this with students in an "advisory group" of mine, they said it added to their sense of belonging, a sign that every voice matters and contributes to collective values that are part of our group culture. You can also have a discussion with them about why they chose certain words.

Here is a list of some of my core values, which I looked to for direction when founding my organization MindWise. My values have been with me for life, driving decisions, priorities, empathy, connection, and my sense of self-compassion and well-being. Even just listing the values makes me more conscious of them; I wrote them recently in a journal in different colors, creating a flow chart of relationships. I wanted to show how each value "shows up" in my daily life—what does it look like to have patience, for example? I like the traits with certain core visible practices that are associated and linked to my values:

Patience → Open, Listen, without Urgency

Clarity → Communicate to Be Understood, Seek to Understand

Trust → Believe in Growth of Self and Others, Believe in Abundance

Optimism → Expect the Best, Celebrate Small Wins

Laughing → Find Humor with Kindness, Invite Others In

Greater-Good → Less Ego, Focus on Community

Gratitude → Appreciate Life

Wonder → Embrace Passion

Risking → Confront Fear as a Teacher

Futurist → See Change as Possible and Necessary

Curiosity → Use Science as a Tool, Invite Intuition as Insight

Reading through this list, and thinking about the elements within it, brings me back to center in an instant. It's not a comprehensive list; it's an exercise in focused self-awareness, and it serves as a pathway. The act of creating it is an engaging artistic endeavor, too, thinking about the words, relationships, and actions and attributes that represent my beliefs. Each of these values, connected with a flow, is something about which I could meditate.

2. Values Bond a Community Group

Wherever I go, I focus on creating community. As I'm motivated to investigate what mindfulness means when applied to systems and organizations, I started a mindful leadership meetup group and began to host gatherings. In conversations together, I would often ask others in the group what they thought the most prominent traits were for an active, wise, mindful leader.

At one meeting, we spent thirty minutes engaged in a design thinking exercise where we grappled with the question: *"What are the traits of a mindful leader?"* We each threw out examples in rapid sequence, just listing whatever came to mind. You can do this using sticky notes, a drawing board, or several notebooks going at once within a group.

After brainstorming, we eventually culled out the following list of values, deciding which ones could rest in the community, representing us. Some of the word associations surprised us; others came quite naturally. We had been especially inspired by several programs with which many of us had engaged, including the Presencing Institute (PI), which grew out of the MIT Center for Organizational Learning, founded by Peter Senge and his colleagues. After the PI, uLab was formed by a team including Otto Scharmer and offered as an edX course online. Another big inspiration came from Frederic Laloux's seminal book *Reinventing Organizations* (2014). The conversation we shared after being impacted by such influences was inspiring. From there, we tried to name people in the world who represent these core values in practice. Having the list of traits gave us the ground from which to work, establishing the necessary criteria for what could be an abstract term. Note, again, that this list is malleable and was our starting point—something with which to work and engage.

Values of a Mindful Leader

Aware	Listening
Advancing	Approachable
Authentic	Flawed
Resilient	Selfless
Focused	Caring
Committed to social good	Honest
Loyal	Positive
Charismatic	Open-hearted
Passionate	Open-minded
Present	Open-willed

The list above is not comprehensive; nor does it exclude additional benefits and traits as outcomes. It offers an anchor and a guide of defining values, which can easily be accessed and addressed.

If I were to ask myself *"Why am I engaging in this activity?"* or *"What is attractive to me about practicing mindfulness and mindful leadership?"* it helps that I have developed and articulated my personal values. I refer back to the list for a reminder of the broader scope of what I believe in, associated with my work and my principles. The core MindWise mission statement of "humanity through connection" also complements my values.

By using values and mission statements as the foundations of our teaching practices and involvement in various activities, partnerships, and groups, it reminds us of our internal compass, and our motivation to connect and feel a sense of belonging with a larger group. It can also remind an organization of what motto and mission it represents, as it looks to form allies, partnerships, and support networks.

3. Values Create a Team: Motto and Mission

Values form the basis for an engaged, committed team, especially in modern systems of holacracy, self-management, and rapid prototyping. Trust within organizations is key, and a unified motto and mission help to establish a community culture in which everyone feels a sense of purpose, even if their specific roles and functions are different.

Serving as a co-founder and core member of an organization called the Center of Wise Leadership has given even more opportunities to co-create initiatives that stem from shared vision. This group decided to start with a unifying motto and values, which became part of our mission-driven outreach. In essence, we started with a purpose, which drove us to define our motto, keystones, and values. Our company evolves to meet the evolving world, inside and out.

Motto

Inspiring leaders to wise action

Keystones

Human Connectivity

Deep Listening

Creating Space

Crossing Bridges Together

Deeper Purpose

Values/Keywords—"What is important to us?"

Connection

Love

Trust

Courage

Equality

Diversity

Integrity

Action

Humanity

Curiosity

Play

Joy

Simplicity

Listening

Space

You can create this exercise, in any group or team, by asking members in a community to think about what really matters to them, or how they would describe the ideal representative of what they believe in. It becomes a foundation upon which you can build your team with confidence. In essence, our classrooms are teams, and we want them to encompass values that each learner feels a part of voicing and creating.

Daring Greatly: Three Exercises for Freedom

The purpose of practice is to expand the range of experiences in which we are free.

—Unknown

Dare more greatly.

—Brené Brown (2015)

Recently, I've had the phrase "the positive power of audacity" in mind—yes, the magical things that happen when we dare more greatly. When we widen the circle of what we think is possible, allowing ourselves to lean toward opportunity, expecting and inviting it, it seems to happen. *Yet this takes effort*—it's a deceptive effort to remember to "stay loose and open" while taking risks.

I was biking in the woods on a spring evening, after a full day of work. There was a lot to think about, keeping my mind occupied as my legs were pumping. The sun was falling golden through tall trees, vines coiled around the trunks, creating a wonderland scene. Right after a recent rain shower, the forest was primordial. As I dodged tangles of tree roots, navigating my bike through a maze of trails, each downhill reminded me of the need to take care, avoiding the wet roots and rocks, following the twists in the path. I knew that, to navigate, I had to hold the handlebars loosely, keep my body in balance, even while letting my brain and consciousness absorb the breathtaking scene. Soon, I fell into a natural rhythm, the pace of my cycling matching my breathing, and I was in balance, my mind and body connected. When I returned home, I realized that the stress of the day had dissolved, and I was able to focus more clearly on the tasks at hand. I had gained back an energy, a strength, and a honing mechanism that allows me to prioritize and pursue my goals.

In order for us to "dare more greatly," and to ask more from our experiences, we must have these opportunities to reconnect with ourselves, with nature, and with stress-reducing activities that bring us back to our own "zone" of flow. It takes intention and time, initially, to defend them, yet they bring us back in contact with ourselves, setting the foundation for daring more greatly.

The following three exercises encourage you to "dare more greatly," expanding beyond what might have been limiting beliefs. They are simple exercises, and you can try each one at different times, to encourage experimentation and play. You can talk about them with students, too, later introducing some practices you have found most helpful and useful. As the quote says, "The purpose of practice is to expand the range of experiences in which we are free."

Mindfulness Skills Taught

▶ **AWARE:** becoming aware of our own needs and connections, strengthening the ties that will sustain our own mindfulness practices

▶ **ADVANCING:** these mindfulness values and practices are not static; they grow within ourselves, and with others in community, stretching and advancing to suit the current situation

▶ **AUTHENTIC:** we learn that, in order to be whole and authentically ourselves, we must, as Parker J. Palmer eloquently writes, work toward leading "an undivided life"—one in which we are not using false fronts or pretenses to separate ourselves from our truth

Practice

1. Get Outside and See What's Inside #SweatSession

This exercise is based on just this premise: the *exercise* is the exercise. The key is to use the sweat session to invite mindful magic to take place internally, using three key guiding points:

▶ **NATURE:** Get outside. This can be any time of day, any weather condition. Running or walking or biking, on hills or flat terrain. It's you and whatever elements surround you, urban or rural, on trails or road. Think of it as an exploration. Don't time yourself to keep a pace or reach a certain distance; that way, whatever you're doing, whatever route you're choosing, you have the freedom to feel it as it comes, and to respond naturally to the environment. Give as much energy to the pace of the experience as you feel is appropriate, feeling connected to your natural surroundings.

▶ **BARRIER-FREE:** No headphones, no phone conversations, nearly no division between you and the natural surroundings. Let yourself hear the birds and stop to smell the flowers; encourage yourself to notice the details as you're doing this exorcise. Don't let the details derail you from the exercise, though. Keep reminding yourself that you're not witnessing a scene from afar; you're part of the scene. And, more than that, you're not *in* nature; you *are* nature. You are meeting an athletic challenge by inviting it and choosing it.

▶ **INVITE SWEAT:** Yes, see if you can break a sweat with whatever you're doing. See what happens when you feel your muscles physically working. Of course, choose health and safety, and if you're recovering from an injury or have any medical concerns, that is something that takes top mindful priority. You're honoring your body and treating it well. You're using sweat to your advantage.

Here's an outlined, eight-step example of one approach to my mindful "Get Outside and See What's Inside" #SweatSession—using the example of a morning run.

1. As soon as an alarm goes off, I get out of bed and drink a full glass of water. I put on the running clothes I had set out the night before, with everything ready to go.

2. When I head outside, I start with a gentle five-minute warm-up of brisk walking.

3. I pause for some dynamic stretching, in a series, giving my quads, hamstrings, calves, arms, shoulders, and hips a good stretch. I keep moving. My muscles are already warm, and the stretches increase my mobility.

4. Now I'm ready to run. I start off slowly and focus on my breath, taking some deep inhales. I get to decide whether I'm heading toward hills or staying flat, on trails or off. Once those decisions are made, I simply let my body follow along.

5. I focus on my breath and my stride. I appreciate the sunrise, since it's morning. I take it all in. I take in my surroundings. For this run, I'm not fixated on a problem. In fact, every time an anxious or negative thought wants to enter my consciousness, or any time my body wants to focus on superficial pain (which is different from injury pain!), I have a mantra that I repeat back instead, choosing to allow the negative thoughts to come and go, flickering away from my mind's screen. I recognize them, acknowledge them, and let them go.

6. The Sanskrit word *mantra* means "instrument for thinking." If we are using mantras to positively fuel our sweat sessions, they can work wonders. My mantras are carefully chosen for these times. They are short, positive, and catchy. They might include the following:

   I run for fun.

   Lean into hills.

   Power arms.

   Breathe and stride, breathe and stride.

   Thank you, legs. (or) Thank you, feet.

   Break the barrier.

   Strong and swift.

   Dare greatly.

   Define yourself.

   The last mantra, "define yourself," is especially powerful for me. It's one that Deena Kastor repeated to herself while winning the Chicago Marathon in 2005. It reminds me that I have the choice about how to see myself, how to be, and what script to choose. I set my own definition of self; I don't receive it externally. It's a simple mantra with far reach.

7. I use my mantras at various parts of the run, reminding myself of my strength, gratitude, and my own positive focus. The thoughts that I *will* allow to enter into my focus, once I have my breath and stride focus down, are positive thoughts, among them: goals, desires, dreams, gratitude, and awe-and-wonder thoughts.

8. After the run, or sometime later that day, I will write down some of these revelations, moments of wonder, and observations in a journal, collecting them as resources and reflective tools. I revisit them from time to time, reminding myself of gratitude, expansion, and dreams.

2. Lose Yourself to Find Yourself #KeepTheBeat

For this stress-burner, you can choose music with a good bass beat, something to which you can move your feet, something that makes you feel happy. I have a whole series of playlists I associate with mindfulness and happiness, and they really get me moving. Some have lyrics and others don't.

Whatever type of music you choose, stand and dance when you hear it. Dance as if nobody's watching. You can be in your living room, you can be with your family and friends, you can be alone—the point is not to focus on anything but your body moving to the music. Your dance is your expression, and it's just for you to feel. You might end up jumping, swaying side to side, bouncing, spinning in circles, rotating your arms in sweeps, or moving your hips in circles. You might be actively laughing; you might be so serene that barely a trace of a Mona Lisa smile rests on your lips. The point is to feel what you feel and to lose yourself in the rhythm of the dance. This dance is all yours to create, and the act of dancing is the gift.

You might dance for five minutes, ten minutes, or an hour. See what you feel; see what moves you. This dance is meant to be a release and an expression.

Martha Graham, widely known as one of the greatest dancers of the twentieth century and an inventor of modern dance, has many inspiring quotes about the power of dance to transform and reinvent. Here are two related quotes of hers that are among my touchstones. I use them in this exercise as a reminder of the power of unique expression—that each movement is a communication of something pure and essentially connected to our individuality, our being.

I wanted to begin not with characters or ideas, but with movements . . .
I wanted significant movement. I did not want it to be beautiful or fluid. I wanted it to be fraught with inner meaning, with excitement and surge.

—Martha Graham

There is a vitality, a life force, an energy, a quickening, which is translated through you into action. And because there is only one you in all time, this expression is unique and if you block it, it will never exist through any other medium and the world will not have it.

—Martha Graham

I keep these quotes with me, reminding myself of them every time I feel the urge to block myself with my inner critic. With this brief dance exercise, it becomes an invitation to find that point of release, to allow it, and to be surprised and delighted at our own impulses to celebrate, express, and dance.

3. Without Art, Earth Is Just "Eh" #ExpressYourself

Years ago, on an initial tour of the school during the interview process, I saw this message on a poster displayed in my future colleague Rainer's art room, and it made an impression right away. I smiled; it's true—a world without art is lackluster, isn't it?

Recently, on a visit to the Museum of Modern Art (MoMA) in New York City, I heard the following quip from an incredible art historian, Jane Royal: *"If you want to know the past, ask a historian. If you want to know the present, ask a journalist. If you want to know the future, ask an artist."* Art has that power to allow us to express something associated with hopes, dreams, and projections. And it lets our minds go from concrete thoughts to the more abstract.

Everyone is an artist.

The process is simple: you can choose your medium, and the goal is to spend about one hour of time set aside to create something that represents a "vision board." You'll then display the vision board at home, somewhere you can see it every day.

A vision board is a collection of drawings, images, etc., that all represent your goals, dreams, and other things that simply make you happy. When you see it, it gives you an immediate positive lift, and a feeling of strength, vitality, and commitment to goals. The vision board is an artistic expression and not meant to be representing what is— rather, it's what could be. I have some colorful, expressive examples of vision boards posted on the companion site at **caitlinkrause.com,** so you can check them out for inspiration, and then get started on your own!

Let loose and get creative with this, using as many media tools as you like—acrylic paints, crayons, watercolors, magazine cutouts, flyers, coasters, anything you like. This is *not* a scrapbook. This is a visualization tool, part of the same mindful technique used by successful leaders and Olympic athletes. It actually lets you craft what you dream, and in the act you envision the possibilities.

Use intention; you might even want to meditate for a few minutes, just breathing, and then journal about your vision board ahead of time, to set the mood. Take an inventory of how you feel—where you're at, and what drives you to dream big and dare more greatly. What words do you associate with happiness? What phrases or hashtags are your current mantras, and what ones can you harness that represent your future self? For the vision board (which can be on a simple piece of paper, a poster board, a cork board for pinning items, or a virtual canvas), I suggest the following key ingredients:

Colors you associate with inspiring themes

Symbols and pictures instead of only text

A few well-chosen words, mantras, hashtags, or sayings

Pictures or objects/symbols that you associate with inspiring themes

Drawings or images that naturally make you smile

For every element on your board, it should have a story behind it so that when you see it, you know what it represents. This board will be a creative representation of your personality, resilience, and commitment to stretch toward your dreams. The artistic exercise, too, has stress-reducing benefits. So it's a win-win, and a great way to #expressyourself!

Pablo Picasso said, *"Art is the lie that tells the truth."* This exercise can serve as a creative way to connect each of us with our truths, beyond limits.

Extensions and Additional Resources

If you want to read up on motivating mantras, a race-training article in the magazine *Runner's World* has good suggestions for mental focus (Aschwanden, 2011).

You can also encourage students to have their own mantras, to call them back to themselves, reminding them of deeper connection, intention, and focus. It's a simple, empowering exercise. You can have students create "mantra cards," colorful index cards decorated with mantras, which can be tucked in a pocket or placed on a desk. They are personal and symbolic, representing something important and inherently liberating, as we choose to reconnect with ourselves, releasing the shackles of stress and anxiety. As an alternative to writing the mantra on a card, you could choose a small object that reminds you of the mantra—a simple bracelet, for example.

EXERCISE
7

Building Solidarity

When spider webs unite, they can tie up a lion.

—Ethiopian proverb

Mindfulness is not a new topic and it's likely a concept that is greeted with a "Yes, *of course!*" response from well-intentioned collaborators in community. Yes, *of course* it's good to be caring. *Of course* it's essential to put kind, empathetic values into practice. *Of course* it's vital to prioritize compassion, prevent stress, and increase focus. *Yes, of course.* Mindfulness. It sounds reflexive—yet it's deceptively hard to practice, and we can sometimes feel alone when we're devoted to it. It takes intention, dedication, repetition. Gently. Curiously. Collectively. This exercise is all about building that strength in ourselves, and also looking for connections in community that can sustain us through the times when we feel we need support. We can appreciate our own resolve and inner strength and also treasure our relationships with others. Relational trust is a pillar of mindfulness-in-community, and it starts with our self-compassion and self-assurance.

Mindfulness is an open invitation, not a mandate. The invitation never expires; it's never too late to start, and we're never done practicing. The experience itself is what teaches me to stay human, stay humble, stay patient, stay open, stay flexible—traits that apply to all of life's challenges. It builds resilience in embodiment. It reminds me every day that *I am alive, and I am not done growing and learning.* The way I might find to use it is one approach; it's *"a way,"* not *"the way."* I am always listening. I remind myself of this each time I share my ideas about mindfulness with colleagues and friends.

Originally, when I started to use mindfulness in my teaching, I wanted to shout about it from the rooftops, proclaiming the joy of such a discovery so everyone around me could know about it. I was elated; so were my students. We had transformed a classroom together. Yet the energy has to authentically build where it gathers, and each individual educator is on a journey that involves a sense of agency in their own way of discovery. As you discover mindfulness, realize that it's free to be personalized, used, and approached in the way you find it best. It can be a revolution. Sometimes, as the song goes, it *starts with a whisper.*

> Mindfulness. It sounds reflexive—yet it's deceptively hard to practice. It takes intention, dedication, repetition.

There's a paradoxical quality to mindfulness, which has hit mainstream in recent years. I've summed up the mindfulness paradox in three parts:

It's often perceived as a clear imperative, yet it can be a hurdle to build in as a priority.

It's viewed as easy in theory, yet it's hard to practice.

It can be stereotyped as soft and an add-on, yet it's truly a foundational element, complementing other practices that can layer on top of it.

In this exercise, I will give three ideas about ways to *build professional solidarity for mindfulness.* I'll also give *three methods for building personal solidarity*—ways for us to keep our own mindful fires burning, even in the midst of hectic personal and professional schedules and increasing demands.

In this way, your entire being is strengthened—with solidarity, and without sweating the small stuff!

Mindfulness Skills Taught

▶ **AWARE:** becoming aware of our own needs and connections, strengthening the ties that will sustain our own mindfulness practices

▶ **ADVANCING:** these mindfulness values and practices are not static; they grow within ourselves, and with others in community, stretching and advancing to suit the current situation

▶ **AUTHENTIC:** living a connected, whole truth means that we must not fear exposure. These practices allow us to see and be seen more clearly, as we choose openness over perceived safety in silence. We might be changing patterns in order to be more authentically whole, and while it is initially challenging, we will find new collective freedom by choosing to live this way.

Practice

Professional Solidarity for Mindfulness: Three Ideas

Try out the following tactics, each of which is sure to give you a boost of connection and confidence in expanding your mindfulness practices and offerings.

1. Build a Scientific "Article Arsenal" of Evidence!

Let's face it, sometimes it helps to have ample research and data on hand that support what we're doing. This appeals to teams because, understandably, we want to feel assured that practices are tried, tested, and backed by science. Mindfulness methods are no exception—and, luckily, there is now a wealth of resources at our fingertips, ready to support all of us. If mindfulness is new to your school or district, this evidence is especially helpful to get the ball rolling. I've included a "recipe" below, which advises the ingredients, types of resources, and other supportive components you can have in your scientific "article arsenal." The specific articles will be most up-to-date if you combine some from this curated list with others that will appear as updated online resources.

Recipe for Article Arsenal

Three to five journal resources, such as the following online articles, each of which received significant media attention (while these are examples, you can find your own, plus additional resources online on the companion website, **caitlinkrause.com**):

- "Mindfulness Exercises for Children: Relaxation Techniques Calm K–12 Students and Staff, Leading to Better Grades and Better Behavior," *District Administration Magazine* (Zalaznick, May 4, 2017)

- "Mindfulness in Schools: When Meditation Replaces Detention," *US News & World Report* (Haupt, December 8, 2016)

- "Does Mindfulness Actually Work in Schools?" *The Atlantic* (Deruy, May 20, 2016)

One to two neuroscience findings, which tend to be denser reading material, talking more about what's happening with brain research and mindfulness practices. I keep these studies in a file, or a list on curation apps (such as Zotero, Evernote, Slite, or even Trello), for easy access and sorting. Here are two examples:

- "Meditation Programs for Psychological Stress and Well-being: A Systematic Review and Meta-analysis" (Goyal, Singh, and Sibinga, 2014)

- "The Neural Correlates of Social Connection" (Hutcherson, Seppala, and Gross, 2015)

One to two talks that can help drive home a point you would like to make in connection to your cause. I have a list of favorite ones, depending on audience, level of humor, and the angle of mindfulness—i.e., am I starting a leadership "kindness campaign" for middle school students or using mindfulness to reduce anxiety and increase focus for adults? Here are two favorites, which happen to be TED Talks, yet they don't need to be TED-specific:

- Sherry Turkle's TED Talk (2012) for discussion of the role of social media and connectivity to mindfulness and presence

- Headspace's Andy Puddicombe (2012) talking about Ten Mindful Minutes

One hands-on example: See if you can practice leading a two-minute mindfulness exercise for colleagues—something that will give them a feel for what you're discussing.

Student feedback: If you've started using some methods in class, consider running an anonymous survey using an online tool so that students can give you some honest, open feedback about what they are experiencing. That way, you'll have even more personal evidence when you seek support!

A note about the above "recipe" ingredients: *Keep them fresh by following current findings related to mindfulness on social networks such as Twitter and LinkedIn, which will help you to make sure the articles you're sourcing are up-to-date. (I post regular updates on these sites, and I find great resources shared there by people in a trusted global network.)*

2. Resist the Superhero; Use Your Superpower

This is a simple practice with a big reward: *get human*. Live by the Brené Brown motto and embrace your vulnerability rather than check it at the school door. As teachers, we often feel it's up to us to carry everyone else's needs and emotions at the expense of our own.

Perhaps we learned this because we're so good at meeting the learning requirements of others, in order to reach them and help mentor and guide them to reaching new levels. This is a skill, after all, and we can recognize it and feel good about it.

Rather than play superhero, though, it's time to invite a little wholeness back into our lives. Do you ever feel as if you get dressed up in your armor to go into work and save the day? It's not a bad image, yet the trouble is that sometimes we can't wait just to relax and "be ourselves," with our own foibles and humanity. What will happen, though, if students see the cracks in the mask?

In truth, they will trust us more. We will feel more engaged, and the entire process will become all the more real. Our lives will be connected.

To start, just realize that every time you want to put on the superhero costume, it's a mindful invitation to be more authentic, revealing your humanity instead. This is through curiosity, understanding, and admitting when we need help and support instead of trying to carry all the weight on our shoulders. It's actually just as proactive, just as heroic, and dare I say, even more creative to be Authentic Me rather than Superwoman.

This is a process that also has to do with Exercise 3, "Invite Partnership: Open the Door."

3. Invite Partnership: Open the Door

Quite simply, keep your classroom door open whenever you can. It sends a message. Invite other teachers to stop by, greet passersby and touring groups with a smile, and take time to have conversations that really allow another person to feel recognized and valued. Go out of your way to make others feel welcomed into the learning environment.

This is genuine and makes an impression, inviting connections and interactions in a learning community that will happen spontaneously. By showing colleagues that you're open, you invite camaraderie and partnership for the future, and you send a subtle message to students about teaming: *no man is an island*. It's a mindset you decide to have ahead of time, and it leads to amazing learning and leadership because students and colleagues see you're interacting with them in live-time, not according to a fixed, immobile schedule. Though it might sound counterintuitive, this engaged practice will actually *save you time*, by allowing you flexibly to adapt to current learning needs, and to rely on your environment for mutual support when needed.

A colleague, Ven, delivered a speech as I was leaving my teaching position in Belgium to move to Switzerland. When he shared such touching remarks, I was deeply moved, realizing that some actions I had thought were unnoticed were actually resonating. This is part of the speech:

> *I don't think there was ever a tense moment in your classroom. . . .*
>
> *Could it be because you have this innate capacity to empathize with [students], to suspend your judgment and just enjoy them for who they are?*
>
> *In short, you taught me the value of slowing down, enjoying the moment, and the value of self-reflection.*

I could never have expected to receive such a special address, and when I did, I knew that much of it was because I acted based on intuition, I left my door open, I invited impromptu interactions, and I took a risk in letting others see my genuine, flawed self. As teachers, we are capable of leading by example, making positive impressions, and establishing solidarity with each other. It shows you always have the chance to make a strong impression, even with a gentle whisper. All that you do matters. All that you are matters. You matter.

Personal Solidarity for Mindfulness: Three Ways

Now that you have three great tactics for building solidarity professionally, here are three ways that you can amp-up your personal solidarity (i.e., beyond school, too!).

1. Address the Common Misconceptions Head-on, without Apology

There's no space for shyness when it comes to defending your rights to freedom, and you don't need to bear the brunt of misconceptions about mindfulness, which can counteract intended effects, adding to stress. Susan Piver has a great post about this, "Mindfulness Doesn't Mean Peacefulness" (2011). I once heard Piver give a longer talk about this, in which she identified three common misconceptions about Mindfulness and Meditation (which I'll call "M&M" here). Here's a summary of notes I made about the talk's key points, along with my own thoughts about how to build strength in responses (rather than reactions):

Three Common Misconceptions about M&M

- **M&M mean you "turn off your thinking" or clear an empty space in your mind.**

  Your mind is not empty; rather, a mindful practice means you are *allowing*. It's a certain freedom. *Everything is allowed.* You operate with a genuine, generous, open curiosity, toward yourself and also toward others. Note that you are not replacing bad thoughts with happy ones, either! There's no good, no bad, no judgment; there's just a simple, pure awareness, allowing these thoughts to be, and calling our attention back to ourselves. In meditation, as one example, we can use a practice of focusing on the breath to help enable and facilitate this, with gentle encouragement and loving kindness for ourselves.

- **M&M is a self-help quick fix for an easy ROI (return on investment).**

  It's not a problem-solver or life-hack. It might end up doing good things, but if you walk in with an agenda in mind, you're creating a high-stakes scenario that's essentially not aligned with the gentle allowing of mindfulness. We don't want to create a game or points system in place of what is a true and authentic journey. The approach is a path of discovery back to your true self, the authentic one who has always been there, who knows you by name, who calls to say *Here I am.* Choose this "path of gentleness and fierceness," as Susan Piver says. It is enough. You are already enough.

• **M&M makes you a more peaceful, happy person.**

Incredible that this is a false impression, right? While a lot of mindful mavens (both women and men) are perceived as happier, and might report that we're at least *10 percent happier*, if we're tuned into the inimitable Dan Harris (2014), this is a misconception because it implies an equation. Mindfulness actually lets you recognize the true suffering, the vulnerability, the pain, the emotion, the realness of what might otherwise be masked or anesthetized. Does that end up making you a more relaxed, open individual? Yes, perhaps, because you are authentic and leaning in . . . yet, you might not be completely resilient, especially at the beginning of such a practice. In the beginning (and in the middle, too!), it might not feel happier. The eventual result, though, is you might find life far more satisfying because you're experiencing "what is."

2. Make Good Art

A key part of mindfulness involves accepting what is—and even embracing it; to keep doing what we're doing well, even in the face of adversity. That's what "make good art" means—to keep doing what we're doing. To keep listening to the internal voice of "the creator." There's a creator in each of us, and if that voice seeks approval, it ends up relinquishing its own drive, energy, and joy in favor of pleasing others. We need to "make good art" and to keep doing what is internally true to us. Not in spite of external challenges or criticism but *because of them*. "*Make good art*" is a mindfulness mantra, and a line from Neil Gaiman's incredibly bolstering commencement address at the Philadelphia Institute of Art in 2012. He said:

When things get tough, this is what you should do: Make good art. I'm serious. . . . Do what only you can do best: Make good art. Make it on the bad days, make it on the good days, too. (Gaiman, 2013)

He goes on to talk about making mistakes, too—about inviting them, expecting them, using them in the process of creating good material, being true to the self. In this message, I see "art" as anything we shape and create—"art" can be our lives, too.

Yes, cheers to making good art, now and always, because this is part of mindfulness. We are all creative. And, as educators, we might forget that it's up to us also to fill our own wellsprings and create the art that makes our hearts sing. Do it. Don't even think too hard or question the impulse. Go for it. Your life will thank you.

3. Water the Plants

Okay, after each day of actively teaching, we're tired, right? We're spending all day making good art and authentically connecting with active learners, and we're just plain tired by sundown. That's no surprise. So, here's the magical third solidarity practice:

Water the plants.

What does this mean? Well, it's back to basic needs; back to biology, in a sense. Plants need some basic elements to survive, including soil, sunlight, and water.

You, too, need to nurture yourself, giving what you need. Your ability to thrive depends on your own self-care. This includes enough rest, time for reflection, nutrition, and a bit of fresh air and light. Yes, there are compromises we make—yet your own awareness knows when you are sacrificing what is essential to your own health and well-being. Show self-love by watering your own plants. And stake your claim to some sunlight.

Extensions and Additional Resources

There's a lot that can grow from here; more resources and extensions can be found online at **caitlinkrause.com** so that we can keep building our mindfulness solidarity practices.

Les Petits Plaisirs: Simple Pleasures for Sustenance

EXERCISE
8

In the French film *Amélie* (2001), there's a scene in which the narrator talks about *les petits plaisirs*, i.e., the simple pleasures, which are gifts to appreciate, activities or other elements that we like for their sheer essence. Amélie is a character who could be called "mindful" in that she notices the details of her experiences, allowing them to bring her a certain happiness and contentment, both in solitude and in community.

This exercise is a great way to remind ourselves of just that fact: at any moment, we have the power to restore and renew. Sometimes, just thinking about these elements brings us back to ourselves, away from stress and anxiety. For each person, these small pleasures will be different. They might include resources we explore, for the pure joy of learning more about the subject itself; for the reward of the experience of growing and stretching . . . and coming back to self.

Mindfulness Skills Taught

▶ **AWARE:** becoming aware of the joyful activities that bring us contentment, happiness, and renewal

▶ **ADVANCING:** using these outlets to promote our own learning about ourselves; ways to advance by refreshing the mind, body, and spirit

▶ **AUTHENTIC:** when we tune in to the goodness of the positive feeling created, it's infectious—others will recognize and feel it, too

Practice

Ask yourself *"What makes me smile? What brings out the best in me? What stretches me, broadening my horizons? What brings me back to center?"* You can do some mindful ideating of your own, coming up with as many activities as you like on your list. Some might be social; others could be reflective and solitary.

In this exercise, I'll share ten of my own petits plaisirs. Notice that they're slightly different from "levity moments" (covered in Chapter 4). These involve specific repeatable practices and pastimes; experiences that we can offer ourselves in order to feel more at peace, whole, and connected. You'll see different angles and approaches in the examples I give. Many of mine are media-based, because I happen to be passionate about #MindfulMedia. I do not call these "hobbies," because the word acquires a diminutive connotation. Though initially labeled "simple pleasures," they are paradoxically complex, linked to our humanity, finding their way into our consciousness, affecting how we approach the world.

1 – **Photography**: I gravitate to photography as an art medium because it requires me to restructure the way my brain approaches a scene right in front of me. I'm thinking about light and dark, framing, angles, and capturing a moment in time that is transitory and therefore ephemeral. It also requires me to move in creative physical ways, to shift my own perspective.

2 – **Humans of Zürich (HoZ)**: So often, I walk around a city seeing faces, greeting them, yet never knowing more about their stories, backgrounds, cultures, and inner lives. Inspired by Brandon Stanton's "Humans of New York" storytelling project (Stanton, 2015), I started an open, curiosity-driven "Humans of Zürich" blog two years ago, and I have also regularly covered the Zürich Film Festival as a presswriter. Still in prototype mode, HoZ is essentially a connective vehicle to let me explore empathy and storytelling, which is also why I love films and all story-driven technology so much!

3 – **Virtual Reality (VR)**: On a similar note, as a writer and artist, I find VR compelling because it allows users to dive into unfamiliar experiences. For me, it's sheer delight to get to see how this new experiential medium is evolving and transforming the way in which we approach stories.

4 – **Poetry**: Yes, poetry must be near the top on my petits plaisirs list. It's an art, it's music, it's philosophy, it's a little bit of everything, and you can carry it around in your pocket. As Mary Oliver says, "Listen, are you breathing just a little and calling it a life?" (Oliver, 1996). When I teach poetry, I teach about the Four S's: *Sound, Structure, Symbolism, Significance*. A poem is not an obtuse puzzle, a thing out of which to beat a meaning—it's a vital language to enjoy deeply. I've included some poems in the "Resources" section; a daily poem happens to make my *journey* brighter. (Incidentally, the word *journey* comes from how far one could travel in a day, or a *jour,* in French. How poetic!)

5 – **Music**: My musical musts for petits plaisirs include anything to which I can drum or move my hands and feet. When I'm creating (writing, art, or other), I enjoy certain music to fit my mood, sometimes instrumental or classical, sometimes not. Everyone has criteria for what music pleases them, and articles have suggested that music can tune with brainwaves along a certain frequency or wavelength. At any rate, I use music as an expressive conduit, combining with movement and dance. And it's healthy. As the Confucius saying goes, "Show me how a community dances and I'll tell you if they are healthy or not."

6 – **Creating and Consuming ART on Social Media**: I use Instagram in this way; it's where I can blend storytelling and visuals, focusing on mindful, artistic, curiosity-driven design. While I do project to an audience, my first Instagram audience is myself—I'm essentially crafting a thing of beauty that brings me personal delight. It's a space for play, whereas I use other social media platforms for more professional development, content, learning, and outreach. Instagram

is a whimsical wonderland for me, though this might change. You get to decide where you might have a space like this, if any, online or offline. You can decide where, if, and how you have such a place. The beauty is wherever it is, it becomes your expressive outlet, and you can also find other like-minded artists and creators with whom to share, so there's an inspiration give and take!

7 – **Water**: Water is an element that brings me a sense of peace and tranquility. Whether it's being near a lake or ocean, strolling alongside a river or burbling brook, or simply contemplating the reflections in a fountain, water is a resource for my mindfulness. I can swim, skip stones, or just be near water to allow some sort of unfolding to take place. Even a perceived chore like doing dishes also appeals to me, but this might be a rare affinity! Choose an element you like, and find a way to incorporate it into your activities.

8 – **Dogs**: I was lucky to grow up with a giant, rambunctious black Labrador as part of our family. He was loving, patient, kind, and filled with irrepressible energy. I can't help but believe that knowing him made me a better person. While we might not all be able to have animals as pets, our relationship with animals, knowing them—observing them and having a reverence for their place in the world—reminds us of the interconnectedness of all creatures, great and small.

9 – **Chocolate**: The ultimate of indulgences! After living in both Belgium and Switzerland, both with cultures that pride themselves on their chocolate legacy, I've become somewhat of an aficionado. At the very least, I'm a master chocolate taster, and I must say that it's a prime delight to revel in a praliné, truffle, ganache, or bar. I enjoy the aroma, the texture, and the rich-sounding "snap" of a dark piece of chocolate as it breaks off between my teeth. Chocolate tasting is a tradition and an art, for sure. Couple this with enjoying a coffee or tea, and it's an instant transportation to a mindful zone.

10 – **Look Up and Look Out**: Looking up and looking out for others is a bit different from "paying it forward" because it's not simply a random act of kindness; it's a way to approach community. It begins by looking up from our mobile phones and daily routines and fixations. We look up from our self-driven activities, and then begin to look out for others, going beyond ourselves. Some of this involves what we might think of as manners, though they're applied to anticipate needs. It might sound odd to place "looking up" in a list of pleasures, yet the ability to look out for others and connect in a way that makes lives better is something that brings enjoyment. You can set this as a mindset, and it can bring you a certain sense of peace and delight in your day. It takes no expense, and just a little effort.

One example of a #LookUpAndLookOut mindset: public transportation. I look out for parents with little children, the elderly, and those who might need help with a seat or an extra hand on/off. In all situations, I try to maintain social awareness. I use others' names whenever possible, and check in with those I know to see how they are. I anticipate emotions, desires, and feelings, using mindfulness as a connection. Note that this is different from intrusive problem-solving or some belief that I know what's best for another person—I'm simply using a heightened social awareness to contribute in small ways to a better world, and this process brings me back to self.

Extensions and Additional Resources

The list does not have to stop with the number ten. In fact, my list goes on and on, and I'm constantly adding to the prime delights, which add to happiness and a sense of greater good. As you create your own list of les petits plaisirs, you can also journal-reflect about them, making it an uplifting reflective practice, adding new ones as you discover what makes your own heart sing.

Conclusion

I often "step back" from my own life situations, taking what I call a "mindful meta-moment" to become aware of my awareness—to embody what Jon Kabat-Zinn calls a *Homo Sapiens Sapiens*—I am a human who thinks, and I am aware of my thinking. Just like at the end of one of those films where the camera pulls away from the protagonist, and we begin to see not just her view but the surrounding landscape and the larger frame of the story, I zoom out a bit from my own emotional conditions, and I'm able to see the grand scope of things more clearly. This viewpoint allows me to view each life situation with less emotional reactivity (yet still colored with wonderful emotions!), and I also begin to see that my work and life have unclear distinctions—there is cohesion and consonance.

In the same sense, as you develop personal mindfulness routines, you will find that these exercises will spill into your "work day," as mindfulness is a practice we cultivate and inhabit all the time. It reconnects us with our bodies and our well-being, and we begin to see that we can *embody* this way of being at any time of day; we no longer have to put on armor to face the challenges of the workplace—nor should we! Living an "undivided life"—one in which we are truly ourselves in our workplace—is not only liberating but physically more healthy, as the body viscerally experiences and senses that deep connection. For leaders, this is a humanizing that involves development of emotional intelligence and "soft skills," now thought to be just as much of a necessity in the workplace as traditional hard skills and raw abilities.

In her 2018 book *How We Work: Live Your Purpose, Reclaim Your Sanity, and Embrace the Daily Grind,* Leah Weiss, who teaches courses on compassionate leadership at the Stanford Graduate School of Business, talks about the great benefits of developing a mindfulness practice, applying it to every day, for a holistic, whole-life benefit. Of course, the more support we have from our organizations and workplaces, the easier it is to integrate mindfulness into our complete life, with a feeling of wholeness. As Weiss says, "There is the biggest challenge: that mindfulness can't ultimately be whittled down to a course (mandatory or otherwise). In order to be effective, it must be woven into the fabric of the workplace. Meditating or meeting once a month won't do the trick—these practices have to be implemented consistently, on a daily basis—especially when things are busy and stressful. . . . There is no magical threshold that separates 'work' and 'life.' All of it is part of the same path" (Weiss, 2018).

As we move to the next section of this book, looking to integrate mindfulness into classroom exercises linked to curriculum, take a mindful meta-moment to step back from your life situations, asking yourself the following questions:

1. In what ways does my daily work routine allow me to be human?

2. Do I incorporate movement and physicality into my day in a way that connects me with my body and mind?

3. How can I encourage myself to "take three breaths" at work, especially when I experience beginning signs of stress?

4. In what ways do I sometimes operate on "autopilot" at work? How can I flip that situation?

5. How do my physical home space and work space encourage mindfulness? What can I do to create even more opportunities to practice mindfulness, by choosing to redesign certain elements?

CHAPTER 4

Mindfulness in the Classroom and Community

Introduction to Mindfulness for Students

Mindfulness is much more than an exercise or a habit to practice and adopt; it's a way to be in the world. *Mindfulness* might seem like an abstract ideal, but it can be quite concrete, if we look at how it takes shape in the classroom.

Being mindful means setting a foundation where all are welcome and honored, and encouraged to use their own authentic voices to connect with themselves and others. I started out focusing on writing, poetry, storytelling, and expression as an entry to awareness and global empathy, across cultures and backgrounds. I looked at all sorts of factors, trying to isolate what brought about the best experiences for learners. Ultimately, I realized that all meaningful exchanges in a classroom are built upon a firm foundation of trust and respect. I listened. Asking my own students to tell me what made a difference for them, I invited them to imagine their ideal classroom spaces. Because mindfulness is rooted in presence and purpose, setting up the ideal classroom space is the foundation for mindful learning in practice. I encourage you to revisit Chapter 2 and **caitlinkrause.com** for more ideas on how to set up a mindful learning space.

Do you remember a classroom that you just couldn't wait to enter, as a student? What did it feel like to be part of it? What qualities made it memorable? What are "a positive place"

"recognized me as a person"

"gave me a sense of belonging"

"challenged and encouraged me"

"made me laugh"

"made me feel as if people cared"

"was a safe space to take risks"

Figure 4.1 • "What Are the Characteristics of a Class That Stands Out in Your Mind?"

the characteristics of a positive class? The answers shown in Figure 4.1 were the most common and frequent responses in my surveys, when I asked my students this question, to tell me what classrooms stood out in their minds . . . and, I listened closely to their responses. I consider the perspective of a learner, recognizing what would make me comfortable and most able to learn and creatively express ideas without anxiety and inhibition. The students' answers mirrored my own—and the more colleagues and collaborators I have queried about this, the more I have heard the same affirmations. Positive classrooms make a difference.

In a design model, feedback is critical—here, the "users" are students. Their input should inform the planning of learning spaces and environments. I used student feedback continually to shape and reshape my approach to designing the optimal learning environment, and I now see an even larger long-term impact, after conducting the student interviews highlighted in this book. Openness, creative invitations, cultivating compassion, and emotional intelligence are all part of the equation of skillful classroom design.

Infusing mindfulness into our daily curriculum content is part of that design. This "Mindfulness Exercises for Students" section offers engaging lessons and exercises to use and apply in your classroom, with examples along the way about how they have worked for me, and where your own imagination could take you. You have ample space for adaptations and personalization, and I have included guidance and tips for various approaches you could take.

The more exciting and hands-on it is, the more a student will enjoy the lessons and expand his mindset. I liked when we did class presentations because they were so interactive and having that sense of being listened to and hearing what others had to say was just a very good feeling of community and collaboration.

—Rafael, *former student*

These exercises directly apply the core principles of mindfulness to our classrooms, across the curriculum, embedded in subjects and topics, rather than treating *mindfulness* as an isolated subject. I choose to incorporate it into the learning environment as a cohesive element. It serves to amplify the classroom experience, and the integration of mindfulness naturally invites creativity, amplifies well-being, and promotes happiness. It's a prime component of an engaging, empathetic, compassionate learning atmosphere and serves as a connected facet of optimal learning.

Notice that, at any time, you can slow down, isolate, and focus on elements of mindfulness with students. You gauge the pace and depth according to the needs and presence in the room. In each individual exercise, I'll give more details about this, as well as guidance about how to scaffold and support the activities.

Mindful Exercise Format

Each of the exercises has the following general format, with some variation:

Title of Exercise

Brief overview and description

Mindfulness Skills Taught

Maps out details about the Mindfulness AAA Mindset, showing how Aware, Advancing, and Authentic elements are embedded, to give an idea of outcomes and benefits

Challenge Tips

Gives considerations regarding challenges and students' reactions to the exercise; amount and types of support that might help to augment the lesson

Creativity Insights

Describes some of the opportunities, within the exercise, for invention, ideation, and open connection

Time Requirement
Resource Materials Needed
How to Teach It

In addition to mapping out the exercises according to the above outline, additional details about student responses and reactions are included, which allow us to envision how the environment can take shape.

For each exercise, elements of journaling are noted. I do recommend the use of journals, sketches, doodles, and handwriting when possible. Incorporating written, verbal, and multimedia expression in student engagement and responses

> *A note on handwriting:* If you haven't seen Clive Thompson's INBOUND Bold Talk "How the Way You Write Changes the Way You Think," it's well worth a watch on the subject of handwriting and note-taking. We already discussed this talk in Chapter 2, yet it's *that good* that it's worth reemphasizing!

boosts the dynamic sharing; it gives a chance for students to reflect and form personal connections before "going public" with formal, often-typed ideas that are intended for mass-public consumption (via blogs or other presentation formats). When appropriate to the nature of the exercise, I also include *"Mindfulness Writing Exercise Prompt(s)"* and *"Reflection Questions"* to enhance the quality of mindful connection.

The Takeaway

Closing messages, lasting impressions, and possible extensions are provided here.

Student Exercises

Sixteen Mindfulness Exercises for the Classroom: All disciplines are covered, adaptable for your grade level, plus you can use the eight "Mindfulness Exercises for Teachers" in Chapter 3 with students, too! The five themes of the student exercises *"Voice," "Care," "Truth," "Nature,"* and *"Lead"* are designed to be able to fit both curriculum areas and interdisciplinary links that align with broad goals, intentions, and values. The outline below details the areas of curriculum focus and also the general themes. Mindfulness is a core component of every exercise.

1. VOICE

Awareness Boosters, Identity Investigations, and Multiple Perspective Considerations

- **Great Debates: "Fire and Ice"** (LA / SCI)
- **Out of This World** (SCI / SS)
- **Story of My Name** (ALL)

2. CARE

Compassion, Empathy, Social-Emotional Learning, Sense(s), and Sensibility

- **Levity Moments** (ALL)
- **Gratitude and Mindful Mentors** (SS / LA / SCI / MATH)
- **Storytelling, Empathy, and Kindness** (ALL)

3. TRUTH

Global Digital Citizens, Pioneers for Truth, and Embodied Ethics

- **Digital Mindful Citizen** (ALL)
- **Dignified Selfie** (SS / LA)
- **The Danger of a Single Story** (ALL)

4. NATURE

STEAM, Biomimicry, Virtual Worlds, and Animated Landscapes

- **Mindful Journaling:** Nature Journals and Moments of Wonder (ALL)

- ▶ **Nature as Teacher:** Bold Biomimicry and Design Thinking (ALL)
- ▶ **Architecture and Virtual Worlds:** Designing Mindful Community Spaces (ALL)

5. LEAD

Community, Courage, and Leadership

- ▶ **What Makes a Mindful Leader?** (ALL)
- ▶ **Sustainability and Poetry Perspectives:** Meditations on "Good" (ALL)
- ▶ **Mirror, Mirror:** Empathetic Partner Exercises that Help to Hone Focus, Leadership, and Listening Skills in the Age of AI (ALL)
- ▶ **The Four P's:** Projects, Passion, Peers, and Play (ALL)

Considerations

Each of the exercises above can also be used as a mindful design module as part of a supportive student advisory program, homeroom, or enrichment class.

Periodically, and definitely whenever you are uncertain or doubt the statement above, I suggest the following considerations:

- ▶ **ADDRESS** your learning outcomes and goals for the unit of study.
- ▶ **REACH OUT** to your community of collaborators for input and support. Sometimes, we might feel "on our own" in taking new risks or designing what we feel is exciting, cutting-edge learning. Now, with an online PLN (personal learning network) that spans the globe, you never need to feel alone, and you're never without resources to help you make this journey as creative as possible! You'll find ample support materials and inspirations online at **caitlinkrause.com** and through many hashtags on Twitter, including #mindfulness, #MindfulByDesign, and #mindfullearning, among others.
- ▶ **IN ADDITION,** circle back to share some of what you're doing and learning with your local network, which could include your technology coordinator and administrative team—that way, you'll have support on the ground, too!

While I've designated some specialized exercises, they all essentially support all areas of curriculum, and underscore communication and relationship-building. Each exercise is designed to be challenging and encouraging at the same time. Practicing mindful learning involves *healthy mental/physical stretching, development of voice, taking ownership of learning, and strengthening resilience.* By promoting the engagement within a diverse learning community, these exercises are a way to enhance both individual appreciation of the learning process, outcomes, and empathetic understanding of self and others. Greater insights are fostered and favored. And it cannot be emphasized enough: *you, as teacher, are empowered to use your classroom as a place of research—to shape, tweak, and design what works best for you!*

> You, as teacher, are empowered to use your classroom as a place of research—to shape, tweak, and design what works best for you!

Over my years of teaching, the above statement is what made the biggest difference in my own experience. I was always changing and shaping the curriculum according to my needs and the needs of the learning community. As theoretical physicist and cosmologist Stephen Hawking famously said, "Intelligence is the ability to adapt to change." I want purposefully to stay open to what I cannot predict, to what emerges in the future. This is adaptive intelligence.

Mindfulness allowed me to be aware of this malleable learning process, with myself as a learner. I keep what works and change what doesn't, and I celebrate the growth mindset and the process along the way. By empowering myself, I also acknowledge my own vulnerability, and the classroom becomes an open space of play and growth, rather than an intimidating arena in which students and I look to prove ourselves. This could be the true nature of a flipped classroom: flip it to empower and engage, from within!

Feel free to use these ideas as a supportive scaffold for your own specialized content—that's truly where the learning comes alive, with your own expertise and personalization to fit your needs. You can also share ideas and feedback, joining our global community of curious collaboration.

I'm devoted to collecting and curating an ongoing set of the most current mindfulness findings, as peer-reviewed research, longitudinal studies, and other links and resources become more accessible. You can refer to **caitlinkrause.com** to extend your PLN and feel supported, every step of the way.

Related resources and links are continually being updated on the companion website. It's a joyful, creative worldwide movement, filled with possibility, and I'm personally grateful to join forces with you as we collaborate to envision and build the best learning environments and communities. Thank you to the wellspring of students, colleagues, and influencers who have helped to shape and define what mindfulness truly means in application and embodiment.

Great Debates: "Fire and Ice"

EXERCISE 1

Who doesn't love an active classroom, filled with voice and (dare I use the term) *engagement*? You don't have to look further than this exercise to see what engagement looks like. The poem "Fire and Ice," by Robert Frost, involves a mix of abstract and concrete terms, with many different angles, interpretations, and applications from the opening lines: "Some say the world will end in fire, / Some say in ice. / From what I've tasted of desire / I hold with those who favor fire" (Frost, 1920). It instantly gets everyone involved—there are no "passive observers" in this reading. It's an activity that can be shortened or lengthened and added into lesson plans already in place. It causes students to step back and consider multiple angles, deciding what they believe and taking a stance. It's easily incorporated into science classes, humanities, and beyond, making for profound interdisciplinary connections. If you wish to involve films, vlogs, and multimedia platforms, it easily lends itself to this style of digital narratives and storytelling. We're sparking a blazing debate from the kindling of a timeless topic.

Mindfulness Skills Taught

▶ **AWARE:** builds awareness of multiple perspectives coexisting; several applications of understanding

▶ **ADVANCING:** encourages students to recognize symbols and to interpret meaning in language; inquisitive, open, positive debate can support a study of rhetoric

▶ **AUTHENTIC:** allows students to develop a personal reaction and point of view; to show respect and nonjudgment toward others

Challenge Tips

Some of the language and interpretation can be challenging, yet it's highly rewarding, and students will feel as if they've deciphered a secret code once they understand Frost's play with language.

Time Requirement: Thirty minutes

Resource Materials Needed

▶ **POEM,** "Fire and Ice," by Robert Frost

How to Teach It

Let students know that this poem is one of the most celebrated debate pieces. As they listen for the first time, they should just focus on enjoyment, to hear the language. Begin by reading the poem out loud. It will help to show the words visually on a projector, pointing out the line breaks and format, as well as explaining definitions of challenging words such as *suffice*.

Then, read it aloud again, even more slowly and deliberately, emphasizing words as you feel them, because students will want to catch details the second time around. The poem is absolutely striking and beautiful in its language, and it's a sensual, pleasurable experience, hearing it out loud and giving attention to the words.

After the second time through, allow students to think quietly for two or three minutes, just letting their own internal thoughts cue them about reactions and interpretations. You might wish to read the poem a third time through. Encourage them to jot down their notes on paper—I have students write in creative journals, marking the date and title "Fire and Ice."

Now, before students share any ideas, let them know they are about to have a debate about which is stronger for destruction: fire or ice. They must choose to take a stance and write about it. You can steer them to include details from science, economics, psychology—virtually any subject that you wish to involve.

Encourage them to write for a full five minutes about why their side—fire or ice—is more destructive. They can use lists, charts, quotes, examples, and more as explanation and evidence.

Once students have had the chance to compose their ideas and reflections, most will be eager to share them with others. Form small groups of four to five students, letting each have a voice to express an opinion in an open roundtable of notes-sharing.

This can also grow to a whole-class discussion; you can choose to bring in a talk about personalities and human kindness. Ultimately, Frost is making a strong statement about the human heart and empathy. This is an entry to connect with students and allow them to bring in their own stories and opinions, helping to make these learning experiences authentic and meaningful.

Some questions below are "starting points" for community discussion. Point students to conduct their own research, sharing answers in small groups or partnerships before engaging in a larger class discussion.

Starting Points for Discussion

▶ Which side appeals to you more, *fire* or *ice*, as the most powerful, when talking about destruction?

▶ In what ways are both fire and ice useful for humans? How did the discovery of fire help ancient civilizations? Similarly, how has ice been beneficial and used in various scientific applications?

▶ Could destruction from fire and/or ice be an environmental concern? How?

▶ Do you think Frost is making a literal argument or a figurative one? Why?

▶ Does Frost take a stance on the issue? If so, what do you think that stance is, and why could you imagine he feels this way?

▶ How does this topic also address human behavior?

▶ What can we do in society to bring about more compassion, recognizing both the fire and ice in human behavior? Can you think of real situations that grow "icy" or "fiery"? In these situations, how can tension be diffused instead of heightened?

Again, depending on your subject area and grade level, complexity can grow, and you can create your own discussion questions. It's an ideal ice-breaker (!) for classes in science and the humanities.

You might also wish to point out several online scholar sites with interpretations of the famous Frost piece (yes, the poet's name always strikes me as all too appropriate, and students will catch the word-play humor!). Have each student play a "historical scholar" role, researching a part of the history of the poem and sharing discovered facts with the rest of the group. This can make for a good blog post assignment, too.

The Takeaway

Students understand the nature of debate, and will grasp the paradox that Frost expresses.

What can be seen as a scientific debate shifts to a discussion about human relationships.

Many students will find the discussion meaningful on a personal level.

Action in class grows, and students recognize a poem that looks beautifully simple in language yet has complex interpretations and many mindful applications! Through reflection, awareness, authenticity, and empathy, this exercise is a true practice in mindfulness, and students will visit and revisit angles of the insights throughout the year. In my experiences using this poem as an exercise in class, this makes for a standout community-builder, and for many students, an all-time favorite expressive event.

EXERCISE 2

Out of This World

Le seul véritable voyage . . . ce ne serait pas d'aller vers de nou-veaux paysages, mais d'avoir d'autres yeux, de voir l'univers avec les yeux d'un autre, de cent autres, de voir les cent univers que chacun d'eux voit. . . . **The only true voyage of discovery . . . would be not to visit new landscapes, but to possess other eyes, to see the universe through the eyes of another, of a hundred others, to see the hundred universes that each of them sees.**

—Marcel Proust (1923)

How can we boost students' perceptive abilities and their sense of freedom and creativity as well? Our awareness heightens when we adopt a perception that travels beyond our "self." Given the necessary resources, students are fantastic at doing this, perhaps due to their naturally rich powers of imagination. This exercise involves a deep amount of play, encouraging students to think from an entirely new viewpoint—*from outer space!* Anyone already enamored with dystopian literature, sci-fi genres, and all sorts of derivatives will love this exercise, which hinges on questioning, dreaming, and a touch of dramatic irony.

Mindfulness Skills Taught

▶ **AWARE:** awareness of surroundings are encouraged; noticing the details

▶ **ADVANCING:** allows students to see how they can work together, conduct research, and build understanding as a foundation for "explaining" the phenomena

▶ **AUTHENTIC:** humor can break down barriers in this exercise, which is also a great vehicle for performance pieces, poetry, and beyond

Challenge Tips

The point of entry here is imagination and wonder; you can easily get the ball rolling by asking students how they would describe something if they did not have the scientific truth to explain it.

Creativity Insights

Students might also get creative, making connections to when they were younger, before they had words and language to explain something they were observing in nature. How could sunsets, rainbows, thunderstorms, and other natural phenomena be extra wonder-full when we imagine a new identity for ourselves? This exercise is brimming with creativity, and there are many links and extensions. One way in which to expand this exercise is to include a mindful sketching activity where students must closely observe and sketch their chosen object, aiming to reflect its shape, contour, and relative dimensions. They can even try a blind sketch, seeing if they can represent the object on paper with their eyes closed.

Time Requirement: Sixty minutes

Resource Materials Needed

▸ **POEM,** "Southbound on the Freeway," by May Swenson

▸ **WRITING JOURNALS**

How to Teach It

Part 1: Alien Discovery

Start by taking students outside, if you have the ability to access nature with your classes. Have them bring their writing journals and pens. Make sure to bring your own journal and a copy of the May Swenson poem. As they sit (in grass, on benches, whatever space is comfortable and available), ask them to look around and notice their surroundings.

Ask students to imagine they are opening their eyes to see the world anew.

Jump right into the first part of this exercise, asking them to imagine they are an alien who has just arrived on Earth as the emissary from a foreign planet. They were sent here on an expedition of discovery, and their job is to observe Earth and report back their findings in a short report to their commandant on their home planet.

For the first report, their job is to look around and choose some detail in the surroundings to write about and explain *as if they have never seen it before*. They must imagine what purpose it serves and how to describe it to fellow aliens on their home planet. For the sake of this exercise, they will be communicating in the English language, though they don't know the names for specific objects, nor do they understand their function.

Still while outside, give a timed five minutes to complete this writing exercise in journals before going back in the classroom. Tell them that these could be loose notes and jottings; they can make it something more polished later. Try to encourage them to focus on one object they can visualize as they write (it can be "natural/organic" or something "man-made"). If you notice anyone struggling, you can simply encourage them to look at *anything*—a leaf, a pinecone, a blade of grass—and imagine how this object would appear to an alien.

Outside, or once back inside, read the following excerpt of the poem out loud:

> **Southbound on the Freeway**
>
> *by May Swenson*
>
> The creatures of this star
>
> are made of metal and glass.
>
> Their feet are round and roll
>
> on diagrams of long
>
> measuring tapes, dark
>
> with white lines.
>
> They have four eyes.
>
> The two in back are red.

Consider reading the poem a second time if this would benefit students and comprehension. At the end, ask them what they think this poem is "about"—and wait for them to go beyond identifying that it's about *cars*. What else do they notice? How is it written? In what style? How does the language tell us that the speaker in the poem is an alien?

Give students time to craft their pieces into something that is "share-able" and encourage them not to give away the name of the object they are describing.

To share, you can choose to have them pair and share, share with small groups, and/or share aloud to the whole class.

Part 2: Digging Deeper

Continuing in their role as an alien, each student must now look a bit more deeply at their chosen object, discovering the answer to the question:

What is its purpose? According to the items they have chosen, you may form them into categorical groups if there are overlaps. Their job, now, is to investigate for ten minutes, using all resources (Internet, observation, talking it out in a group) to discuss the overall function of this object in a system. They might wish to approach this question from the following angles:

- How does this object absorb, store, and also give energy?
- What role does it play in the life cycle of the world, and/or the humans who inhabit it?
- What are its primary functions and secondary functions?
- Who or what benefits from these functions?
- What is its source of creation?

See how many of the above questions can be answered, using a scientific point of view, looking for rational explanations and evidence to support the claim.

As students reflect and record ideas, this can contribute to an active classroom discussion right away. You might also wish to turn it into a formal assignment, letting students draft a creative writing piece for a more structured submission or online blog post.

When students begin to investigate as scientists, with the goal of uncovering truth, this does not diminish their capacity to wonder, create, and dream—in effect, it is a mindfulness exercise in awareness and advancement, and it uncovers authentic truths that then allow us to build even better realms of possibility.

Part 3: A Better World

When we aim to create improvements, often we are making an advancement on what has come before. Students will be interested in the origins of the quote "standing on the shoulders of giants" (Yoon, 2004), tracing back to the twelfth century with Bernard of Chartres and later made famous by Sir Isaac Newton. You can ask them what the phrase means to them, in their roles as aliens. In essence, it's a mindfulness quote that is talking about collective collaboration, building upon knowledge to create something even better. This is also a definition for "technology"—something created to improve conditions of society in some way. It's "the application of science for practical purposes," as defined by the *Oxford English Dictionary*.

Thinking about this mindful definition, their job (either in groups or individually) is to *design some improvement upon the object that they have chosen.* The prompt can be the following:

> *Imagine that, in your persona role as an alien, your home planet has a similar object that plays the same function, but it is an improved version that already has a greater level of advancement. Describe this improvement, and explain that advanced technology to the humans here on Earth.*

Encourage students, even if they are working in groups, to take a few minutes to "mindstorm" in journals. Then they could collaborate and sketch ideas together.

After composing their ideas and reflections, they can share ideas together and hash out how to show this to the group.

They can then give a five-minute presentation to share with the class; at this time, they could also share and summarize some of Parts 1 and 2.

Students can also post their "Alien Reports and Discoveries" on their blogs. Encourage the first "wondering" post to be shared as a blog post. You can see some examples on the companion website at **caitlinkrause.com**—these are colorful, creative exercises that engage the whole class when read out loud!

The Takeaway

At the end, you can have a debrief about the benefits of seeing from other perspectives. Ultimately, this is a universal empathy exercise that also leads to greater discoveries.

Connections might be made to cultural exchange and the benefits of connecting and understanding anything that might be seen as a "foreign" perspective.

Post-Debrief

Here are some debrief questions that serve as useful for a class discussion at the end of the lesson:

- What did you notice about your behavior in the role of an alien? What were your natural character traits as you looked to discover more about the world around you? (Possible answers could be "inquisitive, open-minded, curious, confused, frustrated.")
- Why or how could the traits above be useful in the theme of invention and science?
- Were any of your Alien Reports in Part 1 humorous? Why is that?
- Do we ever feel that same humor about being in a new situation? Have you ever felt this way, encountering a new situation? (This is where I will tell students about my own experiences traveling, and how in Europe there are different light switches, or different electrical devices, and sometimes even the simplest things are hard to figure out and confusing. I can only imagine how an alien would feel, encountering this land.)
- How could traits of mindfulness and empathy help us as scientists making discoveries?
- What global connections can you make about interactions between societies, and ways we can help each other?

Note that if you cannot go outside, you can bring in an assortment of the natural objects, using them as the same source of discovery. You can also (as mentioned in "Creativity Insights" at the beginning of this exercise) provide opportunities for sketching the object as a method of mindful awareness through close observation.

Story of My Name

EXERCISE
3

We use names every day, and they are core components of establishing a community. As teachers, how often do we eagerly pore over our class lists of students' names at the beginning of a course, trying to memorize each one and pronounce it perfectly, to honor each student and show consideration and care? On the first day, we greet each student by name in a way that aims to invite them into a space of mindful learning. We want them to feel as if they belong, and to feel comfortable asking questions, interacting, and connecting with others. For students, too, the start of the year can feature an overwhelming series of name games, and results can be daunting and even tedious. This exercise is an exciting alternative to all of the name games and ice-breakers that might grow repetitive, and it serves as an inclusive community-building activity.

Mindfulness Skills Taught

- **AWARE:** builds awareness of each other's identities, deeper than names, emphasizing their meanings and how we feel about the names we have, which were usually inherited rather than chosen

- **ADVANCING:** encourages the class community to recognize and remember one another's names and also consider where those names come from, acknowledging cultures, histories, and values

- **AUTHENTIC:** ultimately, this is a storytelling exercise that connects to a deeper appreciation of self, heritage, and identity

Challenge Tips

This exercise is fairly straightforward and clear. If students seem to hesitate, it's likely because they are, quite understandably, intimidated or uncomfortable opening up right away and sharing what might feel vulnerable or too personal. I have had adults in workshops who seem tentative at first about this, until they start writing and get the ball rolling.

You can give several modifications to accommodate for shyness or hesitation. The point is to get students writing, and encourage them to share with the class. You might ask them to focus on their middle names instead, or to write about what they would rename themselves if they could choose another name. There are many ways to adapt this exercise in order to invite full participation.

Creativity Insights

The exercise itself is creative by nature, and involves a lot of stretching across boundaries. If you have time, you can also have students create some sort of colorful card, plaque, sign, or virtual heading that displays their name in an artistic, creative way that is a visual representation of the name's etymology.

Time Requirement: Thirty minutes

Resource Materials Needed

▶ **JOURNALS**

▶ **ART MATERIALS** (if desired)

How to Teach It

This exercise is an excellent way to kick off a school term or semester, though it could be done at any time of year. When students come into the classroom, ask them to get out their journals right away, to write down the word *etymology*. Strictly speaking, in linguistic lingo and denotation, etymology means "the origin of a word and the historical development of its meaning." Today, tell students they'll be writing about the *etymology of their names—an origin story we call "Story of My Name."*

In pure stream-of-consciousness free-write style, their writing prompt, for five minutes in journals (you can gauge this timing and shorten to three minutes if you prefer), is the following:

Mindfulness Writing Exercise Prompt

Story of My Name: You have five minutes to write the story about the etymology of your first name. How did you come to receive that name? Is there a background related to it, or a special significance? What does it mean, and who chose it for you? You can write about anything associated with your name—how it came to be, if it's symbolic of anything, and also if you have any nicknames you like to be called. You can write how you feel about your name, and any associations you have with it. You can include ways that you tell other people to remember your name. Feel free to get creative, letting all sorts of connections to your name spill out on the page! The important thing is to keep writing everything that comes to mind. Our five minutes begin . . . now.

The prompt here runs in several directions *on purpose*—students can pick up any thread they like and start writing from there. Because it's all about their name, as soon as they have an angle they like, they can expand and expound in that direction.

This is an exercise that hinges on trust, flow, openness, and time. I will purposefully write alongside students, so that I am also sending signals that I care about the exercise. My participation also underscores camaraderie, and encourages students to give themselves validation instead of asking me for approval and reassurance. They "go for it" as they see I'm also "going for it." I make an announcement, gently, when there is one minute left, prompting students to work their way to a fitting conclusion to the story—at least, for now! At the end of the writing time, everyone is immediately invited to form a circle and share the pieces out loud.

For sharing, I suggest to students that they *read text directly from journals, exactly as it appears on the page*. I guide in this way for several reasons. First, it levels the playing field, in a significant way. It prevents extemporaneous ad-libbing that can actually block the true, authentic writing from being heard from the page itself. Improvising becomes a shield, in this sense. Reading what is written is efficient, clear, and honors the act of response, in which everyone had the same limits and conditions. Also, it lets students practice immediately articulating out loud what they have just drafted, which honors the process of creating something that is filled with life. It does not need to be edited in any way—it can exist as is, and we expect it not to be "perfect"—rather, it fits a deeper, more intuitive truth, because it satisfies what was drafted in the moment. This keeps the vitality in the sharing.

As each student shares, I encourage the rest of the class simply to pay attention by listening—not writing. I will invite each student personally to share out loud; if someone wants to pass and decline the chance to speak and tell their "Story of My Name," I will honor their wishes, but only after several repeated, heartfelt invitations, because this exercise is one that is even better with universal participation.

The Takeaway

This is a simple, foundational exercise that builds community care and presence. It's mindful in the sense that it underscores *inclusion*. Everyone has a voice. Everyone has a story to tell. Our names can serve as the beginning of our roles as storytellers, participating and sharing with each other in a collective, collaborative community. Part of this sharing involves mindful listening, seeing, and recognizing each other and the complexity of our histories, emotions, and intricate lives. This exercise encourages us to reflect upon all of this, and to build our own sense of courage and voice.

EXERCISE 4

Levity Moments

We've all had an experience of levity, at different times in our lives—there we were, weighed down by a heavy thought, and then we noticed something that entirely changed our perspective, lightening the mood. We were busy ruminating when the rainbow appeared—and, luckily, we were aware enough to notice. Sometimes, it helps to recall those small, wondrous moments that make us laugh or smile, or just the quirky things we like that remind us we are human, even while feeling anxious or under pressure. This activity can be started at the beginning of a class and shared at the end. It's especially useful when a class community feels burdened, experiencing stress of some sort.

Mindfulness Skills Taught

> **AWARE:** builds awareness of the five senses, and practices the art of close observation

> **ADVANCING:** allows students to practice sometimes subtle humor and the art of play; helps build listening skills; helps decrease stress

> **AUTHENTIC:** encourages students to check in with their own senses of pressure, to allow for a "lift" to take place, and to appreciate the smaller moments

Challenge Tips

This exercise is an invitation for mindfulness to become part of the day in a way that's engaging, fun, and accessible for all. Some students might need to hear a few examples (see below) before they grasp what it's all about—after all, how often do we collect the "little moments" and lift them up? The challenge can grow from here; this is a perception-builder. I encourage students to keep practicing this art on their own; as their awareness of the details in the world around them builds, the experience of noticing becomes even more rewarding.

Time Requirement: Twenty minutes (ten minutes at the beginning of class; ten minutes at the end, to read the finished piece out loud)

Resource Materials Needed

▶ **EXAMPLES** you create yourself to share as an introduction

How to Teach It

Tell students that during the class time, they'll also create a collective, traveling list of "levity moments." You might wish to read the introductory blurb for this exercise ("Sometimes, it helps to recall . . .") as a warm-up. I usually also add a few of my own as examples, sharing my own quirky side, too. I'll reveal to students that I love it when the expiration date on the milk reads my birthday—for some reason, it gives me a lift, reminding me that my birthday is on its way, coming soon! I also enjoy lying in grass at night in summertime, listening to crickets chirping. I consider these small moments meaningful, even if they might seem quite ordinary.

Setting the Context

You might wish also to tell them, for instance, that the poet John Keats was famous for his great attention to detail, writing odes to "ordinary" things like a bird (nightingale) and a vase (a Grecian urn, to be precise)! He also suffered from myopia, and his near-sightedness might have made him even more prone to seeing things up close, focusing on the beauty of the detail (Townsend, 2011).

In fact, many of the world's greatest minds have made amazing discoveries through their ability to focus on the finer points. This sort of attention to detail can be honed. Sometimes, it involves "levity moments" of recognizing something beautiful; at other times, it might involve simply noticing a detail that others consider unremarkable.

Science is filled with these mindful moments of awareness. In science and medicine, it's this level of "noticing" that is part of the discovery process. For example, in the 1920s, Dr. Alexander Fleming noticed that mold had grown on one of his experimental petri dishes, inhibiting a pathogen. Later, his student, Dr. Cecil Paine, would demonstrate that penicillin, a drug derived from the mold, could effectively combat bacterial disease (Gottfried, 2005).

In a similar sense, many mathematicians will notice their concepts evidenced in nature, or will find themselves "lifted out" of the rut of problem-solving through a moment of levity and release.

Designers operate with a similar sensibility. Graphic artist David Carson (davidcarsondesign .com/), for example, finds himself inspired by travels, local signposts, and graffiti art. The new details he encounters inform his art and perspective.

In mindfulness, this appreciation for the finer, smaller points is part of building awareness. Students can be encouraged to embrace their abilities, which we often have in a heightened state as young children. Finding levity, or lifting, in these moments, is part of the gift that's in our human nature. It's up to us to choose to use it.

Mindfulness Writing Exercise Prompt

Levity Moments: For this exercise, we're passing around a piece of paper—a traveling poem of sorts. When the paper reaches you, add a line that briefly describes your "levity moment," something you see as uplifting, making you laugh or smile. Some people call each moment like this "a moment of wonder" because it takes you out of yourself and reminds you to observe and celebrate the small, special qualities of life. Don't think too hard—these can be quirky and uplifting! Then fold the paper over so the next person can't see what was written before them.

Students can do this on their own, and a separate discussion/course of study can be happening simultaneously in the classroom, as the paper quietly travels. Encourage students not to share ideas or talk about the levity moments until the final product is shared out loud.

Here's a compilation of Levity Moments contributed by students in a ninth-grade class I taught:

Levity Moments

- Popping bubble wrap
- The crunch of the apple when you take the first bite
- Looking for your sunglasses and they're on top of your head
- Silent ripples of waves on the ocean at night
- When a bag of peanuts or a jar of peanut butter says "may contain nuts"
- When you smile at someone frowning and then they smile back
- The smooth top of the peanut butter when you open a new jar
- When you open a fortune cookie and it's relevant to something you're going through
- Chewing to a beat
- Making awkward eye contact with people in other cars
- Watching someone in a passing car dancing and singing to a song on the radio
- The urge to laugh in quiet moments
- Opening a Snapple bottle and pressing the safety button up and down, up and down
- When my cat hears something but turns only one ear, not her whole head
- The white crayon

When class time has ten minutes left, collect the paper, unfold, and read aloud.

The Takeaway

Students understand the need to slow down and notice positive experiences, even (and especially!) during stressful periods.

The exercise builds an appreciation for laughter, an attention to detail, and an honoring of community.

If you like, you can encourage students to snap their fingers a few times if this "levity moment" also reaches them. This serves as a reinforcement, showing students they have a lot in common. The "snap for solidarity" has been around since Roman times, I've heard, and is making its resurgence in recent years. It shows agreement without disrupting the flow of an audio reading or such performance.

I traditionally incorporate this exercise into every school year, and it's a true crowd-pleaser. Not only do students love the writing parts, which feel as if they're part of a secret society, the read-aloud portion becomes similar to a poetry slam experience.

Tips: I encourage you to be the reader/performer, though students might volunteer. My reasoning: you can skip anything that might not be suitable read aloud for the audience, it saves students from having to decipher each other's writing, and it preserves anonymity. If you do feel as if you wish to have student readers, your alternative is to type up the sheets after class, saving the read-aloud part for the next class time together.

The activity builds mindfulness skills, and is a brain-boost as well as a mood-lifter for the whole group.

Gratitude and Mindful Mentors

Piglet noticed that even though he had a Very Small Heart, it could hold a rather large amount of Gratitude.

—A. A. Milne in *Winnie-the-Pooh* (1926)

We've already looked deeply into gratitude and happiness concepts for ourselves in the teacher section (see the full exercise on Grateful Heart and Happiness in Chapter 3, "Mindfulness for Teachers"). The intention and act of fostering mindsets of gratitude have many foundational benefits. "Studies show that gratitude is positively related to hope, forgiveness, pride, contentment, optimism and inspiration," says Open Circle (2018), an organization working with evidence-based social and emotional learning (SEL). Open Circle (2018) developed its own gratitude curriculum components, saying that embracing a consistent "attitude of gratitude" can have the following benefits:

- Improved physical and psychological health
- Higher levels of positive emotions
- More joy, optimism, and happiness
- Ability to form, maintain, and strengthen supportive relationships
- Acting with more generosity, empathy, and compassion
- Feeling connected to a caring community

As we've discovered, mindfulness can be thought of as a lens, and "a way to be in the world." Establishing mindfulness also makes us more receptive to the practice of gratitude. In this sense, gratitude and mindfulness go hand-in-hand (or heart-to-heart, as I sometimes say!). They are allies, and when we act out of a "mindful mindset of gratitude," we naturally reflect empathy and compassion in a way that engages with the world. This is helpful for us to know, as teachers, because our personal practices make a palpable difference, affecting students' perceptions and experiences in the classroom.

The following are several gratitude exercises that address the "full cycle" of relationships. They are useful in all subject areas, and I've included key examples from science, math, and language arts classes, to give a good idea of how the core elements of these exercises can be expanded, adapted, and implemented. Mentoring is also discussed as part of a cycle of gratitude, learning, sharing, receiving, and honoring a legacy of curiosity and appreciation. Consider extending creative applications with pictures, photographs, storyboards, and extension applications.

Mindfulness Skills Taught

- **AWARE:** allows students to recognize all of the experiences, people, and elements in their lives that have played a positive role

- **ADVANCING:** students can better imagine how to use gratitude as a motivation to expand and extend their own realities, surpassing perceived limits

- **AUTHENTIC:** with a sense of community and connection, we begin to see the interrelated nature of all things; gratitude influences this true appreciation for what is right in front of us and what bonds us to others and our environment

Challenge Tips

If students hesitate during any of the prompts, you can step in and give your own examples or sentence starters to keep the ideas flowing. Also, encourage lists, pictures, and anything that unlocks expression.

Time Requirement: Four activities, fifteen minutes each, that can be incorporated into any lesson

Resource Materials Needed

- **JOURNALS**
- **STICKY NOTES**

How to Teach It

Here are four short gratitude exercises, which can be used at the beginning, middle, or end of a lesson. They can be used in any order, though I've included what I think will work well as a building sequence, over the span of several days.

Before starting any of the exercises, think about the overall design of the classroom environment, and have students form a circle where everyone is facing each other (see the "Circles—Everyone Sees Each Other" and "On Designing Mindful Learning Spaces" explanations in Chapter 2 for ways to approach circle formations and design). Ask students what they think the word *grateful* means. You can record responses on a chart or on an interactive surface. How does it make you feel when you are grateful? Usually, being grateful means we are appreciative or thankful for someone or something in our lives. What are some of the things that make us feel a sense of gratitude? Explain that these can be big or small, and mindfulness means paying attention to these elements that we appreciate.

Part 1: Self-Appreciation and Gratitude: What's Your Superpower?

Begin by asking students the following question:

What's your superpower? Today, we're going to create Superpower Gratitude Vignettes. A "vignette" is a colorful description of a brief episode. In other words, it's a short short story that zeroes in on that trait.

Mindfulness Writing Exercise Prompt

My Superpower: Think about a characteristic that is something you appreciate about yourself. This trait can be an attribute, or perhaps something you do that you simply value about yourself. Try to be specific about this. Were you born with this trait, or did you acquire it or inherit it? In your journal, for a timed two minutes, write down a Superpower Gratitude Vignette (short story) that illustrates your superpower evident in a real-life experience.

As the two timed minutes come to an end, tell students

Now, as this quick writing time is coming to an end, close this vignette with a sentence that expresses your gratitude for having the trait. Your sentence can be framed with the words, "I appreciate my _____ because it allows me to _____," or "I'm grateful for having _____ Superpower, as it makes me feel _____."

After students have written down the story, ask them to write down a word on a sticky note that sums up the superpower trait. Have them pair up and share the idea on the sticky note, telling the story from memory. You can also have students each place their gratitude sticky notes on the same board/location, as a display in class. Depending on time, they could also share their closing gratitude sentences out loud as they post them.

Part 2: Grateful Awareness

The following are three ideas for journal prompts that all encourage grateful appreciation for what exists and enhances life. Being prompted to mindfully describe sensory experiences, scientific advances, and well-designed objects leads students to make many positive connections. Sharing afterward, in pairs, groups, and online is optional. Each exercise is a timed five minutes. Online research might help some of the prompts—yet it's not necessary.

Mindfulness Writing Exercise Prompts

Happiness and Senses: Describe a moment that made you happy yesterday. Include as many of the five senses as possible. For example, if you were happy when you went for a hike in the woods, try to home in on one moment during that hike. Describe the temperature, the feel of it, the colors and sights around you. Try to bring yourself back there through the writing. In that way, you can bring the reader there, too.

Tech for a Better Life: Think about your daily routine, and all of the things you do that add to the happiness of your life. Choose one machine or piece of equipment that makes life better or easier in some way. Complete this exercise by describing in detail what this piece is, also giving a brief explanation of how it allows you to live a fuller life. If you already know (or can discover!) anything about its history, you can add this to the writing.

Design Appreciation: *Choose an object around you right now. Observe that object closely. Write for five minutes about how the "design" of the object—its look, feel, materials, shape, dimensions, placement, function, everything—enhances its ability to function. What is its prime purpose? Does it have any others? You can also think about the designer of the object, imagining what their intention might have been, to create that object with those specifications. In your writing, express your appreciation (which is a form of gratitude) for the object existing the way it does.*

Part 3: Gratitude and Mindful Mentors

If we receive something we appreciate from someone else, they might be doing us a simple favor, or wishing to help us in some form, to benefit our quality of life in one way or another. This person can be known as a *Mindful Mentor.*

Ask students to take five minutes to create a list of several moments or experiences when they recall directly benefiting from someone else's help. This can be in big or small ways. The Mindful Mentor can be someone who impacted them intentionally, reaching out to help and offer care, or someone who helped simply by acting out of a general kindness.

See if students can take ten minutes to reflectively create a list of at least ten people who benefited them in some way, big or small. They can include why that person might have reached out, and what they had to give up in order to extend. Students can write this down.

This experience of expressing gratitude is powerful in itself.

At the end of this exercise, encourage students to extend this exercise by writing a short note, on an index card, sticky note, or small card, to express their gratitude to the person. Their note should give details about *what the person did, how it caused them to feel grateful, and what larger impact it made by benefiting their life.* You can post these cards in a prominent place, taking a picture or creating a blog post about them.

You can also invite students to *hand-deliver the gratitude note* to the person, as a way to thank them directly for what they have done. This is a way of completing the expression of gratitude, showing the person it was noticed and appreciated.

Part 4: Kindness Campaign: Paying It Forward

In Part 3, students gave examples of "Mindful Mentors" who recognized a way to extend help. This takes a certain special mindfulness quality, to *see* that there is another who can benefit from your help. In addition to receiving help, we can each give it, too, in this way. Sometimes, it takes looking through a new lens of mindfulness in order to actively see that someone could use our help.

VIDEO 4.1
www.youtube.com/
watch?v=nwAYpLVyeFU

You can show students Video 4.1 (LifeVestInside, 2011) as an example of a circle of gratitude.

Then ask them to write down, in five minutes, ideas for specific ways they could help their local communities—in the classroom, in the school community, in their families, and in their local neighborhood. These can be simple, little things—small acts of "paying it forward"—and they start with intention.

See how many ideas students can come up with in the time limit.

Then create a compiled group list, perhaps using an online shared page or post. Check in from time to time, seeing how these "pay-it-forward" gratitude actions are going over the course of the school year.

Reflection Questions

After these exercises, students might be swimming in gratitude! It's especially helpful to have a post-reflection after the experience of recognizing gratitude.

Preferably in a circle, ask students to take just a few moments to check in, take a few deep breaths, and reflect about the following, sharing together:

- How do you feel after doing these exercises?
- Why do you think we have these feelings when addressing gratitude?
- How does this cause you to think differently about our class? Our school community? Others? The world?
- Can gratitude also be a tool for helping develop even more curiosity? Courage? What else can it enhance?

Extension

What about a moment that might *not* work out in the way we expect or initially see as beneficial? Allowing students to see that these moments can be opportunities for gratitude, too, can be a powerful exercise.

For this extension, tell students: *Sometimes, we are grateful for things we receive—a present, for example—and other times, we are grateful for experiences in our lives that teach us something or shape us in some way. They are unexpected gifts, though they might feel as if they are unwanted. In terms of our own personal "grit" and strength, these experiences lead us to become stronger. They might appear to us as gratitude moments only in hindsight.*

To warm up, before we begin writing, I might give an example, telling the story of one of my jobs in university, as a freshman on campus. I was part of a team that handled "stadium cleanups" on the weekends. This entailed being at the sports arena after the game, walking the rows and picking up everything that was left littered in the stands. Paper plates smeared with ketchup, sticky soda cups, paper straw wrappers—they all went into the bag I carried. I also got to wear a cool dust-blower ultra-powered backpack a few times at the outdoor football stadium, which was definitely fun. I made the experience into a game, viewing my work as play even though I had a job to do, and it taught me about the power of mindset, as well as a valuable lesson about the volume of waste we create. I try to be mindful, now, of the amount of packaging, napkins, utensils, and more that I use when I'm in a restaurant, at a sporting event, or at a theater. I also remember to take my own items to the recycling bins myself—because the experience reminded me that every little thing we leave behind needs to be picked up by someone else, and it adds up! This task certainly made me a stronger, more aware person. Though we might label experiences like this as "clouds with silver linings," implying that the work itself is the negative part and we find positives in it, I can now see the duality, and the goodness of the entire experience, which is my gratitude in reflection. Instead of a cloud with a silver lining, it becomes a silver cloud.

Mindfulness Writing Exercise Prompt

Silver Cloud Reflection: *Think back to an experience when the time itself might not be traditionally associated with the "good," yet it offered something inherently positive, depending on your mindset and perspective. Describe the situation in detail, using a "before" perspective (anticipation), a "during" (experience), and an "after" (reflection). What do you appreciate about it now, in hindsight? How are there multiple perspectives about ways to view it? How do you think it adds some flavor and dimension to your life?*

As with all of these exercises, students can share them—though the nature of this one might cause students to prefer to keep theirs a personal reflection, building awareness.

The Takeaway

This is a universal set of prompts that applies to all curriculum areas. In the examples, you can see the ways in which I customize the theme.

Amplified gratitude yields greater connection capacity and a deeper mindset that can be more embracing of what appears in the here and now. As a class community, everyone benefits from these exercises. They set the stage for a broader way to approach open expression of appreciation. You can revisit these time and time again throughout the year.

EXERCISE 6

Storytelling, Empathy, and Kindness

Children are a wonderful gift. They have an extraordinary capacity to see into the heart of things.

—Archbishop Desmond Tutu (quoted in *Awaken*, 2012)

Naturally, storytelling can be a powerful tool for accessing the human heart, reaching from one experience directly to another.

The art and act of storytelling are about sharing truths, in a certain sense. They allow us to engender empathy, in order to have compassion for others, understanding that there are stories and backgrounds all around us, existing simultaneously, even as we might be most attuned to our own personal experience.

This exercise is important, because every act of storytelling also involves the art of *listening* to each other's stories. We listen in order to feel, to "see" beyond our own view, and to realize the many ways we can use a broader understanding to also make a positive impact on the world around us. We bridge gaps, form connections, and inculcate new models of leadership through these means.

This is a beginning, and a component of mindfulness that can be adapted to many specific areas of curriculum.

Mindfulness Skills Taught

- **AWARE:** builds awareness of the art of storytelling; multiple perspectives and connections in community
- **ADVANCING:** encourages students to listen to others; to celebrate many styles and means of story; to celebrate the community together rather than promote an individual agenda
- **AUTHENTIC:** reveals the impact of empathy, and also the value in being open and vulnerable, flipping fear into opportunity

Challenge Tips

This lesson contains emotional material, and students might be sensitive or reactive to some of the prompts. Instead of shying away from this, I'm open about it up-front, letting them know we're using stories to promote authentic connections. Remind them that to feel is to care, and to care is a good thing, if it motivates us to lead better, more connected lives. Each student must also guard against carrying what can be emotionally draining—in other words, we don't want them to feel burdened by another's pain. The art of empathy is that we can feel what someone else feels (which involves the good and the bad!) in order to understand and connect, leading us to promote a better world. The goal is to encourage a sense of perspective, and also to let students express themselves, journaling about difficult emotions that might come up in this exercise. Having support from the guidance department is always helpful—this is true in all cases, as a counselor is expert support for students who might encounter deep and difficult emotions that are sometimes uncovered by empathy-enriching material.

Creativity Insights

Someone might ask a question about truth-telling here; it's my own nature to question this, too, when it comes to "story"—are they all *authentic*? How can we tell, and know what to judge and trust? First off, all stories are "creative" by their very nature— and not all are fact-based. If a story is authentic, it satisfies what I call the "Picasso condition"—it *tells the truth*. Picasso's full quote, mentioned earlier in "Mindfulness for Teachers," is: *"Art is the lie that tells the truth."*

What does he mean by this? I think he means we point to the human heart when we create something that is moving in a real way, not in a way that is intending to manipulate emotion or malign another. You can have a good discussion with students here about stories and truth-telling, asking them why certain novels (*To Kill a Mockingbird*, for example) point powerfully toward truth, even though they are fiction.

This is true in math, too, when there are conditions set for imagined worlds, and the math itself is consistent with the invented conditions rather than with a physical reality.

Time Requirement: Sixty minutes

Resource Materials Needed

▹ **VIEWING SCREEN** to show videos
▹ **SPEECH TEXT** (if possible)
▹ **JOURNALS**

How to Teach It

Warm-up: On Laughter and Stories

I love to teach laughter coupled with deep empathy. I often tell students that it's traits of *curiosity* coupled with *humor* that encourage me to tell stories and to see them

VIDEO 4.2
ww.youtube.com/
watch?v=w-8ydwV45no

everywhere in the world. Laughter is one connection point that contains empathy—because to see the lightness and humor is also to connect with its source, and to see the humanity underneath.

Have students watch Video 4.2 (Penguin Kids, 2014) about Oliver Jeffers, an award-winning storyteller who illustrated *The Boy in the Striped Pajamas*.

In the film, Jeffers talks about how storytelling is celebrated in his Irish tradition and culture. He also describes his own workflow, using pencils, art supplies, and sketching to record his ideas.

Ask students:

▷ What is your "workflow"? What do you use to record your ideas?

▷ How is storytelling part of your family or culture?

▷ How do you think humor helps Jeffers with his work? How could you use humor with your work?

Beginning with this quick exercise is a great warm-up because it opens up the discussion and literally adds animation! I have used it with middle school and high school students, as well as with teachers, and it resonates across all ages, because it's timeless joy and a passion for his craft that Oliver Jeffers shares, with his own charisma. Consider telling students, as an extension, how "storyboards" are part of a design idea process for storytelling. You can sketch these, too!

Diving Deeper: Empathy and Hidden Stories

Educator, storyteller, digital citizenship and kindness campaigner Darren Kuropatwa is a proponent of stories with heart, connecting people online and offline. I've seen Kuropatwa give incredible talks to educators over the years about opportunities to use compassion in community, teaching students to share stories that matter.

Kuropatwa says, "Kids need more models of empathy and empowerment. Parents do, too" (Kuropatwa, 2015). I couldn't agree more—entire communities need these models, and access through stories. Part of using mindfulness with storytelling is to encourage both voice (empowerment) and empathy (from the Greek *em-pathos,* meaning "in-feeling").

How can we feel what others feel and build a culture of care? The hidden truth is, there are stories everywhere! It's up to us to unearth them. In creating empathetic stories with students, we connect them with their own drive not only to express themselves but to do so with intention, agency, and greater fulfillment.

VIDEO 4.3
www.youtube.com/
watch?v=cDDWvj_q-o8

Have students watch Video 4.3 (Cleveland Clinic, 2013)—a moving video about empathy and multiple perspectives, all within the context of patient care in a hospital. The first time I encountered this was when Kuropatwa showed it during a conference, and it made an impact right away.

Tell students that the video says: "If you could stand in someone else's shoes . . . Hear what they hear. See what they see. Feel what they feel. Would you treat them differently?"

After viewing the video, ask students the following questions:

- How does it change perspective to know that everyone has a story to tell?
- Did anyone's "story" matter more or less than anyone else's?
- What does it mean, to have empathy?
- In crafting and creating stories, how can we use this point of empathy to reach others?

After answering these questions, out loud or in journals, have students write for three minutes (time it!) *a story about kindness from the past year.* This story can be about *anything*—and it can be from their own perspectives, or from someone else's. As you walk around, if you notice certain students having trouble, ask them to write a story of a holiday, or a tradition, or about a piece of advice they were told from someone they look up to and respect. Or about when they gave or received an act of kindness.

Then have students form partners. Their job, in two minutes, is to tell their story out loud to the other person. The receiver of the story must practice *quality listening* skills (which you can practice together)—not interrupting, qualifying, or commenting on the story. Just allowing it, and endorsing it through listening.

At the end of the two minutes, have students reverse storytelling roles.

After both have shared, ask them to see if they can sum up the story in one short phrase or sentence.

See if they can type this out and couple it with a visual picture they take of themselves telling the story. This can turn into a vlog project.

Points for Discussion

- How are stories valuable for the person who writes them?
- Why could a story help a person who hears it?
- What are some traits of a moving story?
- What does "empathy" mean to you?
- How does someone show that they are being empathetic?
- Why is walking in someone else's shoes a powerful metaphor?
- What stories have you heard that impacted you the most, and why?
- How do you think qualities of a good leader link with empathy?

Extension: Indifference Makes a Difference

In these exercises, we are using stories to connect and to show care for one another—even for strangers.

VIDEO 4.4
www.youtube.com/
watch?v=JpXmRiGst4k

The reverse of caring and empathy is indifference.

Nobel Prize winner, concentration camp survivor, and author of *Night* Elie Wiesel talks about the danger of indifference in the powerful speech shown in Video 4.4 (AmericanRhetoric.com, 2016).

Have students watch the video, and then reflect on his words about the dangers of indifference:

> What is indifference? Etymologically, the word means "no difference." A strange and unnatural state in which the lines blur between light and darkness, dusk and dawn, crime and punishment, cruelty and compassion, good and evil. What are its courses and inescapable consequences? Is it a philosophy? Is there a philosophy of indifference conceivable? Can one possibly view indifference as a virtue? Is it necessary at times to practice it simply to keep one's sanity, live normally, enjoy a fine meal and a glass of wine, as the world around us experiences harrowing upheavals?
>
> Of course, indifference can be tempting—more than that, seductive. It is so much easier to look away from victims. It is so much easier to avoid such rude interruptions to our work, our dreams, our hopes. It is, after all, awkward, troublesome, to be involved in another person's pain and despair. Yet for the person who is indifferent, his or her neighbors are of no consequence. And, therefore, their lives are meaningless. Their hidden or even visible anguish is of no interest. Indifference reduces the Other to an abstraction. (Wiesel, 1999)

Reflection Questions

▷ How can indifference be dangerous?

▷ Could indifference ever be seen as an advantage?

▷ About what, in your own life, do you hope you are never indifferent? Why?

See where this takes you; it can also bring about discussions about history, partnerships, economics, and global collaboration toward the good.

The Takeaway

These exercises bring students together with the world. They are stories that involve what Sharon Creech discusses in *Walk Two Moons* (Creech, 1994). What happens when we practice the Native American saying "to walk two moons in someone else's moccasins"? Do we begin to know them better, to use the compassion that mindfulness is all about? How can this make us better problem-solvers, creators, and inventors? How can it make us more empowered global citizens?

Here, students will see that to make an impact on the world, in any area, they must first understand the human condition and the stories underneath the surface.

Digital Mindful Citizen

Hope is definitely not the same thing as optimism. It is not the conviction that something will turn out well, but the certainty that something makes sense, regardless of how it turns out.

—Václav Havel (1990, as quoted in
VáclavHavelLibrary Foundation.org)

Certainly, terms like *alternative facts, post-truth,* and *fake news* might have seemed fabricated themselves in the not-too-distant past. They resemble jargon straight out of an Orwellian dystopia—which is why it makes us pause, as educators, and consider the importance of the online reasoning skills we can build each day in our lessons. We exist in a brave new world—one in which being mindfully aware incorporates the ability to discriminate between fact and fiction, to develop "civic online reasoning" as a skillset, and to work to build digital media literacies programs that establish students as capable, conscious digital citizens.

Being digitally mindfully aware and media savvy is a deep imperative with far-reaching consequences. The goals are high, as we expect students to apply knowledge about rhetorical devices, influences, agendas, biases, and campaigns, using ample filters for detecting what might be false information, all on a quest to disseminate truth and use it toward a practical, mindful end—one that incorporates skills of empathy, global awareness, compassion, and insight about the greater good.

The Center for Media Literacy (CML), included in the resources online at caitlinkrause.com, has said that "the heart of media literacy is informed inquiry." Its four-step building process flows from Awareness to Analysis, Reflection, and Action, emphasizing "navigational skills" for young people. The entire process hinges on a mindful outlook and practice in awareness (MediaLit.org, 2018).

This exercise turns what starts as a daunting task (admittedly complex, too, due to variations in jargon and meaning surrounding what we call "digital literacies") into an empowering opportunity. It's a seed of a beginning—a way for us concretely to introduce concepts of digital mindful citizenship to students in a way that's sensible, digestible, and relatable on an authentic level. Let them sink their teeth into exercises here, ask questions, and feel empowered as they reach out to a global community, fearless and undaunted in the pursuit of meaningful truth.

Mindfulness Skills Taught

▶ **AWARE:** encourages students to become aware of the many facets of media bias, while maintaining a sense of hope and an respect for truth

▶ **ADVANCING:** promotes critical thinking about the messages behind media, using digital tools and resources to stretch understanding

▶ **AUTHENTIC:** students see the use of digital mindful citizenship in relationship to their own life goals, personal values, and identity formation, in this way bridging gaps between false perception and authentic reality

Challenge Tips

This exercise can be challenging because we are addressing applied meaning and consciousness, using reasoning that depends on content and context. We use a pluralized "literacies" because they are not a uniform, singular entity. They are a complex web of abilities driven by context, which include time, perspective, identity, and relationship. As Doug Belshaw says, "Digital literacies are plural, context-dependent, and socially negotiated" (Mortensen, 2015).

Time Requirement: Three exercises, forty-five minutes each, spread out over three days

Resource Materials Needed

▶ **JOURNALS**

▶ **ART AND SKETCH MATERIALS**

▶ **ONLINE SEARCH ENGINES**

▶ **ARTICLE RESOURCES** on hand

How to Teach It

DAY 1: THE NEWS TODAY

Begin by asking students: *"What do you see as your primary goal when you're looking online for information about a topic?"*

See what answers come from this simple question. Some students might share that their goal is to find the answer quickly; others might say their goal is to trust a source. Others might focus on finding a variety of information, using it to reason and seek out truth. You can share the following introduction with students:

How can we tell fact from fiction? This is a growing problem among people of all ages—it's even hard to tell whether a news story on a website is "real" or "sponsored content," which is an advertisement trying to sell us something. How can we maintain hope and a sense of trust in ourselves and the bounty of information online while promoting the best resources and ways to go about finding truth? When we apply mindfulness skills to digital literacies, we boost our own awareness of where the information is coming from, and we thereby increase our capacity to understand how to then make better sense out of what we're accessing as reliable resources. It's a challenge, yet we can face it armed with our mindful mindsets!

Next ask students to form four separate teams. Each team's task will be to research and read an article about digital literacies and also to run a search for reliable information about a topic you will give to them. I provide several articles I like about digital literacies online at **caitlinkrause.com,** and you can also curate your own list, as you prefer. You're teaching students about the research process here, too.

This is, essentially, information + simulation, all in one exercise!

At the end, the students will present their team's findings to the rest of the class, telling about their digital mindful citizen learning journey.

Rather than prescribe restrictive articles and topics, I have suggested a range of sites about digital mindful literacies on the companion website, accessible through **caitlinkrause.com,** so that you can mine the sources and use them to start yourself off on the quest, then customizing to fit your lesson content. In this way, your own list will grow and stay current.

> *Learning to filter out bias is an incredibly important skill to use for the rest of your life. I think it's necessary to teach the students to look at the writer and see if they could be partial. Once students are taught not to believe everything they see, they can start formulating their own opinions, which is the most important skill of all.*
>
> —Claire, *former student*

DAY 2: POINT/COUNTERPOINT AND RHETORIC

On Day 2, you will select one prime issue (that seems to have many facets and associated viewpoints) and divide the class arbitrarily into two separate teams, representing opposing views on the issue—or, at least, views that are not completely in agreement. The team's jobs will be to evaluate the complexity of this issue, understanding that their side has a role to play in influencing how the issue is approached and considered.

Begin the exercise by introducing the terms *Ethos, Pathos,* and *Logos*, which are three building blocks of rhetorical devices (there are others, yet this is a quick triad to get students off and running with their thinking about this!).

Ethos *is an appeal to Ethics, or a sense of right and wrong. We believe what someone shares because that person has established credibility with us as being good and trustworthy.*

Pathos *is an appeal to Feelings, from which sympathy and empathy derive their meaning. We believe what someone shares because they reach us emotionally, in a way that allows us to feel what they feel.*

Logos *is an appeal to Logic. We believe what someone shares because facts back it up, and it makes sense. We have these facts as reliability gauges, and we can refer back to them for credibility.*

> *I think being able to filter through propaganda and bias is one of the best tools one can use. If you can know what is trying to target you and get to you mentally, then you are prepared to combat that and make well-informed choices instead of biased and/or media-influenced ones.*
>
> —Rafael, *former student*

Note that all three of the above terms appeal to us for different reasons, in different ways, and are frequently used by the media to influence us. Students can realize this when looking at advertising campaigns, elections for student government, and even their daily social media feeds. Which one has the most sway? You can have a conversation about this, evaluating the ways that online rhetoric sometimes uses humor or rage (elements of Pathos) to influence social masses.

Next, when students form teams, pick simple, relatable issues that have to do with your current course of study.

In a math class, for example, you could use the following issue as a debate platform:

Time and duration of a school day.

The two sides could be:

▶ The school day should begin one hour later.

▶ The school day should remain as it is.

Within this simple issue lie many positions and complexities that schools have been debating and exploring in recent years. This is part of what makes the issue so compelling. Many of the details involve calculations of hours, time of best focus, health statistics, and various facts and figures that all contribute to an understanding of how a school day should be structured to best benefit societal needs.

Part 1: Researching Your Point

Students on the separate teams can research and collect evidence supporting their assigned sides. Make sure, in these research phases, that the teams can keep track of their sources and use online support, resources, and their own net-savvy skills to ensure reliability.

Part 2: Researching the Counterpoint

The teams can also filter through digital sources to investigate arguments for the opposing side, seeking to understand the alternate viewpoint. The same practice applies for record-keeping and citing reliable sources.

Part 3: Arguing the Case

Teams each compile their best resources, forming comprehensive arguments for their cases, which could involve addressing and disarming the counterpoint.

Teams briefly present their summative arguments to the opposing team. (These summations could be shared with others in the school community, for even more visibility and dialogue.)

Note that this is not intended to simulate a trial—the main goal is to show the strengths and compelling arguments for views in opposition.

Part 4: Reaching Consensus (Agreement)

Is it possible for the two sides to reach a consensus? See what happens when the two sides are encouraged to play improvisation games that include "Yes, but . . ." finding ways to oppose each other's viewpoints, versus "Yes, and . . ." finding ways to agree.

You can start by telling students about the danger of "othering"—a common practice that pits one side against another, forming a bias in favor of one's own view. Mindfulness flips othering around, allowing us to see many viewpoints and recognize the humanity in the "other" side. We become more curious, less oppositional, and more clear-sighted in the process. Even if we disagree with another view, we allow ourselves to see the human condition that represents it.

For example, if the debate topic at hand is the case of "should schools adopt uniforms," the spontaneous improv dialogue could sound like the following:

Example 1: Disagreement

S1: *School uniforms should be mandatory.*

S2: *Yes, but uniforms are expensive.*

S1: *Yes, but so are clothes students would have to buy.*

S2: *Yes, but uniforms show solidarity and a certain school spirit.*

S1: *Yes, but when they're imposed by force it doesn't elicit positive feelings about the school.*

S2: *Yes, but repression is a school tradition.*

Example 2: Agreement

S1: *School uniforms should be mandatory.*

S2: *Yes, and if they were mandatory there should be a way to subsidize the cost of them.*

S1: *Yes, and then students could have a say in what they looked like.*

S2: *Yes, and also the materials used, so they would want to wear them.*

S1: *Yes, and there could be certain variations that would allow for personalization—colors, etc.*

S2: *Yes, and in this way, school uniforms wouldn't have to feel so restrictive.*

See if a compromise can be reached. Have a brief closing conversation with students to talk about how the process to reach the compromise was possible, and/or what made it challenging? How did some of the values of mindfulness help them be more open to the opposing viewpoint? Did they find themselves surprised by an attachment to their assigned side, especially since it had been initially chosen for them?

As Day 2 closes, students might want to process reactions, thoughts, and feelings in a journal reflection at home. There will be lingering thoughts and ideas that might not have ample processing space within the timeframe of one class.

DAY 3: WALK THIS WORLD—THE OUT OF EDEN PROJECT

Harvard University's Project Zero introduced a remarkable program beginning in 2013, united with the Pulitzer Prize–winning journalist Paul Salopek, who embarked on a quest to retrace the origin of human history. He is walking the path, starting in the "Cradle of Civilization," what was once Ancient Mesopotamia, across East Asia, over the Bering Strait, and through the Americas to the southernmost part of Chile, the Tierra del Fuego, traveling step by step (Out of Eden Learn, 2018).

As the Pulitzer Center's Mark Schulte writes, "His journalism project, the Out of Eden Walk, seeks to slow readers down. While so many of us career ever faster through the world, Salopek walks. He lingers and looks closely." It's been an exercise in slow journalism, cultural understanding, and storytelling without bias or political agenda. Thus far, over one thousand classes from over fifty-two countries have been involved in the program. As my students have been involved, they have a different appreciation of geography, story, patience, listening, and curiosity. They recognize connections across cultures, and they have a natural respect for Paul and the people he encounters along the way. The lessons have far-reaching effects.

As a one-day activity, consider having students read one of Paul's many blog posts from the field—found online at NationalGeographic.org. Additional resources are linked on the companion website at **caitlinkrause.com.**

You can decide how deeply you would like to be involved—your class can register on the interactive site as a walking party, joining Paul for part of the journey, and use the platform to join a global community of learners. This was a highlight for my classes, engaging with digital mindful literacies in a way that reaches minds and hearts.

For today's exercise, you have three simple goals:

1. To explore the Out of Eden sites and options

2. To discover slow journalism posts together about Paul's journey

3. To reflect about these practices

As a closing to the day's exploration, gather in a circle for conversation, asking students to respond to the following reflection questions:

Reflection Questions

▶ What surprised you about these exercises?

▶ How can you describe one of the takeaways related to digital mindful literacies?

▶ When you access information online, how can you imagine using Mindfulness AAA Mindset elements as a guide?

▶ What should a learner's attitude be to best approach research?

▶ Why do you think fake news exists in the world?

▶ What has your experience with rhetorical devices been like?

▶ What are some of your reflections about the Out of Eden journey?

▶ Did anything in these exercises surprise you?

▶ What would you like to explore next, in areas of digital mindful citizenship?

Extensions

As extensions, you can also use other digital literacies exercises from the online resources at **caitlinkrause.com** to have students practice distinguishing fact from fiction. Have them search for information from other countries, running searches in other languages. Let them direct their own digital literacies exercises by playing, investigating, stumbling, failing, and getting messy with the material. This is how we learn—not through fear, but through experimentation and *"What if . . . ?"* investigations. Create a safe environment for them to explore and stretch their digital mindful capabilities. Again, it's a mindset, not a skillset!

The Takeaway

This exercise gives students a sense of how informed, mindful approaches to digital media literacies and digital citizenship are paving the way toward an ideal and necessary way to approach a future in which artificial intelligence (AI) and machine learning are commonplace. We've been confronted with the need for digital citizenship in unprecedented ways, due to the explosion of the Internet of Everything. Computers have become a part of every aspect of our lives in a way that is starting to become more seamless, user-friendly, intuitive, and even emotional. And now, it's about how we access information—and how we put it to good use in a world where the sources, algorithms, and analyses devices are more robust, intelligent, and machine driven.

We're steered forward to a ubiquitous computing environment, in which each user has much more autonomy and interconnectedness. On a small scale, in our classrooms, this means students have more digital voice and choice—and greater responsibility.

What does this mean, big picture? As artificial intelligence (AI) builds to integrate seamlessly with human life, augmenting and amplifying it, it is the human voice and choice that will make the most difference. This will define the future of mindfulness: our ability to be human, even while interacting and merging with machines in our daily operations. It's no longer a question of hanging on to control or locking down resources; rather, educators can foster open, clear mindsets that are able to couple reasoning skills with compassion, teaching students to understand how not only to seek out and identify reliable media sources but to put them to good use, with a mindful lens that encompasses the planet.

Dignified Selfie

As we learn and grow in a globally connected community, mindfulness helps us to become receptive and aware of our different backgrounds, cultures, beliefs, and personalities. Mindfulness practices, in this context, help foster a base of acceptance and nonjudgment that can serve as a great fundamental starting point for connecting with others and understanding multiple perspectives.

In simplest terms: *How can we work with others, and seek to understand them, if we don't treat them with dignity? What does dignity mean, and how can we also embody it ourselves?*

In this short exercise, students will self-reflect and see that giving and receiving respect and dignity are not just behaviors that we perform out of duty; they come from natural insights and perceptions about what is fundamentally and universally human.

Mindfulness Skills Taught

▶ **AWARE:** promotes awareness of universal human rights

▶ **ADVANCING:** moves toward promotion of equality in both mindset and action; causes students to look at how they represent and embody ideals

▶ **AUTHENTIC:** fosters deeper compassion for self and others; helps to break down walls

Challenge Tips

This exercise will certainly cause students to feel vulnerable, as they open up and reveal what they believe true dignity means, in presence and action. Gently encourage everyone to participate; if the selfie picture-taking switches to an out-of-class assignment, this could create issues for some concerning access to camera/printer/time. Here, I've mapped out a way for the entire exercise to be completed in class together.

If you participate and make a dignified selfie of yourself to show and share, this adds to the power of the exercise.

Time Requirement: Sixty minutes

Resource Materials Needed

▶ **ACCESS** to a printer

▶ **PHONES WITH CAMERAS**[1] (decide whether you want students to bring and use their own; if not, you can substitute with any camera that can take a selfie)

How to Teach It

Part 1: Introducing Dignity

Begin by asking students what they think dignity means. Likely, answers might include the following words: *respect, rights, treatment, fair, honor, freedom.*

Collect keywords and definitions that students come up with on a whiteboard or shared Google Doc.

Leave open space beside each term and ask if they can fill in quick definitions or phrases they associate with each keyword.

Then show students a quick background explanation and film about dignity, *The History of the Universal Declaration of Human Rights*, in Video 4.5 (ultralized, 2009) and linked on the companion website. Note that this video is also part of "The Danger of a Single Story" exercise, so students might already have viewed it and can use it as a point of reference.

VIDEO 4.5
www.youtube.com/
watch?v=oh3BbLk5UIQ

After students view the United Nations (UN) website and film, ask them if any of the definitions or phrases for the keywords should be added to or changed. Are any words missing that relate to dignity? What does dignity truly mean?

Now you have collectively created a "dignity word bank" that's specially authored by the class, all linking to the concept of dignity.

Students can read aloud each part, and they will also likely wish to share reactions and reflections about the video that relate to the dignity word bank.

Part 2: Dignified Selfie

Keeping the *dignity word bank* visible, ask students if they think people represent themselves with dignity *when taking a selfie*. Why or why not?

"Selfies" are a relatively new phenomenon, actually. People have been creating self-portraits for centuries—but more recently, two technologies combined to make the selfie skyrocket. Can students guess what they were?

---

[1] Tell students the day before you plan to do this exercise, letting them know they will need to bring their phones to class the next day.

The Internet and *the smartphone* (wow!).

So selfies are a wonderful invention of the modern digital age, representing each of us as individuals, able to author our own presence and project our identity in any given place, at any given time, shared with the world.

Selfies are not always great, though. They're even responsible for a significant number of deaths per year, with people trying to take amazing photos and unwittingly putting themselves in great danger in the process.

On top of that, they are not always dignified. Sometimes, they might seem narcissistic; they might even make the person taking them feel *less present* in their environment. This can be okay, for comedy, but what if we were using them to represent ourselves and dignity at the same time?

Vint Cerf, credited with being the "Father of the Internet," has said, "The internet is a reflection of society; it holds up a mirror. If we do not like what we see, our problem is not to fix the mirror, it's to fix society" (High, 2018).

Do we credit the Internet, technology, or human impulse with the nature of selfies? This is an open-ended, rhetorical question that sets the tone.

Ask students the following questions, to answer in journals at the same time you read the questions out loud (allow one minute exactly for each answer—this is a timed set of quickwrites!):

- ❯ What are positive benefits of taking a selfie?
- ❯ Are there any negatives?
- ❯ Some people say that selfies seem narcissistic (self-absorbed) and inauthentic (not the real person). Do you agree or disagree? Why?
- ❯ Do they connect the subject with their environment, or distance them? Why?
- ❯ Do dignity and truth relate?

Last two questions, two minutes each:

- ❯ If you want to represent your dignified self in a selfie picture, what elements (both physical and nonphysical/emotional) would be important to capture?
- ❯ How do you imagine you can accomplish this?

After the quickwrite exercises, students will have an idea of what they want to capture in their selfies.

Taking the Selfie

Without too much lead-in, tell students that their job, now, is to spend the next fifteen minutes taking a *dignified selfie,* and uploading it to their blogs and/or printing them. They must do this on their own. *After taking the selfie, they should include a paragraph, in handwriting (in journals), about how the selfie represents their dignified self.* In this paragraph (about five to seven sentences), they can explain their motivation for taking the selfie the way they did. They can also talk about how it felt to be completing the exercise.

If possible, students can leave the classroom if there are open spaces in the school that could be used for this exercise; they must all be back together by the time the fifteen minutes are up, though!

Once back, make sure everyone has printed or uploaded a picture that's able to be shared with others.

Students should sit down with a partner, someone with whom they don't always pair up. You can use any form of sorting method you wish for making partnerships (there are a range of ideas in Chapter 2).

They should trade the selfies, without any explanation. For five minutes, have students write in their journals to answer these questions: *What comes across in the other's picture? What do they see that makes it dignified? What values come across? How does the picture reflect a side of them that might not be evident in a traditional selfie?* They might even want to write a story that relates to the picture, or a story that is inspired by it.

Then designate "Student A" and "Student B" for each partnership. Begin with Student A's selfie as the focus; for two minutes, Student B should share their interpretation first, and Student A listens. Then, for two minutes, Student A can share the motivation and backstory behind the selfie, and Student B listens.

Then switch, and Student B's selfie becomes the focus, with the same exchange as above.

Post-Debrief

After both selfies have been shared this way, come back together as a class community for a quick debrief. Ideally, form a circle, so that no one's back is to anyone else's. As students wish to contribute ideas, they can also show their selfies to the class.

While some students found sharing to be intimidating because they were revealing parts of themselves that are special and "real," everyone agreed that it is a good exercise because it pushed them to confront the nature of authenticity and think about picture-taking and the act of selfies in a new way.

Simply share these thoughts and reflections together as a class community, holding each other's thoughts with dignity and respect, too. It's a good closure, simply to listen.

One student, when she showed her picture, explained in a caption that it was dignified because it looks as if she has "a relaxed expression. Natural posture, and a soft background." Challenge students to articulate what they think dignity looks like, and how it can relate to their everyday lives. What does it mean to project a dignified view of oneself? What is dignity? Here are two examples of student selfies and personal reflections, shared during classes I taught. It makes for a powerful exercise.

Figure 4.2 • Dignified Selfie Example 1

"This picture shows how free I look . . . like a bird. It's saying women should have their own voices to speak out their opinions and their own rights."

Figure 4.3 • Dignified Selfie Example 2

"I think I look dignified in this picture because I am not wearing anything special. I look like I am going to school, which I am, and I am at my house, which might not be special to anyone else, but it is to me. I was also a bit tired, but smiled, which represents me."

Reflection Questions

▶ Did anything surprise you about this exercise?

▶ What challenges did you face when taking your own dignified selfie?

▶ How did your chosen environment and background inform the message you were sending?

▶ What did you learn when listening to your partner explain what they saw in your dignified selfie?

▶ What do you think is most important when representing yourself with dignity, and looking to see dignity in others?

Afterward, encourage students to post their selfies on the class blog and type up their explanations from their journals to accompany the images.

You might also wish to collect the printed versions and print the others from the student blogs, displaying them inside the classroom. Ask students to vote about this, so that the agreement is unanimous about showing them. Because it's a personal exercise that involves image, it's important to make sure that students feel comfortable with their dignified selfies being shown to the public.

The Takeaway

As shown, this exercise is a quick, colorful way to allow students to represent themselves and "dig deeper" into the meaning of the images they're consuming and projecting, thinking critically about social media. I had many students tell me it was a refreshing exercise, to look at dignity in this way and then be able to represent it with their own captured images. It's a form of self-portrait, with specific angle and meaning. Because we are doing this together as a class community, it creates a safe space to publicize some deeper views about what image and authenticity mean in today's self-promoting, selfie-saturated social media world. Most powerfully, it can also create a genuine first encounter with the topics of dignity and human rights. By forming an intimate connection with dignity first, this becomes less of a lecture and more of a conversation on a personal level.

The Danger of a Single Story

I contain multitudes.

—Walt Whitman

Students have likely heard the term *human rights,* but what does it mean, and where did it originate? Certainly, it links to themes of dignity that are present in other complementary exercises (see "Dignified Selfie" and "Storytelling, Empathy, and Kindness" for two prime examples).

This set of lessons includes several short, powerful videos that make an impact, in different ways. The videos are linked through QR codes in this book and are available on the companion website. This exercise helps to teach students the values of informed voice and leadership. Students will quickly see ways to connect with this exercise and make it their own. There are many ways to personalize, get creative, and extend, with social impact!

This is a three-framed study of speeches, in a sense, because the three videos represent different types of orations made by charismatic leaders:

First Lady Eleanor Roosevelt

Emma Watson

Chimamanda Ngozi Adichie

Students can listen to and read the speeches, and evaluate the themes and impacts the speeches have had on various communities, socially and politically.

Mindfulness Skills Taught

▶ **AWARE:** boosts awareness of audience, intention, and media

▶ **ADVANCING:** moves toward students seeing agency in ability to make impact on a global scale through speech

▶ **AUTHENTIC:** conversations about who we are, embodied in the words we say

Challenge Tips

This exercise involves spoken word and listening. If possible, you will want to create or access a transcript of each speech, using it so students have a visual to follow. They can also highlight the text and evaluate some of the devices at play.

Time Requirement: Two class periods of forty-five minutes each

Resource Materials Needed

▶ **VIEWING SCREEN** to show videos

▶ **SPEECH TEXT** (if possible)

▶ **JOURNALS**

How to Teach It

Begin by asking students to write down in journals three "rights" they have for which they are personally grateful. They can explain beside each item why they have listed it as a "top three" and why they consider it a right. This is something personal to keep in mind during the following exercises.

Part 1: First Lady Eleanor Roosevelt and the Universal Declaration of Human Rights

VIDEO 4.6
www.youtube.com/
watch?v=oh3BbLk5UlQ

Introduce students to the art of speeches. Start by asking them (in open discussion) to think about the speeches they find most compelling. Why do these speeches make an impact? Are they political? Personal? Both? What would motivate someone to make a speech? What traits do they have that make it memorable and influential? How are the mindfulness traits of *Aware, Advancing,* and *Authentic* evident in speeches that have positive social impact?

The first speech in this lesson links to the history of the Universal Declaration of Human Rights (UDHR), which can be introduced by showing students Video 4.6 (note that this short video is also part of the "Dignified Selfie" exercise, so students might already have viewed it and can use it as a point of reference).

VIDEO 4.7
www.youtube.com/
watch?v=_6YNIXPGXKo

First Lady Eleanor Roosevelt helped to bring about the UDHR. Her speeches played a large part in influencing the United Nations to adopt the Universal Human Rights. Video 4.7 (Educational Video Group, 2009) shows her addressing the general assembly.

> Where, after all, do universal human rights begin? In small places, close to home—so close and so small that they cannot be seen on any maps of the world. Yet they are the world of the

individual person; the neighborhood he lives in; the school or college he attends; the factory, farm or office where he works. Such are the places where every man, woman and child seeks equal justice, equal opportunity, equal dignity without discrimination. Unless these rights have meaning there, they have little meaning anywhere. Without concerned citizen action to uphold them close to home, we shall look in vain for progress in the larger world. (Roosevelt, 1958)

In reaction and reflection, ask students to return to their journals where they had written their three rights for which they feel grateful.

Adding to this, how does the Universal Declaration reinforce these rights? What about First Lady Eleanor Roosevelt's speech and her style of speaking make her message about human rights memorable and powerful?

Part 2: Emma Watson and "An Unpopular Word"

Keeping Eleanor Roosevelt's message of universal human rights in mind, ask students to write in journals how they feel about equal rights for men and women. Are these equal rights deserved? Are they evident?

In 2015, actress and activist Emma Watson addressed the UN about gender equality, sharing a message about equal rights and equal voice. As students view the Video 4.8 (United Nations, 2014), ask them to keep journals open, jotting down the words and phrases that make the most impact.

VIDEO 4.8
www.youtube.com/
watch?v=gkjW9PZBRfk

After the speech, ask students which parts of this speech made an impact on them. What phrases did students write down? How are stereotypes challenged and questioned in this speech?

What do students think of the lines:

If not me, who?

If not now, when?

Ask students to answer:

What would you like to do, that you might be afraid to start? How can you mindfully make a commitment to this today?

Part 3: Chimamanda Ngozi Adichie: "The Danger of a Single Story"

The third speech is by a writer who, in May 2017, was elected as a foreign honorary member of the American Academy of Arts and Letters.

Chimamanda Ngozi Adichie talks about stereotypes and expectations, and the complexity of representing more than one story. Certainly, she shares a meaningful message about multiplicity, diversity, and inclusion. It's something to which we can each relate, as we consider our own many stories.

VIDEO 4.9
www.ted.com/talks/
chimamanda_adichie_
the_danger_of_a_single_
story

We all want to live beyond labels; we all are more than one story—and there is a great danger when we put each other in boxes; sometimes, we do this without realizing it, because we have heard "the single story" so often. Being *Mindful by Design* involves understanding the truth of the multifaceted nature of community, and encouraging inquiry through recognizing the individual's multiplicity.

You can watch the speech in Video 4.9 (Adichie, 2009), or on the companion website, **caitlinkrause.com.** My classes loved seeing it, as it prompted a genuine discussion afterward.

Ask students, again, simply to jot down the following, as they view:

What do you find surprising about this speech?

After viewing, ask students to share their moments and snippets of surprise. There might be some common points.

Ask the following questions, to answer in journals at the same time you read the questions out loud (allow exactly one minute for each answer—this is a timed set of quickwrites!):

▶ How does Adichie use humor to amplify the effect of what she is saying?

▶ Have you ever had the experience that she describes, having a "single story" about someone else, and then discovering that they could have more than one story? Or has this happened to you? Describe this experience.

▶ How can a single story be dangerous?

▶ If we don't know otherwise, how can we use traits of mindfulness to see/hear/ understand *beyond* our expectations of a single story?

▶ This speech talks about power and its use in storytelling: how a story is told and who tells it. "Power is the ability not just to tell the story of another person, but to make it the definitive story." How can this power be democratized, giving back dignity? What is the solution that creates "a balance of stories"?

Post-Debrief

Students can share their answers to any of their journal writings from the three different parts. They can also create blog posts from these reflections, sharing ideas online.

Talk about the following reflective questions in this debrief conversation.

Reflection Questions

▶ After viewing these different speeches, what impresses you as powerful about them?

▶ What do the three speeches have in common?

▶ How are they different?

  ▶ How does each speech reflect aspects of dreams and hopes?

  ▶ Adichie says, "Stories matter . . . can be used to empower and humanize . . . to repair broken dignity." Do you agree or disagree, and why?

  ▶ How are stories used to promote powerful results in all of these speeches?

  ▶ How do the speakers embody mindfulness?

  ▶ Are they showing a desire for Awareness? Advancement? Authenticity?

  ▶ Do any of these speeches change your idea about how mindfulness can play a role in social impact?

Extensions with Social Impact

Students can get creative, using these speeches as vehicles to create their own speeches. If you have a Model UN or Student Government/Leadership Forum with which to connect, this could become a partnership project.

Also, students can make many more parallels and connections with the United Nations' Sustainable Development Goals (SDGs) in mind, creating advocacy for reaching a goal of their choice. This project can plant those seeds.

For example, part of the "World's Largest Lesson" web resources focus solely on Goal 5, which is about gender equality. With Emma Watson spearheading this initiative, students can investigate gender issues, take census, and promote equality on a local and global scale. You can find more information about the UN Global Goals on the "World's Largest Lesson" website, posted on the companion website for this book.

The Takeaway

This is a set of exercises with profound takeaways that can be shared in communities locally (in the classroom and school) and globally (through expanding social networks). Students gain an understanding of rhetoric with social impact, conviction, and a message that reflects mindfulness, and they can also reach and reflect about what changes they wish to see in the world. It has myriad applications and extensions. Keep in touch with the Global Goals Educators Network about your own personal reflections—the multiplicity of results and reflections are best when shared, and the theme is certainly foundational.

Mindful Journaling: Nature Journals and Moments of Wonder

You'll certainly notice that journals are a staple of these mindful exercises throughout the book—and that's intentional. It's not an arbitrary choice; nor is it a middle step en route to thoughts reaching the screen or blog post. Journaling as a tool, a process, and an end point has its own merit, and a slew of studies tout its benefits—for inspiration, creativity, catharsis, stress-reduction, and beyond. There are many positive results that come from keeping a journal. The daily habit encourages writers to form a relationship with their own articulated thought process, and to wonder, dream, postulate, and record detail. While journaling can be used as a daily register of happenings, these mindful exercises are mostly designed to promote reflection and ideation. They can be combined with sketching, drawing, and doodling; there's ample space to create.

Here, we'll use a range of nature journaling options, showing what's possible as a full set of activities that each encourage a state of natural wonder. "A moment of wonder," as I like to call revelatory creative moments, can happen any time there's ample space given to contemplate the beauty of the present, natural moment. I use my own nature journal and sketches as examples for students to catch me in a creative play-space, and I have included excerpts here for design ideas, too. When I use nature journaling as a reflection exercise in class, students are encouraged to develop their own journaling styles. You can use one, several, or all of the activities in this exercise, in any order. Design it to fit your timing and purpose. In any way you use it, it's bound to be a memorable mindful curriculum enhancement.

Mindfulness Skills Taught

▷ **AWARE:** encourages noticing small features and recording more sensory details in relationship to natural surroundings

▷ **ADVANCING:** as using journals boosts levels of consciousness, students are able to advance in modes and means of expression

▷ **AUTHENTIC:** amplifies a connection to the environment, deeper relationship with self, and joyful recognition of what is authentically present.

Challenge Tips

When students express challenges with a certain nature journal prompt, I find I can often help by clarifying the details of the exercise, limiting the scope, giving several examples, and/or letting students help design the exercise. This enhances and redefines the roles as partnerships, as they can have a voice in shaping the type of response, better aligned with vision. Sometimes, I take away every restriction, encouraging using an open space in a journal to get outside and record what happens.

Creativity Insights

Nature journaling can have profound results; it's all about letting it happen, in a certain open-flow, unencumbered way. Creative possibilities here are boundless, and I find it enhances my own personal life as well.

Time Requirement: One preview day, which will take about twenty minutes to lead students through a guided introduction

Resource Materials Needed

▶ **NATURE JOURNALS** (You can have students create their own, or find journals that they'll want to use. I'll describe how I selected my journal in the exercise. In either case, focus on finding a journal that has a quality to it that you like—because you'll want to gravitate toward it! I also make sure to use ones that have a variety of paper styles.)

▶ **ART MATERIALS**

▶ **NATURE JOURNAL RESOURCES AND REFERENCES** (You can use examples in this exercise, plus the extra resources provided!)

How to Teach It

Before you begin this exercise, you can have on hand a collection of resources that give an idea of nature journaling examples and how they can be used to animate the learning in and out of your classroom. You might even want to try some of the exercises firsthand on your own, as a warm-up and a chance to mindfully indulge in your own nature journaling—that way, you'll have something to tell students about your own reactions and reflections as someone who has done this "in the field."

It would be good to introduce the idea of nature journaling a few days before the exercises start—that way, students have a chance to gather resources to create their own journals.

The following is a good way to introduce the set of nature journal exercises, with a script you can use to give students a general idea of how nature journals are used with mindfulness.

Script: Nature Journaling Introduction

We're going to take a quick mindful journey right now. Make sure you're sitting in a comfortable position. Feel free to close your eyes. Can you imagine, right now, what it feels like to be in nature, somewhere you consider wondrous, majestic, beautiful, peaceful, or just plain inspiring? Maybe it's inspiring because this place has warm sunshine beaming down through the tree branches, sun through leaves creating variations in the green, or maybe you can see rolling teal waves coming in from a distance, smell the salt air, and feel all of the sounds of the beach.

Maybe you're deep in a forest, surrounded by evergreens capped with snow. Or perhaps this place is wonder-full because you can sit there for a while, hearing the wind moving through tall grass, seeing some vista surrounding you, noticing the way the sky turns bright orange and pink at sunset before fading to deep purple, the stars coming out, so that you notice the placement of constellations, shining down from a place in the sky that tells you exactly what time of year it is. Maybe it's a simple moment in your own garden space, noticing a certain plant or flower that reminds you of the season, tracking the changes in the earth.

These moments in nature are remarkable, in certain ways, and you notice them. As a mindfulness practice, many people keep a special journal to record such moments, and to record details that spark curiosity, awareness, and reflection. Writers, inventors, and all sorts of creative minds have used this type of journaling for centuries, and studies show it has amazing effects.

We're going to take some of these nature journaling practices and try them out ourselves in a combination of exercises you can use in class and outside, too. Your nature journal is a work of art, so the first step is to choose a type that you like.

From examples here, you can see types others have created; now, it's time to use some of these ideas to make your own journal, which you can bring to class to start the exercise together.

The journal has three major considerations:

Craft: *Will this journal be manufactured (i.e., you can buy it in a store) or handcrafted? If you're choosing to handcraft, you'll need to learn how to fold and bind the pages properly. Some places offer handmade book-creating courses; you can also teach yourself using online guides. While it can be a bit time-consuming, it's incredibly fun to create your own journal, and the final product feels even more like a unique, personal, mindful work of art.*

Paper: *The paper you select can be any style, any color, any type. A few considerations, though, will help you make a choice that matches your objectives. If you want to sketch snow or something else light in color, a darker paper is desirable. If you're sketching something that's dark or high contrast, light paper looks fantastic. Some other colored papers, such as blues, grays, lavenders, greens, and pinks, can make for interesting sketch backgrounds without distracting from the image itself—especially if the color fits the theme of the content. In other words, form should match function, and it's all about intention, here. If you want some sort of overlay, choose to include transparent paper or vellum and create layers. Thicker paper is best for watercolors, markers, and other art materials that tend to bleed through thin stock. Note that the thickness of the paper might be a challenge for handbinding. You can choose lined or gridded paper if that's your style, yet most like unlined paper for combining words with graphics. Feel free to get creative and go with what you feel makes your creative heart sing!*

Size: Basically, you'll want a journal that's big enough for sketching, and small, light, and durable enough for realistic transport.

So prepare by having your journal ready and on hand, and let the exercises begin!

Mindfulness Nature Journal Exercise Prompts

The following are prompts for the specific nature journal exercises, inspiring many moments of wonder. You can use these exercises any time of year, in any combination. Some could be done inside the classroom; others require time spent outside in nature. All hinge on open observation and a certain playful quality. You can ask students to complete some of these simple observations and exercises at home, in alignment with what you have planned in the curriculum. The mindful skill-building is universal and can easily apply to themes across all subjects. Each stand-alone nature journal exercise below includes the prompt script you can share directly with students. Enjoy the discovery, and personalize along the way!

Nature Quote

Think of a phrase or a quote you find inspirational, connected to nature in some way. If you can't think of one, search online and see what grabs you! Write this quote in some sort of embellished script on the first page of your journal, and decorate it as you wish. Make sure to give attribution. This is the "epigraph," or introductory quote, for your journal. What will follow is the magic you create!

Trail Map

Take your nature journal outside, and plan a walking route on which you will be stopping in five to seven separate places. Block out enough space on your page to draw each stop so that it fits as part of the whole page. You could even think of the maps at the beginning of fantasy novels, like The Lord of the Rings, *as your map for inspiration. Winnie the Pooh has a map of the Hundred Acre Wood, too, that shows stops along the way. This is the same general idea. As you walk, you'll be recording colors and observations along the way. At each stage, see if you can choose an angle and sketch that lets the viewer feel that he or she is there with you. By the end, you'll have a full-page assortment of pictures that document where you've been.*

Contour, Gesture, Observation

Place an object from nature (e.g., a small stick, leaf, pinecone, acorn—anything like this with a bit of detail works well) on the desk. You'll be creating three types of quick drawings based on the object. The first—contour—is just about showing the texture and exterior of the object. The second—gesture—is a quick sketch of the outline, to give it a basic shape. You could even try this one with your eyes closed, for a memory challenge. The third— observation—is about closely looking at the object from three different angles, drawing each of these.

Figure 4.4 • Mindful Trail Map

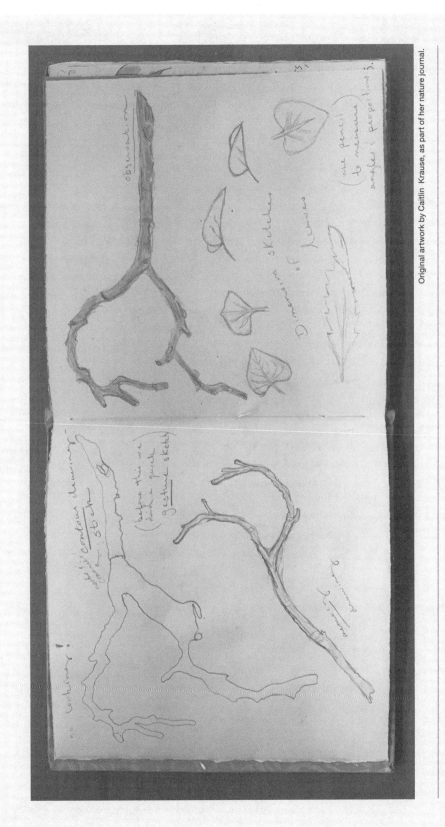

Figure 4.5 • Contour, Gesture, Observation Sketches

Plant Imagination

Find a plant, outside or inside. It can be growing in nature or potted and contained. In any case, imagine you are the voice of that plant, and write from its perspective, about where it has been, what it has endured, and what emotions it's feeling. What is it longing for? Feel free to use hyperbole and be melodramatic; this can be a creative theater exercise, too. Within your writing, or surrounding it, include a drawing of the plant, and add as much color as you like.

Invasives, Survivors

Some natural elements are deemed unnatural, in certain senses, as they are not indigenous to the specific region. The term for these is "invasives". One example of an invasive in the United States is the plant kudzu, which was introduced in the South as a solution for soil erosion and ended up taking over other natural wild plants. When species are threatened and suffer a blight yet manage to survive, we might praise them for their sturdiness and/or adaptability and resilience. There are many ways that plants serve as natural reminders and metaphors of cycles, growth, sustainability, and more. Choose a certain "plant story" to investigate, perhaps looking at examples of invasives or survivors, and write about it in your nature journal, providing a sketch to illustrate the prose or poetry you create. Use a mindful storyteller mindset for this piece, working to engage the reader as much as possible!

Change of Season

Can you feel a certain change of season in the air? Perhaps the mornings are getting darker and colder as you commute to school, or you can feel the ground hardening for winter. There are certain natural signals that seasonal change is under way, and everevolving. In this exercise, you can choose to focus on certain signs that the season is changing, describing the signals, and also drawing certain details that give you clues. This is a prime nature journaling exercise for any time of year. If you live in an area with a relatively constant year-round climate, you can still document the subtle changes that you notice around you, and/or if there is any anomaly, such as frequent rain or drought, you can record what you notice in the ecosystem as a result.

Sound as Colors and Shapes

Spend at least five minutes outdoors, just listening to the sounds around you. Try closing your eyes and imagining each one, picturing the sound and its visual representation. Does it have a shape? Does it have a color associated with it? How would you draw this sound? On a page in your nature journal, create a medley of the sounds combining, representing them just as you picture them when you hear them. For this exercise, anything goes, so let yourself go wild!

Color Palette and Nature Keywords

Choose nature-inspired "keywords"—any tag phrases, rich nouns, or actively descriptive verbs that come to mind as you contemplate your natural surroundings. Create a color palette from

Figure 4.6 • Plants in the Garden: "Invasives" and "Survivors"

this list of keywords, perhaps displaying the words and their colors in a color palette keychart. Then, you can also infuse them into a story, which can be a connected tale, or a series of disconnected thoughts.

Five Skies (in Mornings/Evenings)

For five consecutive days, notice the quality of the sky, and paint/draw/sketch it in your journal. You can note the time of day, the types of clouds you see (if any), and the feeling you have when looking. Maybe there is low cloud cover some days, and it gives you a headache—or the clouds could be racing across the sky, high up, giving you a great sense of motion, too. After five days, you're sure to be amazed at how much there is to notice, just by looking up!

Handwriting

This might not seem to be a "nature journaling" exercise, yet our handwriting is a part of our own natural expression, and it certainly bears an impact, flavor, mood, and style. In nature journaling, we often write alongside our sketches, and our handwriting becomes part of the artistry. We can choose, then, how to portray what we have to share through our choice of script. In this brief exercise, give yourself a chance to play with how you handwrite. Test out all-caps versus all-lowercase; see if you can combine calligraphy, cursive, and print. For a stretch, look at some fonts online, and see if you can copy them in your own handwriting. Graffiti artists have been using text and script for decades to make an impact in urban settings; in the same way, your nature journaling makes its own statement. So it's time to stretch and get even more creative!

After Rain: Taking Stock of the Garden (aka Sketch Petri Dish)

So much can happen, just by looking at a garden up close. In this exercise, you can draw a large circle, imagining it as a petri dish from science experiments, a study space for close examination. See if you can draw at least five natural elements from the garden up close in the petri dish, notating what you examine about them.

One Object, Five Sketches

Bring one natural object into the classroom, to sketch it yourself. Gather in a small group of four to five students per team. After you draw your object, leave it beside your journal, and move to another person's journal and object (travel in a circle so that everyone moves at the same time). On the same page that they have drawn their object, add to that by creating your own separate drawing of the object. Sign your drawing. Repeat this activity until all of the students in your group have drawn on your page. At the end, share your observations about the different perspectives and how they combine to create a unique picture of the object.

Discovery Walk

Head outside for at least thirty minutes, to walk in nature and see what you discover. You can take a friend or parent with you, of course, if you're going somewhere remote and want company

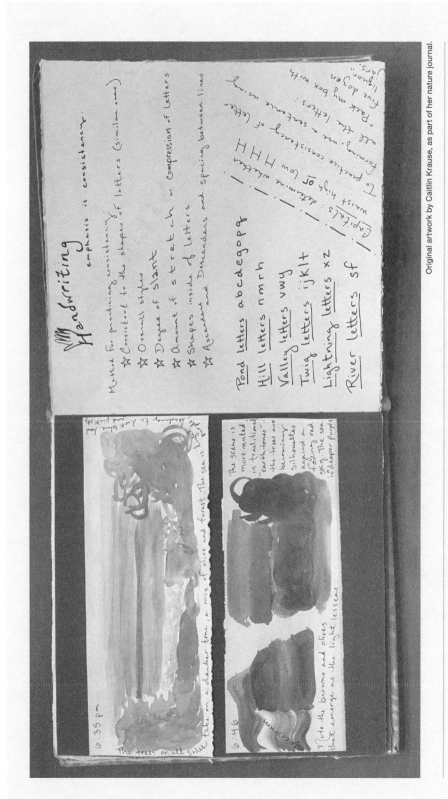

Figure 4.7 • Color Observation Field Studies/Mindful Handwriting: Playing With Lettering

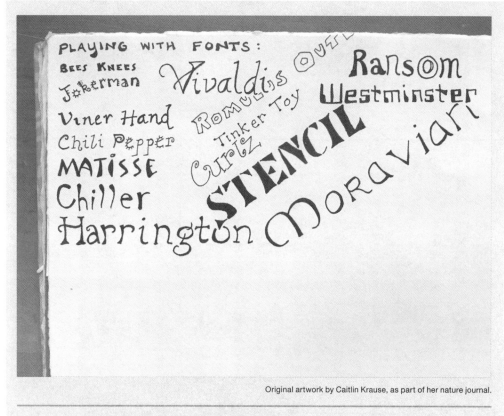

Original artwork by Caitlin Krause, as part of her nature journal.

Figure 4.8 • Mindful Handwriting: Replicating Fonts by Hand

along for the trek! The point is to put away all technology, stay as quiet as possible, and see what sounds, sights, and feelings from nature you can discover. See where the journey takes you. Record it all in your journal, either while you're out there or after you return, spending some quiet minutes writing about the experience.

Landscape

Closely observing a natural landscape around you, create a "window," perhaps using a framing device, or just imagining the edges of your own mental canvas, panorama, or other. On your page of the nature journal, draw this frame. Then map out what will be included in it—trees, rolling hills, a house, a dock, water? A landscape aims to capture the whole scene. You can make notes about this surrounding the frame, adding in what you would want the viewer to see and feel from this landscape.

Close Up, Keats-Style

Did you know that the poet John Keats was famous for his myopia, or nearsightedness could see things very sharply up close, though not from a distance. Some think this could explain

Original artwork by Caitlin Krause, as part of her nature journal.

Figure 4.9 • Mindful Journaling: Recording a Nature Walk

why he wrote poetry that showed such keen observations and attention to detail. In the same way, you should pick a natural object, writing about its details that you notice, using the curious mindset of a poet, celebrating the object for all of its detail, letting everything out on the page. Draw elements of the object that will help you remember how to describe it. Create a visual tapestry on the page.

Reverse Relief with Leaves

Place leaves, grass, and anything relatively flat, yet with its own distinct texture, behind a piece of your journal paper, in order to create a "reverse relief" rubbing. Using crayons or the flat edge of your pencil, press and drag over the object so that its outline, shape, and texture appear on the page. This makes for a natural creation with impact! You can add colors, embellish, and add writing, as you prefer.

The Takeaway

Now you have a wide array of nature-inspired exercises, sure to spark your senses throughout the year. These are springboards—see where your own nature journaling takes you, and have fun with it! As with everything mindful, adopting an attitude of gratitude, with creative curiosity as your guide, is the mindset and the modus operandi.

These exercises contain glimmers of ideas, seeds of inspiration that can be used in different shapes and forms. They represent a range of mindful awareness-boosters, linking students directly with the natural environment. And they can be adapted to fit the timing, location, and theme of the classroom. They can also be used as quick, natural refreshers, easily paired with all sorts of guided mindfulness meditations, breath work, body scans, and so on. It grows and flows from here.

Nature as Teacher: Bold Biomimicry and Design Thinking

EXERCISE 11

Nature offers us all sorts of inspirations, metaphors, and lessons by example. And spending time in nature is a direct conduit to a more mindful, contemplative outlook. How many times have we found ourselves experiencing distractions or stress, and spending a few minutes outside in nature made all the difference, restoring our energy, inspiring us, and gently reminding us that we are all connected? Nature reminds us that we belong. In addition, nature is a skilled innovator, adaptive and resilient.

The following exercise gets students thinking about the inspirations of nature, taking some of the tactics that have been tried and tested over the past 3.8 billion years. As Janine Benyus, co-founder of The Biomimicry Institute and AskNature.org, says, "Life creates conditions that are conducive to life" (Benyus, as quoted by InnovationTools.com, 2005). This exercise puts that quote to use, encouraging students to make profound connections about nature as a guide to imitate.

Mindfulness Skills Taught

▶ **AWARE:** students are encouraged to observe the world around them closely, thinking about the functional aspects and purpose of nature

▶ **ADVANCING:** using nature as a guide and source of inspiration, we ideate ways to improve and grow

▶ **AUTHENTIC:** this exercise reinforces connection inside and out, giving students the chance to view the self as part of a larger whole; it also reinforces social responsibility and a certain respect for nature, and it can pave the way for understanding code and algorithms, too

Challenge Tips

The choices and connections here are intentionally open, so that students have a certain freedom and ability to wonder. If students hesitate during any of the prompts, as in other exercises, you can step in and give your own examples to spark more ideas. Encourage students to make their own connections.

Creativity Insights

Taking students outdoors for even just a bit of this exercise works wonders. They can bring sketching materials, build maps, and get creative by using different media. I will also show my own creative nature sketch journal, handmade and stitched, as an example of what close observation can do and what a maker mindset is at each stage.

Time Requirement: Two lessons, fifty minutes each, with outdoor exercises and extensions possible

Resource Materials Needed

▶ **JOURNALS**

▶ **SKETCH SUPPLIES/ART MATERIALS**

How to Teach It

Since you will be going outside on the first of two days, this is a good lesson to plan in advance, judging weather and telling students to plan ahead in terms of their clothing.

Part 1: Introduction and Nature as Inspiration

Start by asking students what they think *biomimicry* is. You can display the word, parsing it into *bio + mimicry.*

In sustainable design and problem-solving, it's been called "a new discipline that emulates nature's best ideas and blueprints in order to solve human design challenges."

Biomimicry.org calls it: "an approach to innovation that seeks sustainable solutions to human challenges by emulating nature's time-tested patterns and strategies. The goal is to create products, processes, and policies—new ways of living—that are well-adapted to life on earth over the long haul" (The Biomimicry Institute, 2018).

Ask students: *"Why do you think nature can be our best teacher?"* Collect group answers and considerations.

Then, to set the mood, show Video 4.10—a two-minute BBC trailer "What a Wonderful World," with David Attenborough (Wouters, 2011).

VIDEO 4.10
www.youtube.com/
watch?v=auSo1MyWf8g

Introduction to Nature Journaling and Biomimicry

Today, for an initial biomimicry exercise, we'll start by collecting ideas from nature, which is a giant classroom. The first step is to heighten our noticing senses. For this exercise, we'll use nature journals and practice some journaling skills.

Begin by showing students what a nature journal is and what it can be used to track. Exercise 10, called "Mindful Journaling: Nature Journals and Moments of Wonder," serves as a good complement. You can refer to that exercise, too, to show examples of a full range of nature journaling options.

There are examples from my own nature journal there (see pp. 146–153), which I use to record many subjects, including:

- *Weather states*
- *Texture and color of flowers, pinecones, and leaves*
- *Trail map of where I walk*
- *Noises in nature*
- *Animal tracks*
- *Poetry and writing coupled with nature*

Mindfulness Writing Exercise Prompt

Nature Walk and Biomicry Trail Map: Take students outside with sketch materials and journals. (Plan a walking route that has a variety of terrain and ideally takes about thirty minutes total.)

Tell Students: *We'll be spending time going on a nature walk, marking down our own individual trail maps as we go. Your trail map is your path of discovery. We'll walk as a group, pausing at different points and noticing the details around us. At each pause point, you'll be activating your* Mindful by Design *skills, using awareness to notate particular details that follow the specific prompt. Get ready to discover some of nature's hidden magic!*

The total walk will take about thirty minutes, with four pauses of about five minutes each, and time to walk in-between. For each pause point, here are the focus prompts to tell students.

Prompt 1: *Focus on drawing the outline of an object—just to get the shape of it. You might draw it from several angles to give the viewer a sense of its shape, showing if it's round, flexible, skinny, and so forth. See if you can show its proportion; if you like, you can make notations about it in words on the side.*

Prompt 2: *This time, look at a different object and attempt to draw its texture. You can also draw its shape, yet the important part here is to get down its particular texture: Rough or smooth? Firm or soft? How does it feel, and how can you get that across in your sketch? Do* *you need to zoom in and create a close-up drawing, as well as one from farther away? Again, feel free to write a few words beside your sketches, yet try to let the image represent the object.*

Prompt 3: *At this stopping point, focus on a specific object in nature and write about some ability it has.* Have students each think of a subject and the purpose behind the structure it has been given by nature. You can choose how complex the subject is.

First, draw its shape. Next, draw its texture. Last, write what you imagine the use could be, in thinking about its function. For example, you could draw a bird-wing shape, and next, try to capture the softness and certain texture of feathers. Last, you could write that the function it has is to fly, which helps it to navigate.

Here, in this example, if it's an owl's wing, you could encourage students to think about what an owl's wing might be specialized to enable, in terms of functional characteristics. Research Note: When back in the classroom, active online research can provide more insights.

In another example, the focus can be on the roots of a tree, drawn stretching out, branching in all directions, with a texture that is strong yet also porous, to drink from the earth. Or consider a bird's beak, which has a certain shape and texture, ideal for its purpose. By focusing on a beak, you notice how its shape, texture, and purpose are related. You can even make connections to modern technology. The Kingfisher is one famous example of biomimicry (Figure 4.10A).

For this exercise, students can choose any natural inspiration source, completing the three steps with a spirit of curious, mindful attention:

1. Draw shape

2. Represent texture

3. Imagine purpose

The Kingfisher's beak became the model for the nose cone of Japan's 500 Series Shinkansen bullet train.

Source: Andreas Trepte, www.photo-natur.net.

Figure 4.10A • Kingfisher

Source: Shinkansen 500 series at Kytoto Station taken by Nick Coutts, CC BY 2.5 https://creativecommons.org/licenses/by/2.5/

Figure 4.10B • Shinkansen Train

As a closing, reflective reflective part of Prompt 3:

Draw a second image of your whole subject (perhaps the entire tree, with root structure included), and then write down the sentence below, filling in the blanks:

This _____ [subject] has the ability to _____ [ability], which helps it to _____ [function].

Prompt 4: *At the last stopping point, simply ask students to find something they think represents a theme of "change." Have them quickly sketch the object and explain why it can connect to the theme of change.*

For example, a blade of grass could represent change because, when it grows too high in a yard or sporting field, it's usually cut down again. An apple tree can represent change by its bud-flower-leaf-fruit cycle, following the seasons. Another example could be birds' wings, which change in shape and size, to affect a difference in aerodynamics performance (Figure 4.11). You can conduct research later, once indoors, and discover more about why something represents change, using online investigation on sites such as AskNature.org.

When students are indoors, have them reflect with a friend, pairing and sharing about what they noticed in nature. Each student should take about three minutes to show their partner their trail map; then, roles reverse, sharing stories. Together as a class, now that the biomimicry nature walk has led to some authentic insights, check out this compelling article and Video 4.11 (Haubursin, 2017), which shows why nature is often a great designer, and the Kingfisher, as mentioned previously, is a prime model. We're gearing up for applying these biomimicry ideas in Part 2."

VIDEO 4.11
www.vox.com/
videos/2017/11/9/
16628106/biomimicry
-design-nature

Source: Andyworks/iStock.com.

Figure 4.11 • Aerodynamics: Bird in Flight

Part 2: Why Use Biomimicry? Connecting a Design Thinking Challenge with a Natural, Authentic Solution

Today, try beginning with a few simple breaths, bringing students back together to the classroom space, to build on Part 1's discoveries. The following is a short guided awareness introduction that you can use:

> *Start by noticing yourself in your chair, and the way you're sitting, comfortably, relaxed. Notice your breath, traveling in and out, filling your lungs, expanding them, and then leaving as you exhale. Take a breath, more slowly now, breathing in deeply, and then gently exhaling. Let's take three more breaths now, in silence, at your own pace. [Pause here for three breaths.] Now, as we are here together, let's reflect back on the time spent yesterday in nature, creating our trail maps as we walked around, observing. See if your mind can recall the feeling of being outdoors, and the objects you noticed. Focus on shape, then texture, capturing a snapshot of what the objects looked and felt like, to bring those experiences and observations back. Remember the subject you chose that had an ability; remember which one connected to change. See if, right now, you can also feel what it would feel like to be back outside, right there in that natural place, with those elements surrounding you. As you continue to imagine this, bring yourself back to this classroom space, ready and present, ready to share.*

> *The focus today is to use these observations to form authentic connections and solutions.*

Team Biomimicry Design Thinking Challenge for Thriving

Students form teams of about four people in each group, bringing nature journals with them.

Give different teams one "thrive verb" out of the following five (you can allow them to choose, blind draw, or select one for each):

- *Move (navigation, locomotion)*
- *Adapt (resilience of form; maintain flexibility yet keep integrity of shape)*
- *Eat (nutrition, gain energy)*
- *Protect (create a sheltered home and/or temperature for itself)*
- *Interact (discover, communicate, share, and/or gain information)*

Each "thrive verb" is a category that relates to sustainability, keeping a balance. We often have a lot to learn from nature. Each team has twelve minutes total (about three minutes each) to show one another their nature journals. As each person shows, have the group track whether they can make any connections to the way in which any of the objects perform the *thrive verb*. Remember, they won't be using *all of the verbs for their list; each team has only one on which to focus.*

They can write down a collective list together as they go.

Using the nature insights about the thrive verb, and keeping the collective list in mind, each team has a challenge: to create a sketch and functional explanation of an invention for humans that use the same technique, as learned from nature, to mimic what nature is doing well.

Here are the specific challenge prompts for each team; for this exercise, students will be designing for themselves (*unless* they happen to have another user or UX persona in mind!):

1. *Move:* Using what you know about nature's mobility, design a device that could help you get from home to school.

2. *Adapt:* Applying what you know about nature's ability to change and customize itself, design a piece of school furniture that is flexible enough to fit a student's changing learning needs.

3. *Eat:* Using what you know about nature's ability to ingest nutrients and water to refuel itself efficiently, design something you would like to see become part of the school lunch system.

4. *Protect:* Applying what you know about nature's ability to protect itself, design something that mirrors what you observed in nature. This could be a device that helps you in school or something for home.

5. *Interact:* Knowing that nature uses certain means to discover, communicate, share, and/or gain information about the environment, use these examples as inspiration to create a parallel language or means of discovery communication that you could use.

The above can take students a full class period to discuss, sketch out, and write in words. It can become a blog post and a fuller explanation. This will be their first foray into biomimicry. Remind them that this is more about the *process* than the results; any solutions they come up with are fantastic in themselves, as they are going about the steps that a biomimic does.

Reflection Questions

Form a group circle as a class for a discussion together.

You can start by sharing the following reflection from the magazine *GermiNature,* by biomimic Daphne Fecheyr-Lippens (2014):

> The biggest difference between a biomimetic approach and a "traditional" design approach is that the biomimic seeks inspiration from nature. After having defined the problem to be solved (i.e. function to be fulfilled) the biomimic starts digging in his or her brain for biological realities he or she has been exposed to that will inspire solutions to the challenge at hand. The "traditional" designer is also digging into his or her memory for design inspiration, but in this initial brainstorming phase I saw a big difference between what a "traditional" designers vs. a biomimic finds inspiring.
>
> Ideas the designers were shouting out were all related to existing products, designs and services that they have encountered in their lives, from impressive

working engineering solutions, greatly designed products, to small tools they sell at the local store. I was honestly impressed by products and services they knew about that I couldn't even imagine existing. On the other hand, very few were thinking about how spider webs or even our own human body could help solve the challenge.

I realized that in both cases, creativity is based on what you already know and highly limited to how you could connect those things together. Limitations of your own imagination can be widely extended by exposing yourself to more fascinating things.

Then talk through the following questions out loud as a group.

⬩ In what ways did this exercise expose us to "more fascinating things" related to nature?

⬩ How would you describe traditional design versus biomimicry design?

⬩ How do you feel after doing these exercises?

⬩ Can closely observing nature also be a tool for helping develop a better world?

⬩ What are you most curious about now?

⬩ What would be the ingredients in your vision for a shared better world future?

Extensions and Additional Resources

One question, which is actually quite foundational, is *What is sustainability?* For this theme, please check out Exercise 14: "Sustainability and Poetry Perspectives: Meditations on 'Good,'" in which sustainability is a prime topic.

There are also many directions and extensions to jump to from here, including investigating swarms, looking at rules for emergent behavior, and setting up examples that can help to teach students the building blocks for coding and understanding complex algorithms.

Resources and links can be found online **(caitlinkrause.com)** to help further investigations and research, and you can join partnerships, workshops, and community efforts with those who are experts in the field.

The Takeaway

By the end of this exercise, students have a foundation for understanding what biomimicry is and can build from there, later developing a greater appreciation for code and algorithms, which can be perplexing if considered as only abstract concepts. This gives them real shape, and it also shows students that nature is everywhere, even in ourselves! By growing in awareness, self-compassion is also supported, and students can operate out of a state of mindful curiosity, stretching to impact the world.

Architecture and Virtual Worlds: Designing Mindful Community Spaces

EXERCISE 12

How many of us have dreamed of ideal community spaces, or layouts of our classrooms, that would facilitate the most engagement and enjoyment while learning?

This exercise is all about imagination and visualization, quite literally. I remember my own thrill, as a student in high school French class, when we had opportunities to design and create our own cathedrals, modeled after those that made France famous. It taught me so much about the physical space, as well as the religion, social hierarchy, and philosophy that shaped the historical times (thank you, Mr. McGarty!). It was something fun that made the learning sticky—I'll never forget Reims and the mindset and mastery involved in building that grand cathedral.

Now, with the ability to use virtual reality applications in classrooms, technology can enhance this creative process that has applications across all disciplines.

Designing architectural structures and spaces is interactive, imaginative, and practical. In this exercise, we look at creating an ideal outdoor physical space: a "park." It directly connects students with their own capacity to use awareness, presence, and visualization of an environment that fits their needs and goals. As you'll read below, it's filled with various modifications and possibilities, too.

Mindfulness Skills Taught

- **AWARE:** builds awareness of multiple perspectives coexisting; outreach in community
- **ADVANCING:** encourages students to set goals, with community and users in mind; gives them a chance to self-evaluate their progress along the way
- **AUTHENTIC:** allows students to blend ideas, desires, and wishes with what would fit larger community values and needs

Challenge Tips

If you decide to incorporate virtual reality (VR) environments into this exercise, you'll definitely want to first connect with your tech/IT support and/or media specialist in advance, to coordinate a plan to use the best platform that is supported by your school's environment. This could be highlighted on blogs and used as a cross-curricular project, too, depending on your goals.

As your project grows in scope, it could become a vehicle for students to have direct social impact. Start designing, and see where it takes you!

Creativity Insights

This is an exercise with various ways to include technology embedded in the framework of what is created. Remember that *technology* is just a vehicle and a medium—not an end goal. The purpose of this exercise is to get students designing mindfully, and VR technology is a great way to immerse in the environment created. Students could also use some kind of social crowdsourcing platform (either a physical presentation space or online) to share ideas, collect input, and solicit feedback. Just imagine—they're given the freedom to design a space that directly benefits others! This prompt triggers empathy, as students have to put themselves in the shoes of their intended users. They also need to articulate the benefits of their vision, as well as acknowledge challenges in making it happen, not just in VR, but IRL (in real life).

Time Requirement: Ninety minutes+ (which can be divided into several class times, as best fits your timing!)

Resource Materials Needed

▷ **SKETCHING MATERIALS, JOURNALS, AND VR RESOURCES**

▷ **POSSIBLE SUPPLEMENTAL PLANNING MATERIALS** (can include sticky notes, Legos, Play-Doh, and other design-thinking staples)

How to Teach It

Part 1: Warm-up

This is an exercise that starts with a simple, open journal prompt. I recommend bringing the group outside, if you have that possibility and space. They can bring their journals and pens/sketch materials with them.

Have everyone gather in a circle, and ask them to think about outdoor spaces they have visited and enjoyed—community gardens, city open spaces, parks, and playgrounds. What do they like about them? Can they sketch some details from memory and describe a place, using all five senses? What was the experience like to be there?

Then let them know that they will be dreaming up a park of their own, using the *"What if . . . ?"* mindset.

Part 2: Park Values and the "What if . . . ?" Mindset

Once back in the classroom, you can show students a short video that reinforces the message of taking "what is" and dreaming of "what if" possibilities. It's a series of openings, rather than closings.

This *"What if . . . ?"* mentality is one that modern park architects are using to transform spaces and human experiences in a mindful and uplifting way, thinking first and foremost about putting their minds in the perspective of the consumer—the person who will be enjoying the park!

This, by the way, is a tenet of UX design thinking models, the process that designers use to deeply engage their empathetic capacity to understand the user and create experiences that will be of benefit. With mindfulness in focus, it's a perfect complement, as it incorporates the capacity to be aware, to understand others, and to care about well-being on a larger social scale.

VIDEO 4.12
www.youtube.com/
watch?v=76mblYY__PE

You don't need to explain all of this to students—they will be experiencing the process firsthand.

Begin by taking a look at the six-minute clip in Video 4.12, about the creation of the High Line park in New York City, now famous as a paradigm of urban renewal (*Great Museums*, 2014).

At one point in the High Line video (starting just before 2:00), fashion designer Diane von Furstenburg talks about the High Line: "The whole experience is magical. It's slightly elevated, but not too high. So it protects you from the street, yet you feel the energy of the street. And, also you're near the water. . . . That also adds yet another dimension, and another sense of air, and space, and hope, and freedom, and all the things we like." After von Furstenburg says this, pause the viewing.

Have students make a list (in journals, right near the descriptive writing they completed outside) of "all the things we like." Have them think about the word *we* and recognize community—they are speaking for themselves, certainly, yet also representing a larger group.

This list can be a poem, a series of bullet points, or sentences. The points can be abstract or concrete. What will result is a list of values, and these values can become touchstones, pointing toward the "why" intention behind what they will be creating. The reflection itself is an exercise in mindfulness.

Diane von Furstenburg's list of values for a park, for example, could be:

> *Protected*

> *Energetic*

> *Near water*

> *Air*

> *Space*

> *Hope*

> *Freedom*

See what students come up with as their own list of "park values" in three minutes of quiet, reflective writing. You can compile a list together once they are finished, and/or have them share with two to three people around them.

Note: It could be important to give space for the reflection to be personal, at this stage, as each student will be designing a different park that is their own imaginative creation. It's highly individual, and these values are subjective.

Then continue to watch the rest of the film, noticing the part that focuses on photography at the end.

After viewing the film, ask students what they noticed about the park's evolution. You can have a discussion (full class or in small groups) around the following focus questions:

High Line Discussion Questions

- What challenges did the founders encounter along the way?
- What inspired them to save the High Line from demolition?
- How did photography play a role in helping them?
- When the photographer talks about his relationship to the project, what kind of language does he use? Is he involved based on an emotional motivation or a practical one (or both)?
- What are some of your motivations for creating your park?
- At the end of the film, the High Line is called "a real New York park." In what ways does it reflect the culture of New York?
- What community would you like to serve, and how will you reflect its culture in what you create?

Give students at least fifteen to twenty minutes to focus on these questions and reflect upon answers. You could focus on some of these questions in a larger group, and then some in individual reflection and journal responses. Remind students that, with changing times and a push for more environmental awareness and nature conservation in urban spaces, parks are more and more important and critical to the well-being of a population.

Students can also brainstorm about the types and purposes of parks—there are so many functions a park can serve. Ultimately, you build a space and then imagine how humans will use it. You create an experience as the architect of a space.

Part 3: The Human Scale and User Experience

Next (on Day 2, preferably, as you space out content), you can view the trailer in Video 4.13 for the critically acclaimed Danish documentary *The Human Scale* (Metropole, 2013).

VIDEO 4.13
www.youtube.com/
watch?v=BxywJRJVzJs

The trailer opens with the words "The mega-city is a reality," comparing our modern cities to works of science fiction, in sharp contrast to the warm and social human nature.

Check out some of the statistics and data that the film posts:

Fifty percent of the world's population lives in urban areas. By 2050 this will increase to 80 percent. Life in a mega-city is both enchanting and problematic.

After viewing the film trailer, use the following as discussion points. You can have students individually write thoughts down in journals in response to the points, before forming small groups to talk about their ideas. Then, form a circle for a larger group discussion.

"The Human Scale" Discussion Questions

- How is city planning operating with "an incomplete toolbox"? (Let students just imagine what they think is missing.)

- Do cars and traffic help social planning or hinder it? What are some positives about transportation, and some negatives?

- What type of a social space do you imagine makes people happier and healthier?

- The trailer mentions that 89 percent of Times Square isn't a "square." What do you think it is, both geometrically and purpose-wise?

- Is it our job to "take care of lives of others"? Whose job is it to design social spaces in a community?

These become complex philosophical questions and considerations—this is a topic with great impact. You might find students actively debating these answers—encourage them to really take a stance and use real-life examples to back up how they feel.

Some say design is the language of a place; it informs how people will interact, the experiences they will have, and how they will ultimately reach happiness and well-being in a social, interrelated community.

You might find even more resources to share with students; the next step is for them to think about how to go about designing their own parks, in ways that fit the values and reflections they have expressed.

Part 4: Design-a-Park in Action

At this point, you have effectively introduced a mindful designer mindset, and the reasoning behind the need for well-designed public spaces.

The goal, now, is for each student to design a park that will benefit the user community, and they can use their sets of values as anchor points and guides.

I recommend a portfolio-style project, including the following:

- Warm-up Reflection Journal Entries (these can become blog posts)
- Set of Values Motivating Park Creation

> ▶ Users in Mind for the Park (i.e., the intended community it serves)

> ▶ Sketches of the Park Layout; Architecture

> ▶ VR Landscape of Park (design a prototype or model using virtual reality technology)

> ▶ Post-Reflection Journal Entries (these can become blog posts about students' experiences)

In setting up the requirements for what students will produce and include in the portfolio, you can decide about the possibilities and parameters, with the following considerations (it's up to you to decide):

> ▶ Is the park an imagined application for the school or the local community, or is the location wide open?

> ▶ Are there limitations for the physical size of the park? When designing the space, how much geometry and math will you incorporate?

> ▶ Will students have a budget consideration, which could involve mock fund-raising and crowdfunding?

> ▶ For the VR component, what setup will you use? (see "VR Setup" section below)

> ▶ Will there be a contest or presentation fair at the end? If so, who will be the audience/judges?

These considerations shape the scope of the exercise. From there, jump in with an open mindset, per Howard Rheingold's advice.

VR Setup

This is where partnering with your IT specialist will help. I have seen great VR programs in dynamic learning environments right now, using all sorts of variants of headsets and devices, from Google Daydream to Samsung Gear VR to Oculus Rift to HTC Vive. There are also different VR education applications and programs already in place, and your school might already be using one.

For me, form fits function, and I recommend starting by looking at all of the possibilities involving the materials and technology that your school has on hand. Adopt a mindset of curiosity and playfulness, and seek others to form communities as you learn!

Believe me, VR is a hot topic, and there are many other teachers looking to learn about it. There are also quality online groups for VR/AR integration that can be part of a supportive community—I recommend using Twitter and also resources from global conferences (World VR Forum [WVRF] and International Society for Technology in Education [ISTE], among others) to glean a feel for what's current in VR, as there are technology trends and advancements every week in the VR/AR arena.

If you keep the focus on the immersive experience of VR, the exercise has an intrinsic value in itself, giving users the chance to feel as if they have truly entered this imaginary world. It has a magical element to it, and everyone involved can derive happiness from the sheer freedom of creative expression.

Keep in mind that you don't need to be the expert in the technology. Often, as David Weinberger (2011) says, "The smartest person in the room is the room," and everyone can pursue knowledge and understanding together as a community, helping each other, co-learning, and teaching.

What if I'm Not the Expert in Media and Technology?

Words from Howard Rheingold, Learning and Connections Expert

In 2016, I interviewed luminary Howard Rheingold about leadership and learning, asking what it means to be a good leader, and he gave the following response—so valuable to keep in mind when any new media or technology is being used (it's universal!):

> My advice about being a good leader in the classroom is to be a good and visible learner. . . . The more I revealed about what I didn't know, the more I made mistakes in public and then looked at why I made them, in public, the better teacher I became; the more attentive the students became. Because I was teaching social media, I used a lot of media, and quite often it would break.

> Those were opportunities for me to tell students, *You're not really on the edge if you don't fall off it from time to time.* I think that falling off the edge, in public, and using that as a teaching moment is a great form of leadership for teachers. . . .

> In my experience, the more you reveal about what you don't know, and about how you go about learning, the better you are as a teacher.

The Takeaway

This exercise presents a series of opportunities to bring mindfulness into practice, with real-world context and applications. Students use their imaginations and creativity playfully to engage with the prompts, learning about design thinking process and user experience. They also gain valuable insights about community, empathy, and values.

EXERCISE
13

What Makes a Mindful Leader?

Leadership is a topic that stretches into all areas of learning, and applies to all ages. Because of its ubiquitous nature, it can also fade into the backdrop of curriculum content. This quick lesson brings leadership back to the forefront of a discussion that actively incorporates examples and student-led discussion. In many ways, it attaches to mindfulness and the idea of "doing good" to contribute to the world in positive ways.

Dr. Paul Grossman, who founded the European Center for Mindfulness and is part of the Mind and Life Institute, wrote a paper in which he talked about mindfulness as an "embodied ethic." As Grossman (2014) says, mindfulness "also constitutes an embodied ethical act, process, and practice."

The article is a useful overview of mindfulness practices worldwide and also addresses interpreting mindfulness within a context of wise action. Grossman explains, "Ethics is meant and defined here, not as part of a system of religious imperatives, but, more generally, in terms of a coherent set of values relating to human conduct, with respect to rightness and wrongness of certain actions and to the goodness and badness of the motives and ends of such actions."

In this age of searching for truth and trust, it's this ethical aspect of mindfulness that can bring it alive for students, showing them it is a way to be, actively and openly, in the world. Applying this ethical embodiment to leadership is a natural fit. Here, students play a role in defining what it means.

Mindfulness Skills Taught

- **AWARE:** students gain self-awareness and also can openly consider what it means to be leaders in the world

- **ADVANCING:** making connections between ideas of active leadership; discussing the ways in which it can help a community to advance

- **AUTHENTIC:** without judgment, thinking about ethics and values of true leadership

Challenge Tips

This is a quick exercise, without a "right" or "wrong"—all sorts of ideas will naturally emerge, especially during the drawing phase, with students gathered together. You can keep this initial exercise simple, building it into larger frameworks as it naturally fits.

Creativity Insights

There are "daily moments of leadership" everywhere, waiting to be recognized, in every field. Using mindful curiosity, students will get creative with their investigations of leadership. As educators, our role is to encourage that spark, seeing what develops from here.

Time Requirement: Thirty minutes

Resource Materials Needed

> **LARGE POSTER-SIZED PAPER,** potentially in an assortment of colors
> **MARKERS**
> **JOURNALS**
> **STICKY NOTES**

How to Teach It

Start by asking students the simple-yet-complex question:

What is a leader?

Using journals, they have two minutes to write down all the qualities they can think of when they think of a leader.

Sharing out loud, have a mini–group discussion about what a leader is to them, creating a class list of attributes. Next, ask the students:

What is a mindful leader?

When I asked this in my seventh-grade class, one student was quick to offer, "A mindful leader is someone who has the qualities of a leader, and is using them *for good.*"

Have students form teams of three to four people, each gathered around a table with a large, poster-sized piece of paper (and several colorful markers) in the middle.

Their quick challenge is the following:

"Attributes of a Mindful Leader" Prompt

In ten minutes, decide as a group a list of at least ten attributes of a mindful leader. Draw a picture of this leader—what you imagine—in the center of the poster, including the ten+ characteristics surrounding them.

As you time the activity, you can walk around the room watching the teams create. Be intentional as a quiet observer—not altering the dialogue, just listening in. You'll hear a lot, and it's an energizing exercise, without a doubt!

After the ten minutes are up, some groups might be finished, and others might wish they had even more time. This is as it should be with a quick-fire exercise!

Their second challenge, however, is to move on and use ten minutes to *create a story.*

"Mindful Leader in Action" Story Prompt

As a group, decide on a story you can tell that features your mindful leader in action! This story can involve elements of what you have encountered in real life; it can also incorporate elements you imagine. Write down some of the key elements of your story, or create a picture storyboard so you can share it.

At the end of this time, have each team share their ideas with the rest of the class. They can swap ideas together, too. You might decide, for the final reflection, that gathering in a circle makes sense.

Reflection Questions

After each team has shared the stories, allow students to reflect a bit, personally, about what they have experienced in this exercise about mindful leadership. Ask them to respond individually to the following questions (in journals). I like to read each question out loud, giving about one to two minutes for each response before gently prompting the class to move on:

- In working together as teams to generate ideas about mindful leadership, what challenges did you encounter, and how did you overcome them?
- Do you imagine it's a challenge to embody a mindful leader? Why?
- Have you ever come across someone who performed an act of mindful leadership? Try to describe this event in detail.
- How can using mindfulness and being a mindful leader offer personal benefits?
- In what ways do you imagine it could change the community? And the world?

Extensions

As an extension, it is helpful for students to visualize mindful leaders and also find them actively in the world. Aim to have a Mindful Leadership ongoing search, looking for change-agents who are empowering "for the good" both locally and globally. You can investigate how they formed their missions, how they inspire others to join them, and also reach out to contact them and involve them in your classroom.

You might come across inspirations in your own active Personal Learning Network (PLN); one personal example that affected my own learning was discovering Paul Salopek, the mindful leader who is featured in "Walk This World" as part of the "Digital Mindful Citizen" exercise. Showing students examples of active leaders gives them concrete visions of leadership. Inventors, Nobel Prize winners, Fields Medalists, and local community heroes can be used to demonstrate leadership.

One open extension idea is to ask students to build an ongoing project involving leadership, perhaps even using it as one channel on their blogs. Leadership, social justice, and human rights themes can be linked to leadership.

In addition to in-the-classroom extensions, students might consider forming community task initiatives with leadership and action in mind. The areas they could impact could link to the UN Sustainable Development Goals (aka "Global Goals"), for example. And they can make active strides in the school and local community toward achieving these goals by focusing on certain ones and creating campaigns. Links to these resources, and ways to get started, are included in the References, and also on the book's companion site. Let students take it to the next level!

The Takeaway

Before actively using the term in my curriculum, *leadership* seemed like an empty, nebulous word to some of my students. It was understood that we all knew it was important, yet/and/so we never talked about it concretely. "Everyone is a leader," they might have said. This exercise brings leadership to light, giving it better active definitions, allowing students to come to an understanding about what leadership means. They are challenged to think about the intention and foresight necessary to embody leadership; the insight to act upon values that involve mindfulness; and the open, reflective enthusiasm that allows mindful leadership to inspire and empower others. Takeaways impact the classroom and school environment in profound ways; you're certain to see aftereffects!

EXERCISE 14

Sustainability and Poetry Perspectives: Meditations on "Good"

Sustainability is a topic that's undoubtedly linked to mindfulness, yet the term itself—*sustainable*—might be somewhat elusive. This exercise gets students thinking about the nature of "good" and what they might be willing to do to create a better, more sustainable world. Though the topic might be massive, this is a light, playful exercise that invites students to make big connections. As you find your own useful resources, videos, and supplementary materials, you'll certainly want to incorporate them, as this topic is ever evolving and being updated with new supportive platforms and media. You can find valuable ideas and connections online, including on the United Nations Sustainable Development Goals site (sustainabledevelopment.un.org), which has many education initiatives.

Mindfulness Skills Taught

▶ **AWARE:** awareness of what "good" actually means, put into practice

▶ **ADVANCING:** urges students to think about small and big-picture changes

▶ **AUTHENTIC:** in terms of sustainability as a mindset and a goal, allows students to look past individual perceived needs and ego, looking instead to connect in a true and authentic way with a united world

Challenge Tips

This topic is both simple and dense, in that it involves deep consequences and considerations for the planet. If students seem to wish to take the issue lightly, they might be at a stage of beginning to consider some of the implications of sustainability as a topic. Allow this to happen. Give reflective space, and appropriate challenge along the way to stretch thinking more deeply about the topic. It does not need to be all at once, at the same pace. The group discussions will illuminate what students are thinking; their ability to journal and use blogs as a reflective tool will also give them creative outlets. Keep communication open; nothing is a mandate. This is an invitation, instead, for curiosity to drive the learning.

Creativity Insights

Through the extensions and activities, there are many ways to publish and share students' creative responses. With this exercise, it's wide open!

Time Requirement: Two exercises, forty-five minutes each

Resource Materials Needed

- **JOURNALS**
- **MATERIALS ABOUT SUSTAINABILITY** as a term and practice
- **POEM,** "Meditations on Good," by Caitlin Krause
- **POEM,** "What We Would Give Up," by Marie Howe

How to Teach It

DAY 1

Part 1: Sustainability as a Term

Recent developments in humans' way of living have spawned today's "sustainable" movement, which is popularly linked to environmentalism and economics. It's a complex term, and a challenge that can be approached in ways related to:

- *design*
- *science*
- *economics*
- *social movements*

- *personal choice and decision-making*
- *leadership*
- *. . . and more!*

Gathered in a circle, with journals open, ask students if they have heard of the word *sustainability,* and if so, what are some associations? Students can discuss with those beside them before sharing with the whole circle.

Begin by talking with students about the term's complexity, sharing the following explanation:

> *Sustainability is most often defined as meeting the needs of the present without compromising the ability of future generations to meet theirs. There are three main pillars: economic, environmental and social. These three pillars are informally referred to as people, planet and profits (UN Documents,* Our Common Future, *Chapter 2: Towards Sustainable Development).*

▶

Note that, in the above definition, the equations are *people = social; planet = environmental;* and *profits = economic.* The three can be seen as interrelated and linked, in concentric circles.

A simplified definition for sustainability, using the above as a guide, is "Let's avoid actions today that will make life tomorrow worse." In discussing notions of "worse" and "better," inevitably, we confront the nature of good, and invite students into a conversation about their own personal values—what is "good"?

This beginning discussion should last about ten minutes, before students open journals to a blank page, writing at the top: *Meditations on Good.*

Part 2: A Force for Good

Ask students to create, on this open, blank page, a quick "list poem" of things they think are "good." It's an often-used term, just like "sustainable"; yet what does *good* actually mean?

Tell students they have three minutes to create a list of "good"—and then issue an open invitation to share it out loud with the classroom circle.

I use the poem "Meditations on Good," which I wrote during this exercise with my eighth-grade class, as my personal example to share with students. (Yes, you can and should write alongside students during this exercise—and share away!)

Meditations on Good
by Caitlin Krause

Good dog,

Good morning, Sunshine,

Good grief.

To be *good*:

don't disturb,

I'm perturbed by the word—

It's absurd!

Goodie goodie gumdrops,

Good for me is wicked

Wiki-pedia, symmetry,

ice, and

everything nice.

Sugar and spice,

and silence

after heavy rain.

Thick clutch of a net

(continued)

when the basketball sinks.

Good is go,

red is stop,

fast or slow?

Good . . . someone once

told me to *be good.*

And I thought *No! Fall down!*

It's okay if they frown!

But, I didn't dare act on it

'cause I wanted the *goods*

That *good* people *get.*

(Oh, regret!)

Good morning,

Good day,

Good night

Moon.

> *It was a world opening up; I learned about all the things that could be represented in a poem. Up until that point, it was about fitting what a poem should be. Then, your class opened my eyes.*
>
> —Charlotte, *former student*

Students are invited and encouraged to share their own "Meditations on Good" with the circle. The process of sharing and voicing opinions and ideas is a great mindful exercise. It's a beginning, also, of contemplating multifaceted perceptions about a relatively simple-sounding concept.

Note that, as students are sharing, we'll see that "good" can be interpreted in different ways: Is it behaving correctly? Something that makes us feel good? And/ or something that benefits others? The community? The planet? There are many considerations.

Back to the "sustainability" topic at hand, people have also called it a "human decision challenge"—in which, using some broader decision-making, we can change our own capacity to thrive in a modern context, as we pursue actions that are "good." In Day 2's reflections, we'll explore this more deeply.

DAY 2

Part 1: Sustainability as an Embodiment

After the first day of discussing sustainability and the nature of "good" as both abstract concept and concrete detail, this second day allows us to investigate some of our actions that might possibly bring about a mindful, sustainable life.

Again, gathered in a circle, introduce students to the concepts of *"enoughism"* and the related *"minimalism."*

It's been said that we now live in an "Age of Enoughism," an age of inequality in which some have a surplus of "things" yet perhaps (not necessarily in consequence, yet as a by-product of lifestyle) a shortage of *happiness*. Could this be true? How can we focus on what truly matters and makes a difference, and in what ways does a Mindfulness AAA Mindset engage with this?

In 2016, a documentary called *Minimalism* (The Minimalists, 2016) explored the growing trend to have less and do more with what you have. You can share the trailer in Video 4.14 with students.

What have students heard about these ideas? What do they think about them? The open discussion is an exploratory talk about possibilities, and you can bring up the concept of freedom as well:

VIDEO 4.14
www.youtube.com
/watch?v=0Co1Iptd4p4

Is freedom about having more, or less, and why?

You can also track spending trends over time, using resources and data online as a way to deepen the discussion. A 2012 article in *The Atlantic*, for example, analyzes the past one hundred years of spending in America, showing that a century ago, more than half of a person's money was spent on food and clothing, whereas today, our values have changed and our wealth allows us to spend more on homes and cars. It's interesting to consider the changes in expectations and perceived happiness (Thompson, 2012).

There are no "right answers" in this discussion—just an open and provocative dialogue. The next part involves a writing exercise that expands and underscores the topic.

Part 2: What Would You Give Up?

Marie Howe's book of poems, *The Kingdom of Ordinary Time,* features a remarkable poem, "What We Would Give Up." I ask students to open journals to a blank page, putting the letters *WWYGU* (for the question, "What Would You Give Up?") in all caps at the top. I don't explain more at this point—I leave this part as a mystery, a curiosity-builder.

Then I read the following poem excerpt out loud to them, choosing a conversational, chatty, open style that the poem seems to invite. It sings and rings with a dynamic tone, and students love that it's a real representation of what we go through every day. I suggest having the full collection on hand. Here is an excerpt from the poem, kicking off the discussion.

What We Would Give Up

by Marie Howe

One morning in Orlando Florida, I asked a group of college students—What would we be willing to give up to equalize the wealth in the world? Malls, a red-haired young woman said right away. Supermarkets, the young man in a black T-shirt said—where you go to buy bread, and there's a hundred and fifty loaves on the shelf. Imported fruit, the young woman sitting next to him said—berries in winter. A car, the guy with the nose ring said. I don't have a car anyway.

Travel? Jet fuel? Well, we'd all be together, someone said. TV, said the guy without a car, I don't watch TV anyway. What about coffee, I said, looking down at my double tall half-caf soy latte. Ok, everyone said, but I wondered about that one. Ten pairs of shoes? Yes. Movies? Maybe.

Immediately after reading the poem to students, ask, "What Would You Give Up (abbreviated *WWYGU*) to equalize the wealth in the world, as Marie Howe says in her poem?" If students point out that Howe uses the pronoun *we,* I let them know that now, I'm turning the question to each of us, individually, and eventually those reading their poetry responses might, in turn, feel as if they are being asked the same provocative question. The *you* pronoun is personal, inviting, and collective.

Give students five minutes to create a response in any style—poetic, prose poem, pure prose, conversational, formal, or other. The response should be a reflection about what they think they can do without. The hidden-yet-important understanding is that these things we could give up all come with varying levels of convenience or inconvenience, due to our own feelings of need and attachment. Students will come up with all sorts of answers. Encourage them to let it flow!

Then, after five minutes of steady-stream writing, let the sharing begin. As you encourage students to share, you could also introduce that idea of snapping discussed earlier in Exercise 4, "Levity Moments," in which fellow students snap their fingers if they have a response in common with the person who shares. For example, if someone shares that they could give up commuting to school by car, and I've responded the same way, I would quickly snap once or twice to show my connection and solidarity.

All sorts of surprising results emerge with this exercise. You might also point out to students that it can often trigger our impulse to judge, and when we step away from that reaction, listening openly, we're also being more mindful and responsive to others.

After sharing out loud, students can also document responses online in blog posts, getting creative with the look and feel of them.

In the final fifteen minutes of this exercise, as a discussion in a circle (which can also include journaling), address the following reflection questions:

Reflection Questions

> What does "sustainability" mean for you, at the end of this exercise?

> Was there anything that surprised you that we discussed or did as exercises?

> How did it feel to hear others' ideas about "good" and *WWYGU* ("What Would You Give Up")?

> In what ways can we relate sustainability to the Three A's: Aware, Advancing, Authentic?

> Considering big-picture global goals for a sustainable future, are there any small steps we can take right now?

> What topics do you feel personally drawn to, or curious about investigating further, after this exercise?

Extensions

As an extension exercise, you can observe the Dalai Lama's "A Force for Good" campaign—as well as other sustainable movements—with students, evaluating how they positively impact the planet.

You can also use online sharing platforms to look at social impact through storytelling and shared curriculum campaigns. I share links to these global platforms online at **caitlinkrause.com,** as they serve to connect students to other global classrooms, allowing them to investigate ways to become more actively involved in sustainability initiatives.

There are many resources and tools for extensions and developments in this arena, which can all be customized to your content area. Fundamentally, the Mindfulness AAA Mindset is at the base.

The Takeaway

As noted, Mindfulness AAA Mindsets are foundational, and this exercise gives students an initial chance to familiarize themselves with the sustainability concepts while connecting at a personal level. Because the poetry is engaging and relatable, it brings a larger global concept up close, which then allows you to build lessons that will stretch even further in impact, because they build from an emotional core connection. Students refer back to these exercises as ones that allowed them to visualize themselves as active agents for change while also engaging in some deep philosophical wonderings about the nature of concepts like *good* and *need* versus *want*. Talk about important takeaways!

Mirror, Mirror: Empathetic Partner Exercises That Help to Hone Focus, Leadership, and Listening Skills in the Age of AI

EXERCISE
15

In our ordinary experiences with other people, we know that approaching each other in a machinelike way gets us into trouble.

—Peter Senge (as quoted by Alan M. Webber, 1999)

While we are living in an age of AI, robots, and machines, we are undoubtedly human, and what sets us apart just might be our greatest leadership asset. One key trait of a mindful leader is the ability to listen to others and work as part of a collective team, sensing others' feelings and understanding multiple viewpoints and perspectives. In a way, anyone can be a leader and active collaborator by practicing mindful leadership skills.

In learning environments, we want to foster ways for students to be more aware of themselves and in tune with others. Psychologist and writer Daniel Goleman, known for his work with leadership and emotional intelligence, cites a "triple-threat" focus as a key leadership skill that can be developed (Goleman, 2015).

Throughout the student exercises in this book, we practice developing aspects of this triple-threat focus across three dimensions of empathic learning and leadership:

1. **Self awareness (focus on yourself):** knowledge of our own thoughts and how they affect our actions and learning

2. **Community awareness (focus on others):** attention to those around us, with the aim of understanding others' thoughts and feelings, using empathy and compassion for connection

3. **Global awareness (focus on systems):** a broader view of our context and how we interrelate with and impact the larger world, including organizations, economies, technologies, social systems, and industries

Here, in this exercise, students specifically focus on the second part, *community awareness,* in building awareness and listening skills.

This in-class exercise involves working with a partner. It is an entry point that can lead to deeper awareness and understanding—and, ultimately, powerful connection capacity!

Mindfulness Skills Taught

- ▶ **AWARE:** awareness of self, others, and the interrelated nature of what drives us
- ▶ **ADVANCING:** causes students to go beyond comfort zones, actively stretching possibilities
- ▶ **AUTHENTIC:** gives the opportunity to take a quick look at self and others, without veils or projections; also, lets students simply play with collaboration

Challenge Tips

This exercise is quick, yet it involves some level of closeness and connection with a partner. Thinking ahead of time about how to partner students in a way that streamlines the process will help the exercise run smoothly.

Creativity Insights

For the exercise, students can create diagrams, reflective art, and vlogs describing the experience. Encourage them to get creative with their feedback and connections to this. It's the ripple effect, and the more enthusiasm you show, the more they will reflect, too!

Time Requirement: One forty-five-minute exercise, with different segments

Resource Materials Needed

- ▶ **JOURNALS**
- ▶ **AMPLE SPACE** to move around
- ▶ **TIMER** (to make flow of exercise easier)

How to Teach It

Part 1: Discussing Empathy

Form a large circle with students and ask them if they know the definition of *empathy.* Tell them they will be working with a partner to practice what it means to use empathy embodied in an awareness activity.

In theory, empathy means "to feel what another feels," and it's useful for awareness and understanding. In a famous line from Harper Lee's *To Kill a Mockingbird*, Atticus Finch tells his daughter Scout "You never really understand a person until you consider things from his point of view . . . until you climb into his skin and walk around in it."

Ask students if they have ever had a situation that required them to give or receive empathy from another individual. How did it feel to be understood, or to understand another's situation? They don't have to describe it out loud; they can just be thinking about the experience.

To be empathetic is to practice mindfulness, because one has heightened awareness of a human condition outside of their own experience. Sometimes, this can feel heavy or burdensome, to feel what others feel, especially if the experience is one that involves suffering. However, using compassion, we realize that the larger aim is to help to relieve that suffering, not to ignore it or deny its existence. Empathy can be about feeling another's curiosity, joy, and happiness, too—there's a full range of feelings!

This exercise, you can tell students, is one that simply boosts the awareness capacities of being receptive to another person.

Part 2: Mirror, Mirror

This mirroring exercise might seem familiar to those who study Theater Arts. At recent Wisdom 2.0 summits (in San Francisco and Silicon Valley), a variation was used as an introductory exercise. It has a way of bringing people together and immediately engaging participants. The description I give here is my own version, which I've used across all ages of participants, from kindergartners to adults.

Begin by having students form partners. Each partnership should position themselves somewhere in the room where they have ample space to move. You can start out demonstrating this with a chosen student. Stand facing your partner and decide who will be the leader and who will be the follower. Imagine, as partners face each other, that an invisible wall separates them. This wall is the "mirror." As the leader begins to move hands and arms and makes gestures, sometimes so slowly it is barely perceptible, it's the follower's job to mirror back exactly the same motion.

The goal is to see how closely they can mirror each other, so that as you walk around the room, it's hard to tell who is the leader and who is the follower. Start with two minutes timed for one student to lead; then switch roles. Switch roles several times, so that students have multiple chances to lead and follow. As the exercise builds, see how creative they can get with their motions. See if they can complete this exercise in complete silence while holding eye contact with each other. Consider filming the exercise while walking around the classroom, if you are able to do so without being obtrusive.

After this part, have students take a break, recording for three minutes in journals how the exercise felt. Ask them to address the following: *What was challenging about it? What was easy? Was anything surprising?*

Then have students step up for the "Mirroring 2.0" exercise (taking the art of mirroring to a new level)!

Part 3: Mirroring 2.0—Breathing in Sync

Students stand facing each other, in a comfortable position. They are instructed to breathe together, in synchronous fashion, aiming to have a completely connected frequency of breath. They might be able to do this in one minute; it might take several minutes. They might even laugh while attempting this! Everything is welcomed; as one of my favorite mindfulness quotes goes: *Everything is permitted.*

You might choose to play music during this time, or simply have it quiet, so that students can feel the pace of each other's breathing, slowly, in and out. You can talk as they do this, instructing them to feel and follow their breath. After about three minutes of peacefully breathing in and out, you might notice that the buzz of this exercise changes into a calm, meditative state.

Bring students back together, into a collective class circle, to have them answer the following questions as a discussion:

Reflection Questions

> What was surprising for you about this experience?

> What will you take away with you?

> How can listening and empathy begin as something very simple?

> What can we do to encourage more listening and awareness when building leadership skills?

These are responses a group of seventh-grade students in my class gave (in written responses, through a survey) after completing the exercise together.

What was surprising for you about this experience?

- I thought it was very surprising doing the mirroring activity and learning a lot more about empathy and putting myself in someone else's shoes.
- One thing surprising was how we had to copy one another [in the] movement exercise.
- I could feel other people's emotions.
- We can exercise empathy just like we can exercise sports.
- That if you try hard you can tell what someone else is thinking.
- How you can get so connected through breathing in sync with another person.
- It was interesting to see another person breathing at the exact same time and it felt really relaxing.
- That I enjoyed learning some relaxation techniques.

What will you take away with you?

- Always be caring and try to step in their shoes.

- I will take away the meaning of empathy with me.

- Feeling what others feel.

- I will take away that anyone can be empathic if we try hard and empathy is something that we should all aim to get better at.

- I will take with me empathy. I will really try to feel what another person feels and help them if they need it.

- That you should always empathize with someone because you might not know what they're going through.

Extension

When students are in partnerships, you can also have them practice telling each other about an experience, with one acting as the "sharer" and one as the "listener." Practicing active listening, the listener can demonstrate attentiveness to what the speaker shares, mirroring back a detail about what the listener heard *after the sharer finishes*—this is not a judgment. Then students can switch roles. The key, in this exercise, is for the listener to *stay absolutely silent* for the entire duration of their time as listener, without interrupting, not even to echo agreement with an "Uh-huh" or "Yes, I understand." They show their agreement, respect, and encouragement as a leader by listening alone.

The Takeaway

Listening is a powerful tool, and it is no coincidence that it shares the same letters as the word *silent*. When I have interviewed capable leaders around the world, my general observation (this is not yet quantified by data, though it's been a noticeable trend!) is that *listening* seems to be the number one skill identified as most valuable, most needed, and most elusive. The ability to listen is what builds effective mindful leaders, contributing to better global communities. This skill takes practice, and students get a chance to play and experience firsthand the many challenges and rewards of mindful awareness skill-building.

The Four P's: Projects, Passion, Peers, and Play

en·gi·neer·ing noun

The art or science of making practical application of the knowledge of pure sciences

Mindful learning is about connection, not isolated subjects. In this active mindful STEAM-infused project, we are engineering authentic connections and real results! STEAM (science, technology, engineering, arts, and mathematics) is an education acronym that underscores the interdisciplinary nature of modern learning approaches, hinging on a mindset that embraces curiosity and tinkering. Much of this mindset owes its development to the work of Seymour Papert. Mitch Resnick, LEGO Papert Professor of Learning Research at the MIT Media Lab, calls Papert "the biggest intellectual influence on my life" (Resnick, 2012). Resnick helps to impart Papert's legacy with four guiding principles to guide learning and development as a creative thinker (and each one starts with the letter *P*!): *Projects, Passion, Peers and Play* (Resnick, 2014).

As Resnick says, the focus should be on projects rather than problems. Students will learn more if they focus on solving problems (i.e., "challenges" to positively reframe) in the form of a project, using ideas in authentic context. Papert wrote the book *Mindstorms* in 1980, changing the education landscape by upending the premise that students should be passive receivers of information (Papert, 1980). Like developmental psychologist Jean Piaget before him, he believed in constructivism, that we learn best as active agents making connections and personally reacting to and reflecting on what we investigate in the world around us. Children are not empty vessels to be filled with knowledge. They are active, curious personalities who need a certain open environment to learn. In this way, Papert changed thinking about thinking and has been at the epicenter of revolutions in understanding of child development, artificial intelligence, and education technology (Ackermann, 2001).

We can use the "Four P's" to drive learning forward. This exercise adopts a "maker mindset," using what Neil Gershenfeld (director of the Center for Bits and Atoms at MIT) terms three tenets of an active maker community: communication, computation, and fabrication (Gershenfeld, 2017).

This exercise applies a *design approach* to the project framework, encouraging students to ideate and share in community.

Mindfulness Skills Taught

▶ **AWARE:** using mindfulness skills allows students to draw from their own prior knowledge (constructivism) and make new connections, using awareness as a tool

▶ **ADVANCING:** students are designing and creating solutions in this exercise, stretching their own ways of thinking about possibilities

▶ **AUTHENTIC:** the social engineering can be the hardest part of creating learning communities; this exercise encourages students to play with peers and form authentic connections with the material

Challenge Tips

This is one of those exercises that can frustrate students who are not used to iterative learning processes and complex situations. It is not a linear process. Encourage students to adopt a "fail forward" mentality, which complements a mindful mindset. You might also want to encourage them to mindmap and draw pictures/expressive text to document their journeys, encouraging open questions and reflections along the way. To quote Papert from *Mindstorms* (Papert, 1980):

> Many children are held back in their learning because they have a model of learning in which you have either "got it" or "got it wrong." But when you program a computer you almost never get it right the first time. Learning to be a master programmer is learning to become highly skilled at isolating and correcting bugs. . . . The question to ask about the program is not whether it is right or wrong, but if it is fixable. If this way of looking at intellectual products were generalized to how the larger culture thinks about knowledge and its acquisition, we might all be less intimidated by our fears of "being wrong."

Creativity Insights

The process of this exercise can be easily repeated with different content and focus. It's the structure—and, most important, the mindset——that makes the difference.

Time Requirement: Two activities that will last full lessons, fifty minutes each

Resource Materials Needed

▶ **LARGE PAPER** (one shared poster-size per team)[2]

▶ **MARKERS**

▶ **STICKY NOTES**

▶ **ALL SORTS OF "MAKER MATERIALS"**—see "maker kit" ideas (both analog and digital) to get some ideas flowing

---

[2] If you wish to pre-draw a chart on the poster for this process, you can map out different sections for "Team Name," "User Personas," "Storyboard," etc., so that teams know where they fit on the poster board. This way, a template is set in advance!

How to Teach It

Begin by *choosing a theme topic* that fits your curriculum. I will describe the structure of this process using one challenge example topic: *water*. This relates to the United Nations Sustainable Development Goal (SDG) 6: "Ensure availability and sustainable management of water and sanitation for all." It's a prime topic also featured online in education task forces, and there are plenty of resources provided in the "Extensions" section below, plus extra links and supportive tools on the companion website at **caitlinkrause.com**.

Why this topic, as a broad example? With STEAM, there are many active, engineer-minded tracks to take, fitting the curriculum in innumerable ways. For this topic example, I was choosing one example from many possible topics, including city planning, smart fabrics, prosthetics, nutrition, and solar power/alternative energy. You can choose the customized topic that fits your classroom needs. And you can access the support of online and in-person STEAM communities, including Fab Lab hubs, with an online network at fablabs.io, to get a global community boost, stretching across oceans.

Which brings us back to the chosen example topic. Water is essential; it's at the core of sustainable development. It is a resource that everyone needs, yet there is widespread inequality of clean water access. Moreover, improvements are not always safe. In 2017, an estimated 2.1 billion people lacked access to clean drinking water at home (World Health Organization, 2017). It's identified by the UN as one of the SDGs because it's important—and it has many extensions that make it an interdisciplinary subject!

This qualifies as a prime project topic and lets students get creative about ways to approach it within STEAM framework. The key here is to look with mindful awareness at the structure of how the exercise is run so that you can adapt it to your own classroom, using that "Four P's" mindset as your foundation.

DAY 1

Part 1: Connecting the Peers (ten minutes)

Before sharing the topic, begin by forming teams of students. I recommend teams of about four to five people in each, so there is a diverse assortment of voices present. Tell them they will be *addressing a challenge with a Four P mindset*. You can briefly describe the Four P's and promote a group discussion, evaluating the benefits of each element in learning.

Note: If you're not sure of why the Four P's are connected to learning, I recommend watching Mitch Resnick's five-minute Video 4.15 (The Brainwaves Video Anthology, 2017), which sums it up nicely!

VIDEO 4.15
www.youtube.com
/watch?v=ZoczAscGYeQ

Next, as teams are grouped together, they have two timed minutes to agree about *a team name, and to each come up with their own alliterative superpower member name*. For example, I could be "Catalytic Krause" for "Team STEAM." Students can write down the team name and their alliterative nicknames on sticky notes, to attach to the common poster space. Everything they create is shared together on the poster board.

Part 2: Defining the Project (ten minutes)

Announce the following:

> ▶ **WHAT:** the STEAM topic

> ▶ **WHY:** sentence briefly identifying the reason it's critical/the reason it's part of current study

> ▶ **SECOND WHAT:** sentence clarifying the challenge invitation!

> ▶ **WHO/WHERE:** nouns that give the project a scope

Using our example:

> ▶ **WHAT:** water

> ▶ **WHY:** there is a global crisis for safe, clean, open access to water

> ▶ **SECOND WHAT:** our challenge today is to build a better device for sanitary local water transport (using hand-carrying methods)

> ▶ **WHO/WHERE:** people living in one district in Uganda (you can be more specific if you wish)

Given these conditions, students will be investigating the "how," creating possibilities that will address what they envision as possibilities to solve the challenge needs.

The team challenge is to come up with a feasible device idea that can solve the "Second What" question for the scope of "Who/Where" defined.

At the end of the two days, the teams will be presenting their ideas. Their presentation has two parts:

1. A five-minute presentation to the group

2. A storyboard that describes their solution in pictures

Your job is to *guide students through the project process, encouraging them in their focus on the topic at hand, mindful about the nature of their team interactions.*

Part 3: Understanding the Topic and the User Who Will Benefit from Your Ideas (thirty minutes)

This is the quality research phase. Teams should start by imagining what it would be like to be faced with this situation themselves. Using empathetic skills, they are actively researching the geography, climate, culture, and values that are part of the community their topic is contained within. Through investigating the full multifaceted dimensions of the topic, they will have a better understanding of a user's needs. Representing a Mindful Mentor in this stage, you can remind students about the difference between primary sources and secondary sources. See if they have an assortment of sources that give a full scope of views (keeping "The Danger of a Single Story" in mind)!

Now, the ironic key with this part of the exercise (and throughout the process) is *limits. Limited time*, to be specific. Encourage students to be mindful of this. Students are urged to practice sharp online research to home in on their area of focus and to sketch findings on the poster in a section they can label "User Personas."

They might already be familiar with the term *persona* from the story exercises. Using that same idea, they should then create a set of *three personas,* each of whom needs this solution. They should be specific about each persona's name, age, and *personality.* You can think about "primary human emotions" to address a persona sketch—I also have posts about primary human emotions and storytelling on the companion site, **caitlinkrause.com.**

You can explain to students, as they sketch these user personas, that the term *UX* in design simply stands for "user experience." A designer must imagine the person whom the project is serving. In that way, it comes to life. The Mindfulness AAA Mindset of Awareness, Advancement, and Authenticity is part of understanding a UX and the user's needs. In this way, mindfulness is intertwined in a good designer mindset.

DAY 2: PASSION AND PLAY, WITH A TAKEAWAY

On this second day, emphasis is on the action and the building. Resources and art materials are close at hand, as are the posters. Greet students and let them know the themes of the day: passion and play. Sure, they are problem-solving, yet with a "plastic" (flexible!) positive mindset.

They will already know the mindfulness values as part of class, yet it's always great to reinforce them with reference to AAA Mindset and design principles of rapid ideation.

You can display a poster with the following six principles of design. This one was created by Cindy Chang. The six ideas sum up the main mindfulness values that underscore the values of the exercise.

Source: Cindy Chang | cindychang.org.

Figure 4.12 • Effective Brainstorming Techniques

Part 1: Ten "Quick-fire" Ideas—No Censorship! (five minutes)

Each student, separately, has a timed five minutes to come up with ten separate ideas for solutions, sketching each on a sticky note. They can use one or two words, yet the majority of the sticky note should be visual. Encourage rapid ideation, without any self-critique voice. Just go for it!

Part 2: Combining Forces (ten minutes)

At the end of five minutes, have the teams gather the ideas together, looking at all of them, seeing if some can be grouped together and perhaps combined to support one another.

For ten minutes, let them talk out their proposals and encourage some combinations. Allow them to explain the way the visions would work. As students explain, if they want to sketch diagrams or even build prototypes, they can do that, too.

Much of the design process can involve simply stepping back and allowing some great ideas to happen.

Part 3: Selecting a Storyboard (five minutes)

Teams must narrow their solutions to three top choices. From the top three, they must choose the one for which they would like to create a script and a storyboard, designing the description of the solution and mapping it out in story form.

Part 4: What's the Scenario? (ten minutes)

Using writing, students should pick one persona and insert them into an imaginary scene that shows them using the sketched solution.

Part 5: Storyboard (fifteen minutes)

Using pictures only, the teams synthesize that scenario from Part 4, drawing it in a fluid set of eight to twelve story frames. They might put captions for the frames, or speech bubbles for the characters—*if* words are necessary. The focus is to emphasize the nature of the solution through the story frame.

Part 6: Presentation (five minutes)

Teams narrate the storyboard to the class. If there is time, they might take a picture and project it onto a whiteboard, so that the class can view it clearly. They can walk through what their visualization entails, using presentation skills, and also inviting audience engagement.

After the excitement of these dynamic design processes, gather students together for reflection, sharing responses to the following questions which they might take time to individually reflect about in journals first.

Reflection Questions

▶ What was the most challenging part of this process?

▶ How can we better understand certain user needs through this design thinking and empathy?

▶ What was the most rewarding part of the process for you?

▶ What do you think are the conditions for "great ideas" to happen?

▶ How might having a mindful mindset complement design?

Extensions

Consider posting the storyboards on a blog and also having students write posts about the design process and the Four P's that are part of the "mindful maker mindset."

To have an even broader authentic connection, you can contact other schools, partnerships, your own online community, organizations, and places that are potentially looking for crowd-sourced ideas for solutions. Looking deeply into your topic, and using the vast online network, is a great way to start. This way, student-driven solutions have a larger audience, and community engagement is reinforced. And, who knows? One of their solutions just might be the one that helps build a better world!

You might decide that this initial exercise is so wonderful (and it is!), you want to incorporate more of this process and build an active "mindful maker mindset" into your curriculum.

The Takeaway

In this STEAM-powered playground of Four P's, students get exposure and practice with principles of design and teamwork to come up with a solution together.

They learn about the process of good design, how to start with a general idea and challenge and then build from there. They learn to experiment with new ideas, collaborating with others; they discover how to find and fix mistakes, practice grit and persistence, and take pride in their own sense of innovative play.

They develop a maker mindset, and they hone their skills across STEAM fields, practicing putting science knowledge into action, which is the trait of an engineer. While applying scientific concepts specific to the chosen topic, they also use engineering skills of understanding processes, techniques, structures, and practical applications. And they engage in all of this while they are using a lens of mindfulness, inspiring confidence and curiosity as creative thinkers, designers, experimenters, and explorers.

PART III

CHAPTER 5

The Future of Mindfulness

We've traveled on quite a journey in this book, from exploring approaches to the philosophy of mindfulness, linking the mindset to learning goals and curriculum standards, and applying mindfulness to exercises for ourselves and our students, in and out of the classroom. Our approaches have led us to innovate ways to act as our own experience designers, creating practices that fit our intentions, styles, routines, personalities, and preferences. We've focused on awareness, stretched and advanced in our engagement, and made our Mindfulness AAA Mindsets real and authentic to us. We have brought the *Mindful by Design* methods to life through our activities and contemplations related to this book, and the dialogue continues to grow. We are now connected in a meaningful community.

Along the way, we have discovered a great deal about ourselves and the world around us. We learned about what is inside, with open hearts and minds, and with enough inspiration to drive us to action. We can take mindfulness exercises that focus on anchoring breath, or connect in a body scan, or dive into an observation that heightens awareness of our emotions and thoughts. We can bring mindfulness practices on a walk and into conversation with colleagues and collaborators, and we can also simply observe our own mind-state and its attachments, reminding ourselves that we don't have to dwell, ruminate, or catastrophize about anything that threatens to add toxic stress to our lives. We can choose to observe our thoughts and emotions, and let go of what is not necessary, as we prioritize thriving. This is a mindful superpower, in many senses.

A great deal of mindfulness practice is about waking up to the luminous quality of the present moment—the time that is always an opportunity to dwell in appreciation and awareness. The word *mind* has a relationship to the word *heart* in its Buddhist origins. Because of this, I think of mindfulness as "mind-heart-full-ness," which has nothing to do with cluttering or overwhelm. It is a dwelling in abundance of the purely connected mind-heart, that essence that allows us to abide deeply in the now. There is joy and happiness here, as we realize that we are gifts with immeasurable worth. Life itself is a treasure—and it has called us to a vocation that involves giving many gifts to students, too, in the learning experiences we make possible.

Part of what I most enjoy about mindfulness is the chance to form connections, inside and out. We connect deeply with ourselves and the interior landscape, and we reach out and connect with the surrounding world and each other in community. We begin to see how mindfulness can affect our daily life—the life that is neither grand nor unimportant. It's the daily life we lead, including the travels, the interactions, the despairs, the joys. It is a life that is. As Mary Oliver eloquently states in her marvelous poem "Wild Geese" (Oliver, 1996), it's about belonging, and about curiosity: "the world offers itself to your imagination . . . over and over announcing your place / in the family of things."

We are all united in that family of things, all together, and mindfulness reminds us of that connection. In current times, as over 40 percent of adults report suffering from loneliness (and research suggests the true number might be much higher), mindfulness can alleviate that sense of alienation and disconnect and also serve to prevent the rise of toxic stress and burnout (Murthy, 2017). We've seen and felt the innumerable advantages of mindfulness, and the beauty is that it's adaptive, not prescriptive. It's up to us and our creativity to decide how we want to apply mindfulness to our daily lives and learning worlds. This is what it means to embody *Mindful by Design*. This book gives many ideas and tools for how to bring that about.

Our *Mindful by Design* learning worlds become places of relational understanding and connection, and this is critically important. In an ongoing Harvard study that spans eighty years, researchers have investigated health, happiness, and longevity. Over seven hundred men have participated in the study, which began when they were teenagers in 1938 (Harvard Health, 2017). Findings show that, over the course of a lifespan, socioeconomic status didn't make a significant impact on health and well-being—the major difference in quality of life appears to be the quality of connections. Dr. Robert Waldinger, a psychologist at Harvard-affiliated Massachusetts General Hospital, says, "People who are more socially connected to friends, family and community are happier, healthier, and live longer than people who are less well-connected." Dr. Waldinger's TED Talk (Waldinger, 2015) highlights the study, and he shares his thoughts about what makes a good life. You can view his TED Talk by scanning the QR code for Video 5.1.

VIDEO 5.1
www.ted.com/talks/robert_
waldinger_what_makes_a_
good_life_lessons_from_the_
longest_study_on_happiness

While correlation does not necessarily define causation, it's undeniable that positive relationships bring about greater happiness, and this adds to our gratitude measures, too! I would suggest that, along with this point about external connections of relationships, a person's internal connection—their relationship with the self, including cultivating mindfulness and self-compassion—matters just as much. As the saying goes, befriending others begins with befriending ourselves. The mind and the interior landscape offer up many ways to explore, to appreciate, to question, and to discover the wondrous nature of our own state of being. And then we expand outwards in deep, soulful connection.

At an education conference that focused on innovation and creativity, I led a session for educators looking to connect and apply current brain research to education design. Many shared that they were suffering from feelings of isolation while looking to make positive changes and adopt powerful leadership models to fuel school reform and help to build the best learning environments that meet future needs as technology becomes more robust. They were curious and eager to contribute to a larger, collective initiative. In a sharing exercise, we worked with the ideas of "passion, problem, and purpose" to ground our open conversation. It's these types of healthy, ambitious exchanges that seem to be most needed in learning environments.

We talked about passion and what "brings us back to ourselves" when we're feeling disconnected—what passions fuel our fires spiritually, creatively, essentially? We discussed problems that seem to be obstacles or blocks right now, and we shared our sense of greater purpose, the "why" intentions underpinning our values and choices. Research also shows that those who have a purpose guiding their life and vocation are more satisfied, with greater well-being (Neighmond, 2014).

After a brief ninety minutes together, group participants shared the following reflections:

- "Though I sat with a table of relative strangers, I immediately found reason to continue the conversation, to learn more about those around me."
- "I was inspired by what others have accomplished regarding education, exchanging ideas and learning from those different ideas."
- "I felt like I was able to make real change in my school, and there were all of these great supportive people there with helpful ideas and words."

We are not alone. We are designed to be connected, and the group exercise in community-building was one more example of what was helpful and necessary. Mindfulness was embedded in the design, with the AAA of Awareness, Advancement, and Authenticity as foundational elements. Listening was present: listening to each other, listening in community, listening to our students, and listening to the world.

When our group reflected about "What the world seems to need right now," responses included the following arenas:

- Deep listening, motivational interviewing
- Significance, valuing ourselves
- Resources and environmental awareness
- Restoration of civility
- Thoughtful decision-making
- Communication, respect
- Empathy and understanding

What does your world seem to need right now? How can mindfulness help us to realize it, meeting some of those needs? We can certainly add to this list, and this journey has invited us to operate with resolve, peace, happiness, and appreciation, even in the midst of what might seem daunting.

The context and conditions of our world add an extra sense of urgency to our missions. Teen depression is on the rise and has been correlated with time spent on social media.

According to the Pew Research Center, by 2015, 73 percent of teens had access to a smartphone, up from 50 percent in 2012 (Pew Research Center, 2015). Not only did smartphone use and depression both increase, but time spent online was linked to mental health issues across two different data sets.

There are many studies linking screen time to deteriorating mental health, and feeling socially isolated is cited as a prime risk factor (Twenge, 2017). Our screens and smartphones vie for our attention, dividing us from those who physically surround us. And we can become so entrenched in these patterns and behaviors involving technology that we condone and even rationalize them, thinking they are a form of deep connection. Yet technology is not a vice—it's *how* we use it that matters. I feel mindfulness is directly linked to these issues of wholeness, as it's a critical time to address our ability to be present, both with ourselves and with other humans. With the rise in capabilities in robotics and artificial intelligence, it's not a question of "if" or "when" our lives will be augmented by technology and artificial, simulated realities, it's a question of what impact they will have on our quality of consciousness and connection. As someone who works with VR and AR (virtual reality and augmented reality), I'm often questioning our ability to use these brave new mediums to express ourselves and connect with others in a way that is authentic and sustaining. I think it's possible, as long as we operate with care, setting priorities and parameters in place that are based on the same principles that guide our mindfulness practice. Listen to ourselves and our human nature, and use technology to amplify humanity, not to replace what is human.

Humanity reminds us that the quest for perfection is elusive, no one can claim to be an expert on everything, and impermanence and change are certainties. Students are wonderful mindfulness teachers, as they have a great ability, in the midst of these exciting times, to dwell in the present moment, appreciating it for what it is. As we listen to students, we learn so much.

In current models of redesigning schools, learning environments are being created that have mindfulness mindsets embedded in their values. Many have their own innovation and design centers, as well as curriculum models that encompass time spent outdoors in nature. Beyond buzzwords, whether these schools have cutting-edge pioneering practices that embrace maker stations, fab labs, impact hubs, coding dojos, or poetry slams, they all seem to have creativity, exploration, social-emotional learning models, critical consciousness (meaning the quest for truth), and qualities of openness built into their approaches. Students and teachers thrive in these capacities, as it's an organic model of inquiry and discovery. Mindfulness can be found in each of these future-forward learning models.

Bringing us back in touch with our humanity, allowing us to better connect with ourselves and with each other, mindfulness is organic and at the heart of effective human social systems. When I met with education creativity expert Sir Ken Robinson in early 2017 for a conversation about leadership, Sir Ken said,

> Organizations, which include creative schools, are not like mechanisms, they're like organisms. They're living, breathing communities of people. They thrive in certain conditions, and successful organisms in the actual world are successful because they adapt and are synergistic with their environment . . . and it's exactly the same with human organizations. The only way they survive is by adapting.

Adaptive intelligence is the survival sine qua non, and mindfulness goes hand-in-hand with enhancing this ability. The practices of mindfulness that we make manifest in learning worlds are adaptive, building our capacity for wholeness—that is what *Mindful by Design* means. It's an inside-out design journey, a way to be, starting within and expanding out in connection. It's about adaptation, intention, and non-judgment, and it's ever evolving. This way of being shifts to meet our conditions and our needs. Like stones cast in a lake, our mindfulness practices have effects beyond the acts themselves. There will be many ripples that are lasting and meaningful, affecting students, colleagues, and others who are part of our daily interactions. Mindfulness influences our experiences—and our perceptions of these experiences—in myriad ways, helping us to lead lives that are open and in tune with our passions, our callings, our very beings. We salute each other, connected and conscious, as the journey continues and worlds of possibilities open.

References

Ackermann, E. (2001). Piaget's constructivism, Papert's constructionism: What's the difference? *Constructivism: Uses and perspectives in education.* Retrieved from http://learning.media.mit.edu/content/publications/EA.Piaget%20_%20Papert.pdf

Adichie, C. N. (2009, July). *The danger of a single story.* [Video file]. Retrieved from https://www.ted.com/talks/chimamanda_adichie_the_danger_of_a_single_story

Amélie. (2001). [DVD] France: Jean-Pierre Jeunet.

AmericanRhetoric.com. (2016, March 17). *Elie Wiesel: The perils of indifference.* [Video file]. Retrieved from https://www.youtube.com/watch?v=JpXmRiGst4k

Aschwanden, C. (2011). The magic of mantras. *Runner's World.* Retrieved from http://www.runnersworld.com/race-training/the-magic-of-running-mantras

Awaken.com. (2012). *Notable living contemporary teachers: Desmond Tutu.* Retrieved from http://www.awaken.com/2012/12/desmond-tutu/

Basecamp. (2018). *Basecamp3 app.* Retrieved from https://basecamp.com/

Biomimicry Institute. (2018). What is biomimicry? *Biomimicry.org.* Retrieved from https://biomimicry.org/what-is-biomimicry/

Brainwaves Video Anthology. (2017, March 21). *Mitchel Resnick—on Seymour Papert.* [Video file]. Retrieved from https://www.youtube.com/watch?v=ZoczAscGYeQ

Brown, B. (2010, June). *Brené Brown: The power of vulnerability.* [Video file]. Retrieved from https://www.ted.com/talks/brene_brown_on_vulnerability

Brown, B. (2015). *Daring greatly: How the courage to be vulnerable transforms the way we live, love, parent, and lead.* New York, NY: Penguin Random House.

Brown, V. (2015). *Pilgrimmage of El Camino de Santiago: Mindfulness in motion.* Thousand Oaks, CA: CorwinConnect. Retrieved from http://corwin-connect.com/2015/11/pilgrimage-el-camino-de-santiago-mindfulness-in-motion/

Buechner, F. (1973). *Wishful thinking: A theological ABC.* New York, NY: Harper & Row.

Center for Courage & Renewal. (2018). *The circle of trust approach.* Retrieved from http://www.couragerenewal.org/approach/

Chang, L. (2006). Wisdom for the soul: Five millennia of prescriptions for spiritual healing. Washington, DC: Gnosophia Publishers.

Chappuis, S., & Chappuis, J. (2008). The best value in formative assessment. *Educational Leadership, 65*(4). Retrieved from http://www.ascd.org/publications/educational-leadership/dec07/vol65/num04/The-Best-Value-in-Formative-Assessment.aspx

Cheuk, T. (2013). Relationships and convergences among the mathematics, science, and ELA practices. Refined version of diagram created by the Understanding Language Initiative for ELP Standards. Palo Alto, CA: Stanford University.

Cleveland Clinic. (2013, February 27). *Empathy: The human connection to patient care.* [Video file]. Retrieved from https://www.youtube.com/watch?v=cDDWvj_q-o8

Common Core State Standards Initiatives. (2018a). English Language Arts Standards. Introduction. Students who are college and career ready in reading, writing, speaking, listening, & language. Retrieved from http://www.corestandards.org/ELA-Literacy/introduction/students-who-are-college-and-career-ready-in-reading-writing-speaking-listening-language/

Common Core State Standards Initiatives. (2018b). *Myths vs. facts: Myths about implementation.* Retrieved from http://www.corestandards.org/about-the-standards/myths-vs-facts/

ConnectSafely.org. (2015). *ConnectSafely.* Retrieved from http://www.connectsafely.org/

Creech, S. (1994). *Walk two moons.* New York, NY: HarperCollins.

De Tocqueville, A. (2018). Quote: "Gratitude is a habit of the heart." A Network for Greater Living. Retrieved from https://gratefulness.org/resource/what-is-gratitude-angeles-arrien/

Deruy, E. (2016, May 20). Does mindfulness actually work in schools? *The Atlantic.* Retrieved from https://www.theatlantic.com/education/archive/2016/05/testing-mindfulness-in-the-early-years/483749/

Dweck, C. (2006). *Mindset: The new psychology of success.* New York, NY: Penguin Random House.

Educational Video Group. (2009, 22 October). *First Lady Eleanor Roosevelt addresses the United Nations and Carnegie Hall.* [Video file]. Retrieved from https://www.youtube.com/watch?v=_6YNIXPGXKo

Emmons, R. A. (2010.) Why gratitude is good. *Greater Good Magazine: Science-Based Insights for a Meaningful Life.* Retrieved from https://greatergood.berkeley.edu/article/item/why_gratitude_is_good

FabLabConnect. (2018). *Seymour Papert quotes.* Retrieved from http://www.fablabconnect.com/seymour-papert-quotes/

Fecheyr-Lippens, D. (2014, March 28). List of links about biomimicry. *GermiNature.* Retrieved from https://germinature.wordpress.com/2014/03/28/list-of-links-about-biomimicry/

Frost, R. (1920). Fire and ice. *The Poetry Foundation.* Retrieved from https://www.poetryfoundation.org/poems/44263/fire-and-ice

Gaiman, N. (2013). *Make good art.* New York, NY: William Morrow.

Gershenfeld, N. (2017). Professor Neil Gershenfeld: The third digital revolution: Fabrication. *National Aeronautics and Space Administration.* Retrieved from https://www.nasa.gov/ames/ocs/seminars/neil-gershenfeld

Gilbert, L. (2014). Dear ones—Yesterday, I was talking with two of my dearest old friends about vulnerability and love. *ElizabethGilbert.* Retrieved from https://www.elizabethgilbert.com/dear-ones-yesterday-i-was-talking-with-two-of-my-dearest-old-friends-about-v/

Glacier Lake School. (2018). *Glacier Lake School: Life is not standardized, so why should schools be?* Retrieved from http://www.glacierlakeschool.com

Goleman, D. (2015, October 4). Emotional intelligence. *DanielGoleman.* Retrieved from http://www.danielgoleman.info/daniel-goleman-how-self-awareness-impacts-your-work/

Gottfried, J. (2005). History repeating? Avoiding a return to the pre-antibiotic age. LEDA at Harvard Law School. Retrieved from https://dash.harvard.edu/bitstream/handle/1/8889467/Gottfried05.html?sequence=2

Goyal, M., Singh, S., & Sibinga, E. M. S. (2014, March). *Meditation programs for psychological stress and well-being:*

A systematic review and meta-analysis. Retrieved from http://jamanetwork.com/journals/jamainternalmedicine/fullarticle/1809754

Great Museums. (2014, May 26). Great museums: Elevated thinking: The high line in New York City. [Video file]. Retrieved from https://www.youtube.com/watch? v=76mblYY__PE

Grossman, P. (2014, December 19). Mindfulness: Awareness informed by an embodied ethic. Springer Link. Retrieved from https://link.springer.com/article/10.1007/s12671-014-0372-5

Groupsort.com. (2008). Groupsort.com: The site that sorts people into balanced groups! Retrieved from http://www.groupsort.com/

Hamilton. (2015). Retrieved from https://hamiltonmusical.com/new-york/

Hare, R. L. (2016). The space book—with co-author Rebecca Hare. EdTechTeam Press. Retrieved from https://www.youtube.com/watch?v=RzonblEuHBl

Harris, D. (2014). 10% happier: How I tamed the voice in my head, reduced stress without losing my edge, and found self-help that actually works—a true story. New York, NY: HarperCollins.

Harvard Health. (2017, June). Can relationships boost longevity and well-being? Harvard Health Publishing: Harvard Medical School. Retrieved from https://www.health.harvard.edu/mental-health/can-relationships-boost-longevity-and-well-being

Haubursin, C. (2017, November 9). The manmade world is horribly designed. But copying nature helps. Vox.com. Retrieved from https://www.vox.com/videos/2017/11/9/16628106/biomimicry-design-nature

Haupt, A. (December 8, 2016). Mindfulness in schools: When meditation replaces detention. US News & World Report. Retrieved from https://health.usnews.com/wellness/mind/articles/2016-12-08/mindfulness-in-schools-when-meditation-replaces-detention#close-modal

High, P. (2018, March 26). The father of the Internet, Vint Cerf, continues to influence its growth. Forbes.com. Retrieved from https://www.forbes.com/sites/peterhigh/2018/03/26/the-father-of-the-internet-vint-cerf-continues-to-influence-its-growth/#7af5b08d49e5

Hutcherson, C. A., Seppala, E. M., & Gross. J. J. (2015, March). The neural correlates of social connection. Retrieved from https://www.ncbi.nlm.nih.gov/pubmed/24984693

InnovationTools.com. (2005). Convergence 2005 report: Biomimicry offers amazing opportunities for innovation. InnovationManagement.se. Retrieved from http://www.innovationmanagement.se/imtool-articles/convergence-2005-report-biomimicry-offers-amazing-opportunities-for-innovation/

International Baccalaureate Organization. (2018). The IB Learner Profile: A singular capacity for invigorating campus life. Retrieved from http://www.ibo.org/globalassets/publications/recognition/learnerprofile-en.pdf

ISTE.org. (2018). ISTE standards for students: Knowledge constructor. Retrieved from https://www.iste.org/standards/for-students

Jacobs, H. H., & Alcock, M. H. (2017). Bold moves for schools: How we create remarkable learning environments. Alexandria, VA: ASCD.

Kabat-Zinn, J. (2005). Coming to our senses: Healing ourselves and the world through mindfulness. New York, NY: Hyperion Publishers.

Kagan, S., & Kagan, M. (2009). Kagan Cooperative Learning. San Clemente, CA: Kagan Publishing.

KhanAcademy. (2018). Khan Academy. Retrieved from https://www.khanacademy.org/

Kralik, J. (2011). A simple act of gratitude: How learning to say thank you changed my life. New York, NY: Hyperion.

Kuropatwa, D. (2015, February 24). A difference: You, your kids, and your phones. Retrieved from https://adifference.blogspot.com/2015/02/you-your-kids-and-your-phones.html

Laloux, F. (2014). Reinventing organizations. Brussels, Belgium: Nelson Parker.

LifeVestInside. (2011, August 29). Life vest inside—kindness boomerang—"one day." [Video file]. Retrieved from https://www.youtube.com/watch? v=nwAYpLVyeFU

Lutz, A., Dunne, J., & Davidson, R. J. (2007). Meditation and the neuroscience of consciousness. In P. D. Zelazo, M. Moscovitch, & E. Thompson (Eds.), Cambridge handbook of consciousness. Cambridge, England: Cambridge University Press, 19–497.

Markova, D., & McArthur, A. (2015). Collaborative intelligence: Thinking with people who think differently. New York, NY: Penguin Random House.

Mead, M. (1935/2001). Sex and temperament: In three primitive societies. New York, NY: HarperCollins.

MediaLit.Org. (2018). Center for Media Literacy. Retrieved from http://www.medialit.org/

Metropole. (2013, August 12). The human scale—official trailer. [Video file]. Retrieved from https://www.youtube.com/watch?v=BxywJRJVzJs

Milne, A. A. (1926). Winnie-the-Pooh. London, England: E. P. Dutton & Co.

MindfulSchools.org. (2018). Evidence of the benefits of mindfulness in education. Retrieved from https://www.mindfulschools.org/about-mindfulness/research/#reference-15

The Minimalists. (2016, January 29). Minimalism: A documentary about the important things (official trailer). [Video file]. Retrieved from https://www.youtube.com/watch?v=0Co1lptd4p4

Mortensen, E. (2015, 19 August). Small blog on networked learning: Web literacies—a part of digital literacies. Retrieved from https://elnamortensen1.wordpress.com/2015/08/19/web-literacies-a-part-of-digital-literacies/

Murthy, V. (2017, September). Work and the loneliness epidemic. The Harvard Business Review. Retrieved from https://hbr.org/cover-story/2017/09/work-and-the-loneliness-epidemic

Neighmond, P. (2014, July 28). People who feel they have a purpose in life live longer. NPR: Morning Edition. Retrieved from https://www.npr.org/sections/health-shots/2014/07/28/334447274/people-who-feel-they-have-a-purpose-in-life-live-longer

Nhat Hanh, T. (2005). Call me by my true names—the collected poems of Thich Nhat Hanh. Berkeley, CA: Parallax Press.

NoTosh. (2018). NoTosh: Think differently and change the way you choose to do work. Retrieved from https://notosh.com/

November, A. C. (2008). Web literacy for educators. Thousand Oaks, CA: Corwin.

Oliver, M. (1996). Dream work. New York, NY: The Atlantic Monthly Press.

Open Circle. (2018). Open circle: Getting to the heart of learning. Gratitude Curriculum Component, Wellesley Centers for Women, Wellesley College. Retrieved from https://www.open-circle.org/

Out of Eden Learn. (2018). Free online learning program for youth around the world: Slowing down, sharing stories, making connections. Retrieved from http://learn.outofedenwalk.com/ultralized

Palmer, P. (2009) A hidden wholeness: The journey toward an undivided life. Chichester, England: John Wiley & Sons.

Palmer, P. J. (1997). The courage to teach: Exploring the inner landscape of a teacher's life. San Francisco, CA: Jossey-Bass.

Papert, S. (1980). Mindstorms: Children, computers, and powerful ideas. New York, NY: Basic Books.

PassageWorks. (2014). Publications by Rachael Kessler. Retrieved from

http://passageworks.org/about/remembering-our-founder/publications-by-rachael-kessler/ https://www.ted.com/talks/chimamanda_adichie_the_danger_of_a_single_story

Penguin Kids. (2014, April 4). *Oliver Jeffers, picture book maker.* [Video file]. Retrieved from https://www.youtube.com/watch?v=w-8ydwV45no

Pew Research Center. (2015, April 8). Teens, social media & technology overview 2015. *Pew Research Center: Internet and Technology.* Retrieved from http://www.pewinternet.org/2015/04/09/teens-social-media-technology-2015/pi_2015-04-09_teensandtech_06/

Piver, S. (2011). *Mindfulness doesn't mean peacefulness. Susan Piver.* Retrieved from https://susanpiver.com/darn/

Project Zero. (2016). *Project Zero: Harvard Graduate School of Education.* Retrieved from http://www.pz.harvard.edu/

Proust, M. (1923). *In search of lost time: The prisoner* (Vol. 5). Paris, France: La Nouvelle Revue française (NRF).

Puddicombe, A. (2012, November). *Andy Puddicombe: All it takes is 10 mindful minutes.* [Video file]. Retrieved from https://www.ted.com/talks/andy_puddicombe_all_it_takes_is_10_mindful_minutes

Resnick, M. (2012, July–August). Reviving Papert's dream. *Educational Technology,* 42–46.

Resnick, M. (2014). *Give P's a chance: Projects, Peers, Passion, Play.* Retrieved from https://web.media.mit.edu/~mres/papers/constructionism-2014.pdf

Rheingold, H. (2000). *The virtual community: Homesteading on the electronic frontier.* Boston, MA: MIT Press.

Ricard, M. (2018). *What changed in my mind after decades of meditation.* Retrieved from https://www.youtube.com/watch?time_continue=8&v=eVW9BFvX6PA

Rief, L. (2015). Read write teach: Choice and challenge in the reading-writing workshop. Portsmouth, NH: Heinemann.

Robinson, K. (2018). Personal communication.

Rogers, C. (2018) *Chris Roger's homepage.* Retrieved from http://emerald.tufts.edu/~crogers/

Roosevelt, E. (1958). *In our hands.* Speech delivered on the tenth anniversary of the Universal Declaration of Human Rights.

Ruesch, J. (2018). Bringing wonder into mathematics. *Edutopia.* Retrieved from https://www.edutopia.org/article/bringing-wonder-mathematics

Scharmer, C. O. (2009). *Theory U.* Oakland, CA: Berrett-Koehler Publishers.

Scharmer, C. O., & Kaufer, K. (2013). *Leading from the emerging future: From ego-system to eco-system economies.* San Francisco, CA: Berrett-Koehler Publishers.

Shapiro, S. (2001). *What is the "Harkness Method"?* Retrieved from https://katherinecadwell.com/what-is-the-harkness-method/

Sinek, S. (2009). *How great leaders inspire action.* TEDxPuget Sound. Retrieved from https://www.ted.com/talks/simon_sinek_how_great_leaders_inspire_action

Stahl, B., & Goldstein, E. (2010). *A mindfulness-based stress reduction workbook.* Oakland, CA: New Harbinger Publications.

Stanton, B. (2015). *Humans of New York.* Retrieved from http://www.humansofnewyork.com

Swenson, M. (February 16, 1963). Southbound on the Freeway. *The New Yorker.* Retrieved from https://www.newyorker.com/magazine/1963/02/16/southbound-on-the-freeway

Team Shake. (2016). *Team Shake.* Retrieved from https://www.rhine-o.com/iphone-apps/team-shake/

Thompson, C. (2015). *INBOUND Bold Talks: Clive Thompson, "How the way you write changes the way you think."* Retrieved from https://www.youtube.com/watch?v=89vzfTFu1Vw

Thompson, D. (2012, April 5). How America spends money: 100 years in the making of the family budget. *The Atlantic.*

Retrieved from https://www.theatlantic.com/business/archive/2012/04/how-america-spends-money-100-years-in-the-life-of-the-family-budget/255475/

Townsend, A. (2011). Myopic Keats. *The Kenyon Review, 34*(2), 167–172. Retrieved from www.kenyonreview.org/journal/fall-2011/selections/ann-townsend/

Turkle, Sherry. (2012, February). *Sherry Turkle: Connected, but alone?* [Video file]. Retrieved from https://www.ted.com/talks/sherry_turkle_alone_together

Twenge, J. (2017, November 14). With teen mental health deteriorating over five years, there's a likely culprit. *The Conversation.* Retrieved from https://theconversation.com/with-teen-mental-health-deteriorating-over-five-years-theres-a-likely-culprit-86996

Ultralized. Human Rights Video Education. *The story of human rights.* (2009, September 26). [Video file]. Retrieved from https://www.youtube.com/watch?v=oh3BbLk5UIQ

United Nations (2014, September 22). *Emma Watson at the HeForShe Campaign 2014—official UN video.* [Video file]. Retrieved from https://www.youtube.com/watch?v=gkjW9PZBRfk

United Nations. (2018). Sustainable Development Goals: 17 goals to transform our world. Retrieved from https://www.un.org/sustainabledevelopment/sustainable-development-goals/

VáclavHavelLibraryFoundation.org. (1990). *Disturbing the peace.* Retrieved from http://www.vhlf.org/havel-quotes/disturbing-the-peace/

Waldinger, R. (2015, November). What makes a good life? Lessons from the longest study on happiness. [Video file]. Retrieved from https://www.ted.com/talks/robert_waldinger_what_makes_a_good_life_lessons_from_the_longest_study_on_happiness

Webber, A. M. (1999, April 30). Learning for a change. *Fast Company.* Retrieved from https://www.fastcompany.com/36819/learning-change

Weinberger, A. (2016). *The global mobility workbook.* Zürich, Switzerland: Global People Transitions GmbH.

Weinberger, D. (2011). Too big to know: Rethinking knowledge now that the facts aren't the facts, experts are everywhere, and the smartest person in the room is the room. New York, NY: Basic Books.

Weiss, L. (2018.) How we work: Live your purpose, reclaim your sanity, and embrace the daily grind. New York, NY: HarperCollins.

Wheatley, M. (2001). Listening as healing. *Shambhala Sun.* Retrieved from http://www.margaretwheatley.com/articles/listeninghealing.html

Whitman, W. (1892). Song of myself. *Leaves of grass.* Philadelphia, PA: David McKay, Rees Welsh & Company.

Wiesel, E. (1999). Excerpts from speech delivered to President Bill Clinton April 12, 1999. Washington, D.C.

Wiggins, G., & McTighe, J. (2005). *Understanding by design.* Alexandria, VA: Association for Supervision and Curriculum Development.

Williams, M., & Penham, D. (2011). *Mindfulness: A practical guide to finding peace in a frantic world.* London, England: Piatkus Books.

Wouters, D. D. (2011, December 9). *What a wonderful world with David Attenborough—BBC One.* [Video file.] Retrieved from https://www.youtube.com/watch?v=auSo1MyWf8g

Yoon, J. (2004). *On the shoulders of giants.* Retrieved from http://www.aerospaceweb.org/question/history/q0162b.shtml

Zalaznick, Matt. (2017, May 4). Mindfulness exercises for children: Relaxation techniques calm K12 students and staff, leading to better grades and better behavior. *District Administration Magazine.* Retrieved from https://www.districtadministration.com/article/mindfulness-makes-difference-school

Index

Confident Teachers, Inspired Learners

No matter where you are in your professional journey, Corwin aims to ease the many demands teachers face on a daily basis with accessible strategies that benefit ALL learners. Through research-based, high-quality content we offer practical guidance on a wide range of topics, including curriculum planning, learning frameworks, classroom design and management, and much more. Our books, videos, consulting, and online resources are developed by renowned educators and designed for easy implementation that will provide tangible results for you and your students.

GRAVITY GOLDBERG

In *Teach Like Yourself*, Gravity Goldberg applies ideas from fields of psychology, education, and science to name five key habits involving core beliefs, practice, relationships, professional growth, and teacher courage.

SERENA PARISER

This handy guide offers 50 proven best practices for managing today's classroom, complete with just-in-time tools and relatable teacher-to-teacher anecdotes and advice.

LISA WESTMAN

Full of step-by-step guidance, this book shows you how to build collaborative student-teacher relationships and incorporate student voice and choice in the process of planning for student-driven differentiation.

JOHN ANTONETTI AND TERRI STICE

This book will teach you to use the Powerful Task Rubric for Designing Student Work to analyze, design, and refine engaging tasks of learning.

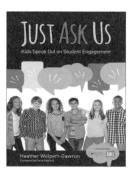

HEATHER WOLPERT-GAWRON

Based on over 1000 nationwide student surveys, these ten deep engagement strategies help you implement achievement-based cooperative learning. Includes video and a survey sample.

VICTORIA LENTFER

Whether you're new to teaching, working with at-risk students, or simply looking for new strategies, the CALM method provides an actionable framework for redirecting student behavior.

corwin.com

CORWIN

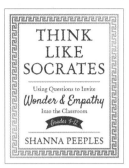

SHANNA PEEPLES

Shanna Peeples, 2015 National Teacher of the Year, shows you how teachers can create an engaging atmosphere that encourages student questions and honors their experiences.

KIMBERLY L. MITCHELL

This book provides the opportunity to do inquiry as you read about it. Learn what inquiry-based instruction looks like in practice through five key strategies.

CARLA MARSCHALL AND RACHEL FRENCH

Concept-Based Inquiry in Action provides teachers with the tools and resources necessary to facilitate the construction and transfer of conceptual understanding in any K–12 classroom.

JAYME LINTON

Designed to help K–5 teachers develop and implement a personalized plan for instruction in blended environments, this resource identifies key competencies and strategies for development.

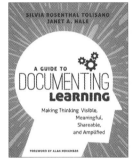

SILVIA ROSENTHAL TOLISANO AND JANET A. HALE

What is learning? How do we capture, reflect on, and share learning to foster meaningful, active engagement? *A Guide to Documenting Learning* answers these questions.

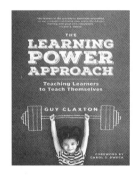

GUY CLAXTON

Written by a renowned cognitive scientist, Guy Claxton's powerful resource will help teachers understand how "every lesson, every day" shapes the way students see themselves as learners.

corwin.com

CORWIN
A SAGE Publishing Company